P9-CDM-690

CULTURE SHOCK!

Australia

Ilsa Sharp

Graphic Arts Center Publishing Company
Portland, Oregon

In the same series

Bolivia	India	Philippines	Chicago at Your Door
Borneo	Indonesia	Singapore	Jakarta at Your Door
Britain	Iran	South Africa	London at Your Door
Burma	Ireland	Spain	Paris at Your Door
California	Israel	Sri Lanka	Rome at Your Door
Canada	Italy	Sweden	
Chile	Japan	Switzerland	A Globe-Trotter's Guide
China	Korea	Syria	A Parent's Guide
Cuba	Laos	Taiwan	A Student's Guide
Czech	Malaysia	Thailand	A Traveller's Medical Guide
Republic	Mauritius	Turkey	A Wife's Guide
Denmark	Mexico	UAE	Living and Working Abroad
Egypt	Morocco	USA	Working Holidays Abroad
France	Nepal	USA—The	
Germany	Netherlands	South	
Greece	Norway	Vietnam	
Hong Kong	Pakistan		

Illustrations by TRIGG
Photographs from Ilsa Sharp

This book is published by special
arrangement with Times Editions Pte Ltd
Times Centre, 1 New Industrial Road, Singapore 536196
International Standard Book Number 1-55868-094-2
Library of Congress Catalog Number 91-077246
Graphic Arts Center Publishing Company
P.O. Box 10306 • Portland, Oregon 97296-0306 • (503) 226-2402

Printed in Singapore

*This book is dedicated with respect and affection
to Australia,
a country which has had the foresight to welcome
the strangers knocking at her door,
and the courage to embark on an experiment
with multiculturalism.*

CONTENTS

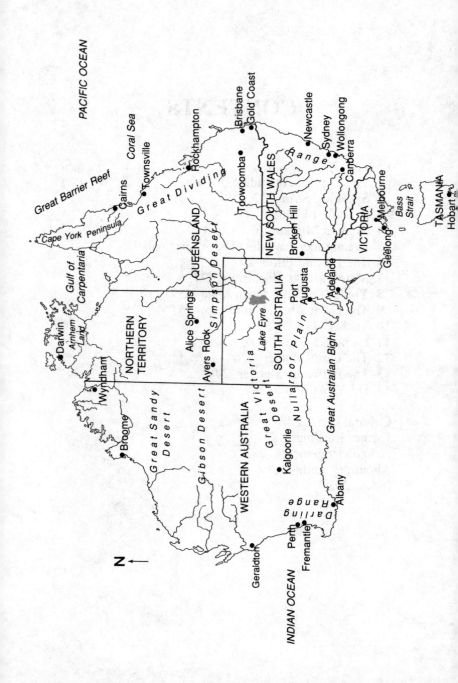

PREFACE

I would like to think that this book may help explain Australia to newcomers and visitors and thus bridge any 'culture gaps', improving the chances of mutual empathy and friendship. It is my particular, personal wish that Australia and Asia should draw closer together.

I hope too that the book will help Australians understand themselves and what it is that makes their culture unique, by holding a mirror up to them and asking them to see themselves through outsiders' eyes.

Finally, I must beg Australia's pardon if any of my interpretations have been skewed somewhat by my own 'Sandgroper' bias, due to being located at Perth, despite my best efforts to avoid such imbalance, and for any other inadvertent 'greenhorn' errors.

Chapter One

THE TYPICAL AUSTRALIAN

'He is a very nice fellow, certainly nobody would ever guess he was born in Australia.'
—British playwright and wit, George Bernard Shaw,
in his play *Major Barbara*, 1907.

Images, Stereotypes and Misconceptions

I can't count how many times my decision in the late 1980s to set up home in Australia, particularly Western Australia, was greeted with curling lips and an amazed 'But, why on earth would you want to live *there*?'

This told me more about the enquirer than about Australia.

Australia seems to be one of those countries that nobody feels neutral about. Everybody has strong views, for or against. Depending on where you are coming from then, geographically, psychologically and culturally speaking, you are sure to harbour in your heart one of a well-defined range of stereotypes depicting 'the typical Australian'.

So let's clear the air first by spelling out some of these stereotypes from the start. The most widespread, unfortunately, is 'The Ugly Australian', which seems to come in approximately three models:

European Model

If you are of continental European origin, this means the Aussie is barbaric, loud-mouthed, ignorant and uncultured, hopelessly provincial.

He is physically outsized but mentally minuscule, somewhat naive, and nearly always extremely badly dressed (this gaffe weighs particularly hard on the minds of the Parisian French). He cannot hold his wine, and has the temerity to claim that his own country produces this celestial ambrosia on a par with the French original. Worst of all, he cannot understand menus written in French. Basically, he is a peasant.

But actually, most Europeans are blissfully unaware of the existence of Australia or the Australians.

British Model

If you are British, you probably see your Antipodean cousin as a rather alarming, alien being bereft of the (hypocritical) courtesies of the mother country, far too frank (which other country could have produced a foreign minister who used the F... word in public while on an official tour of South Africa?), frequently obscene; a naive colonial boy in shorts, an insular sheep-farmer sporting a big hat with corks hanging off it to keep the flies away.

You find the way he tends to 'get physical' rather terrifying, although you secretly admire it too. And the way he puts himself on first-name terms with you from the word go is quite beyond the pale. He's notorious as a bloke fond of a booze-up, most often culminating in a 'technicolor yawn' or 'chunder' (in low Australian patois, a vomiting session)—which he performs in a back-garden 'dunny' (outshed toilet).

The Australian accent, furthermore, is execrable by British standards and unfortunately slots the Australian firmly into 'the lower classes', since it best resembles working-class Cockney from East End London, or Irish-dialect English.

Many of these British images derive from the Barry ('Bazza') McKenzie comic strip, which ran for years (1963–74) in the British satirical magazine *Private Eye*, lampooning the worst traits of an Aussie on the loose in Europe.

Asian Model

If you are Asian, you probably share the European and British concern at the Australian's admittedly blunt ways, since calling a spade a spade is hardly an Asian trademark. His predilection for semi-nakedness will not have endeared him to you, either.

And most likely, you have been persuaded that the typical Australian is a dyed-in-the-wool racist, besides being lazy or on the dole and totally incompetent because he can't seem to make as much money as you can—and even more irritatingly, for some reason, does not seem to *want* to make money, anyway.

He has no drive and to all intents and purposes, has parked himself in the world's KIV tray, his nation quite literally 'a basket case'.

Although it is true that where there is smoke, there usually are at least a few glowing coals, in fact, many of these images derive from a hostile Asian press, egged on by Asian governments intent on preventing their best and brightest from emigrating to Australia. (The

11

Aussie media have, however, more than held their own, exchanging insult for insult, and then some.)

The culture gap is at its widest between Australia and Asia, a cause of enduring sadness to all concerned, for Asia is where Australia is located and where Australians eventually must, willy-nilly, make their psychological, cultural and economic home.

The Great Suburban Bore

A kind of sub-category within 'The Ugly Australian' classification is the Australian as 'The Great Suburban Bore'.

By definition, this view of the Australian can only be held by someone who thinks he himself or she herself is the opposite, i.e., sophisticated, intellectually dazzling, exciting, glamorous, etc. Well, we know what we think of people who think this of themselves, don't we? That would certainly be the Australian reaction to such pretentiousness, at any rate.

It is true that the vast majority of Australians lead simple lives, putting great store by their homes and families, and the general philosophy of *cultiver son jardin* (with the gardening bit taken quite literally). But then, what is so reprehensible about such simple values in our troubled times?

As chief Australia-watcher Professor Donald Horne, himself a native son, has said, describing Australia as the world's first 'suburban nation' in his seminal *The Lucky Country*, 'The profusion of life doesn't wither because people live in small brick houses with red tile roofs.'

Crocodile Dundee

Another, more positive, image of Australians bases itself on the 'Australian Pioneer' stereotype, one which many Australians themselves have taken to their bosom, along with sundry others, particularly the Americans. You can tell how much Aussies fancy

The goanna—diet of the Australian pioneer. Photo courtesy of the Northern Territory Tourist Commission.

themselves in this role by the number of them who don bush hats, cowboy hats or 'Digger'-style Aussie army hats, especially when showcasing themselves on trips abroad. Former labourer-turned-comic actor Paul Hogan's sell-out *Crocodile Dundee* films of 1985 and 1988 did much to fuel this myth.

This stereotype has it that every Australian is fit, tanned and courageous in the face of hideous adversities daily encountered in the bush and deserts of a harsh continent. He is attuned to the secret voice of Nature, thanks to his Aboriginal mentors, consumes goanna steaks most dinners and spends an awful lot of time fighting bush-fires, that is, when he's not locked in mortal combat with either crocodiles or lethally poisonous serpents. He is the original frontiersman (alias Davy Crockett) reborn.

Americans really relate to this myth, because many of them live its American counterpart, nursing the idea that they are all cowboys at heart, still conquering the Wild West.

A subdivision within the Australian Pioneer category falls into the *Rural Idyll* box: here, most Australians make their living herding

13

Fitting into the landscape, the author on horseback in the Avon Valley, Western Australia. Photo by Siva Choy.

cattle or sheep, spending much of their time on horseback, bathed in pastoral peace and romantic sunsets.

These fantasies of course completely ignore the fact that the overwhelming majority of Australians—close to 90 per cent—in reality huddle together in urban centres, in mortal dread of the outback beyond, terribly disturbed by the thought of having to deal with the Aboriginals and blithely oblivious of their own burgeoning paunches. If anything, the nearest they have ever got to the desert is burying their heads in the metaphorical sand most of the time.

The Honey-Coloured Facts

As with all extreme stereotypes, the truth lies somewhere in between.

'The truth' is also changing rapidly, almost minute by minute, as Australia itself changes, under the impact of the geo-politics of the Australasian region, and of very varied immigration inflows, particularly from Asia.

How inadequate black-and-white statements are, about any country or culture! The truth in between is in fact not so much grey as honey-coloured when it comes to Australia: the country's distinguished first ambassador to China, Stephen Fitzgerald, has declared that this will be the national skin colour one day soon, thanks to Asian immigration and mixed marriages.

A fifth of Australia's 17.7 million people today were born outside Australia. By the middle of the 21st century, perhaps 20 per cent may be of Asian origin. And this is not to forget the more than 200,000 original Australians—the Aboriginals.

Australia is no longer a bastion of white or Anglo-Saxon culture. The Anglo-Saxon foundations were in fact undermined long ago, with the influx of southern European immigrants after World War II, notably from Italy, Greece and Eastern European countries such as Yugoslavia. But as I shall explain shortly, the foundations cannot be ignored, even today.

Self-Image

What do Australians think of themselves? Fortunately, like their British ancestors, they are blessed with a limitless capacity for self-mockery, always a healthy trait. Home-bred intellectuals are at times far more critical than outsiders would be.

But one mocks only when the foundations are secure, and the fact is, the vast majority of Australians believe that their way of life is the best, and the right one. In fact, they are blissfully unaware that there could be any other way.

Their biggest failing, however, is that few of them realise just how lucky they are. They take their freedoms and the welfare system for granted, among other perks of the Australian way of life. For all their detestation of the 'whinger', they themselves are capable of whingeing about the most minute infringements of their rights. They need to travel more, to bring back sobering lessons from the tightly 'guided democracies' and outright dictatorships of the developing world.

Call it smugness and complacency if you will, but there is an attractive sense of security, pride and identity in the ordinary Australian's conviction that he has got it right.

The Cultural Cringe

The only chink in this armour is the famous 'Cultural Cringe'. This originates from an uncomfortable suspicion that anything British, from the original motherland, was *per se* better than homegrown Aussie stuff. In these post-British Empire days, there are now variations on this theme, focusing on Europe: I have met Australians who are obsequiously obsessed with the notion that anything French must automatically be superior, for instance.

I have met Australian diplomats, ostensibly charged with the job of promoting their country, who were only too eager over a private dinner table to dissociate themselves from what they saw as the unspeakable yobbos of their homeland.

This inferiority complex, which for a moment showed happy signs of diminishing during the 1970s, has revived with a vengeance now that a heavily indebted Australia is plainly in dire economic straits, particularly in comparison with its non-white neighbours, such as the 'Mini-Dragons' of Hong Kong, Taiwan, South Korea and Singapore.

This has led to extensive self-flagellation in public places. At the end of 1990, it was even announced that the Federal Government would sponsor annual lecture tours of Australia by disgruntled expatriate Australians, to give 'an objective viewpoint' of the nation. Announced by the Federal Employment, Education and Training Minister, John Dawkins, these lectures are the brainchild of Professor Donald Horne. The lectures were to take place on Australia Day itself, usually a case for national celebration and self-congratulation.

'The Cringe', still a topic of eager discussion in the Australian press, learned works and the like, permeates Australian culture and indeed its economy (which is importing too many foreign goods for its own good, in preference to those made in Australia). There is still the lurking worry that Australian-produced cinema, literature and fashions—the whole gamut of creation—may not be as good as 'the real thing', from Hollywood, Britain or France.

The Colonial Past

Such discussions will ring a clangorous bell with other 'developing' nations who share Australia's colonial past—similar debates on the worth and universality or otherwise of local literature occur from time to time in Singapore and Malaysia, for example.

In short, he who wishes to understand the Australian mind, needs to study the country's history and to take both convict-hood and the 'colonial factor' into careful account.

The Australians who called England 'home' and valued a pukka British accent are still with us today, albeit dwindling in numbers and influence. The Queen of England is still the Queen of Australia, albeit perhaps not for too much longer, judging from the gathering momentum of the Republican movement in Australia.

Despite all the overlays deposited by post-World War II migration, the key to mainstream Australian culture still lies in the 19th century, working-class London and Ireland from which the first, convict, Australians were unwillingly torn—to the extent that you still hear forms of the English language in Australia which are no longer currency in modern England itself.

I would go so far as to say that a good way to understand Australia, especially for non-Europeans, might well be to spend a couple of years in London first. A tortuous route for some, perhaps, but a worthwhile soft landing, compared with going in cold.

In this context, I continually marvel at the bravery of the thousands of Asian and other non-English speaking migrants who every year struggle to bridge the enormous cultural and linguistic chasm separating them from 'the real Australia'. Without my own British background, I do not know how I could possibly have begun to understand Australia. But even a British grounding is still only a beginning.

The Battler

The typical Australian also invariably likes to see himself as that national icon, The Battler—a working-class underdog who struggles to survive, the salt of the earth. This is the model he emulates. Hence his odd celebration of a major military defeat like the Battle of Gallipoli in 1915, during World War I.

The Tall Poppy

However, should the battler actually win and come out on top, achieving success, fame and money, he immediately transforms into a Tall Poppy, a most undesirable thing, begging to be cut down to size. The typical Australian tries not to shine too obviously and does not much like those who do, although he also prides himself on his ability to give everyone 'a fair go'.

Street-Friendly

It is true that Australians have 'country ways' for the most part; this is a large part of their considerable charm. They take a direct, simple approach to things and people, and can be quite child-like at times. Their most delightful characteristic is a willingness to talk to strangers in the street, on the bus, anywhere, and to spend time with you—they are rarely in a hurry. (This principle may not apply in the centre of Sydney at rush hour; however, capital cities will be capital cities.)

Singaporean journalist Chai Kim Wah nutshelled this quality neatly in an excellent travel report in the *Sunday Times* of Singapore, November 26, 1989: 'A trait I came across often (was) a readiness to give you the time of day, to be matey. It is not the American gushing-on-all-eight-cylinders friendliness, but a laid-back variety you can take or leave.'

Never be afraid to greet an Aussie in the street or to talk to a taxi-driver; always take the initiative if you can, because you will inevitably be rewarded with a smile and friendly conversation. This presupposes, of course, that you can speak English. Most Australians are not comfortable at all with foreign languages; and good English is still the *sine qua non* key to their hearts.

Mateship

Once your friend, the Australian is characteristically your friend for life, for better or for worse. Loyalty, 'mateship', still counts for much.

And there probably can be no better friend in a physical crisis than an Australian. The Australian somehow seems to revert to the 'Pioneer' stereotype at the sight of fires, floods or crime—he will always roll up his shirt-sleeves (or more typically, take his shirt off) and charge in to help, oblivious to his own personal safety.

I shall never forget how my Australian neighbours demonstrated this quality when a serious fire broke out in the wooden-hut village down my road in Singapore. By the time I got to the scene, having dithered around putting on the 'right' clothes and shoes, and then dousing myself in water first, the Aussies were already running in and out of the flames, stripped down to their underwear, carrying the villagers' sticks of furniture out of harm's way.

Proud and independent they may be—and they expect others to be likewise—but Australians do know how to band together in times of crisis and are quick to lend a helping hand to their fellowman, a habit learned in the bad old days of bush settlement. Asians, and others too, have often wrongly labelled the Australian 'individualistic'.

Mateship is what makes the difference even to the most conservative Australian. The same Australian who has just made disparaging remarks about Asians to white friends over the dinner table, will the next minute deck any white who insults the Asian friend and neighbour with whom he has been enjoying a pint of beer at the pub for the past few years—'cause mates are mates, see? He himself is unlikely to perceive the paradox.

Scout's Honour

The Australian can be naive—long may he stay that way. It is only yesterday that most, even in the cities, kept their front doors open to visitors and never locked their cars. All that has changed, but it is still all too easy to take advantage of the Australian's innocence. He takes you at your word, and expects it to be your word of honour too.

It seems inevitable, although lamentable, that the Australians will be pushed into the harsh real world. Already, it is not as easy as it was to walk into a bank and open an account in the name of Mickey Mouse without showing any identification whatsoever. But that, too, was only yesterday.

You can phone up and open a Telecom Australia account without any paperwork or further ado, sight unseen. You leave your passport at the Immigration office but get no receipt for it to prove that they have it. Why? Because this is a matter of trust between you two, right? You wonder if anyone else who asked for it could get it over the counter. But you are not supposed to worry about this, because it is all a matter of trust. Just as you are supposed not to worry when the passport comes back to you complete with your desired visa, but by ordinary (not registered) local mail. Neither are you supposed to worry when you deposit a large amount of cash into a bank account and get no documentation to prove you have ever paid it in – no worries, the clerk is your mate, right, he/she would never dream of siphoning a bit off for himself/herself.

The two most famous Aussie catch-phrases, 'She'll be right,' and 'No worries' assume the essence of the Latin *mañana* or Oriental fatalism at such times.

Naiveté is why Australians have had some trouble doing business in Asia. They are not used to hidden meanings behind words. As far as they are concerned, words mean exactly what they say.

This attitude hardly fits them for the arcane shadow-play of business in countries like Indonesia or China—no wonder Broken Hill Proprietary, or BHP, Australia's huge steel corporation, irritably announced its withdrawal from most China investments in April 1989, pronouncing itself thoroughly frustrated with 'a continuing series of negotiations and attempts at building and maintaining relationships'.

The Soft Underbelly

Lastly, I have observed that, contrary to the machismo pervading the nation's self-image, Australians are incredibly soppy sentimentalists. It's a short step from slap-on-the-back mateship to blubbering on each other's shoulders at the pub.

You have only to study the Australian creative style in film-making, whether for advertising or for the cinema, to be struck by its lingering, lyrical quality, its preference for tear-stained soft focus. (Those familiar with the famous 'Singapore Girl' advertisements patented by Singapore Airlines, which fit very much into this genre, might remember that the image-creator behind them is an Australian.)

The Australian's shell is rough and tough, a protection born of his violent past in a harsh land; but if handled sympathetically, he will turn turtle and show you his soft underbelly.

Chapter Two

SPEAKING STRINE

'To employ more than the most limited of vocabularies is not only ostentatious but anti-democratic. If the teachers are half right, little has changed since I attended primary school in the 1940s, when to show an interest in words was to damn yourself as some sort of deviant. As a wimp, or worse.'

—Columnist Phillip Adams in *The Weekend Australian*,
July 27, 1991, on the Australian attitude to words.

An English-Speaking Country?

Nothing distinguishes the Australian more sharply from the average Anglo-Saxon than his very special brand of English.

Many English-speaking newcomers to the country make the awful mistake of imagining that operating there will be a breeze because 'They speak English there, don't they?' Well, not quite. Like English in other former colonial outposts, from the West Indies to South Africa and Zimbabwe, from India to Singapore and Malaysia, the language has mutated in Australia's desert soils.

The extraordinary thing is that many of the central features of Australian English were well in place by the late 19th century, hiving off from the mother-tongue very soon after the original convicts' and settlers' arrival in Australia. The language of a rebellious subculture.

Unfortunately, the lingo is extremely hard for the outsider to penetrate, or to imitate, (for practice, try saying 'Australia' the Strine way—'Orst-ri-ya'). If you are a new migrant, you may gain comfort (or despair, depending on your point of view) from the certain knowledge that your children will be fluent 'Strine' speakers within months of setting foot on Australian soil. ('Strine' is an approximation of how the word 'Australian' sounds, coming out of an Australian's mouth.) It's definitely catching.

There is still an older generation of Australians, particularly the more educated ones, which was brought up to speak 'English English', but this cohort is fast dwindling. There are also some distinctly well-moderated, gentler accents to be found among educated and well-travelled Australians, especially in the eastern states, in major cities such as Sydney, Melbourne and Adelaide.

Although the trend is definitely for a more earthy Australian accent to take over the airwaves, out of a sense of increasing national pride, there are still quite a few such moderated accents to be heard on 'Auntie', the Australian Broadcasting Corporation's radio programmes.

No Plums Please, We're Australian

Generally speaking, though, you will be considered suspect and a bit 'up yourself' (an obscene but commonly heard reference to sexual gratification of yourself; 'wanker' is another frequently heard insult of the same breeding, referring to masturbation) if your English comes with too 'plummy' an accent. ('Plummy' refers to the over-careful speech you would produce if you had a plum in your mouth.)

Not only does the majority of the nation favour 'Ozspeak' but there is now also a subgroup of youngsters whose dialect of choice is sarcastically alluded to by older journalists as 'Wayne-speak', this term being a reference to today's 'in' names for Australian children, Wayne (or Jason; female version, Bron), rather than the good old Bruce (or Jan). (There was also a brief hippy interlude during the 1960s, which produced Amber, Jasmine, and Sky for some.)

Much of Wayne-speak is plain old lousy pronunciation, rather than just dialect English. Examples are *heighth* for height and *esculator* for escalator, as noted by journalist Deborah Bogle in an article for *The Australian Magazine*. In the same category can be bagged the increasing tendency to pronounce 't' as 'd', thus, *qwordah* for quarter and *wor-dah* for water. Overlaid on this is the growing impact of American English.

Today or To Die?

True-blue Australian English differs from the 'mother-tongue' both in terms of its accent and in terms of its vocabulary. The accent is best gauged from old jokes which run thus ...

Wounded soldier to nurse in Australian hospital:

'Have I come here to die?'

Nurse: 'Now, love, yer came 'ere yesterdie!'

And a punning headline in *The West Australian* newspaper, 30 April 1993, would not have been possible were it not for the Aussie accent: referring to Princess Diana of England, the newspaper headlined 'Diana—Princess of Wiles'.

... and the national form of greeting, 'G'day, mate!' (not common currency between the sexes or among women, it should be noted), which could be transcribed roughly as 'Ger-die, mite!' Woe indeed were my two migrant friends desperately looking for Hay Street— they would have been better understood if they had said 'High Street' like everybody else in Australia.

Be very careful whom you label an Australian on first hearing. It is difficult for the beginner to tell an Australian accent from a New Zealand one, but New Zealanders do not like to be taken for Australians, not one bit (the feeling is mutual). As a general guideline, Australians open their mouths wider, while New Zealanders are said to speak through their clenched teeth and semi-closed lips. Typically, a New Zealander will say 'yis' for 'yes', and 'fush n' chups' for 'fish and chips', somewhat like the Scots' accent.

The contortions that Australians can perform with diphthongs are a marvel to the ear. Often they are extended to double-diphthongs, to the point that a simple 'no' may well become more like 'nah-oh-oo-u'. For reasons I do not quite understand myself—probably sexist ones—the essentially nasal accent sits particularly uneasily with the female voice, which in Australia also seems to be higher-pitched than it would be in most of Western Europe (although not so much higher than is common among Asian females).

A commentator in the 1940s once surmised that the Australian accent was attributable to a permanent inflammation of the nose, due to the excessive pollen to be found in the air. Australian vocal delivery is most often slow and rather flat by outsiders' standards, without great light and shade contrasts, tending to a monotone in some cases. An Australian is capable of saying something extraordinarily interesting and lively in such a low-key manner that you may not notice he has said anything out of the way at all.

Ups and Downs
For this reason alone, never mind the accent, you need to concentrate

on what Australians are saying (try hard not to fall asleep), in case you miss something. Since the Australian also has a penchant for terse understatement, the risk of misunderstanding is great.

Clearly, there is a corollary here to guide you on how you in turn should converse with an Australian. Loud, assertive delivery will not go down too well. Lower your voice and flatten it like his, erase all excitement or emotion, and you should be able to get your point across without too much offence.

There is one interesting exception to this rule: the infectious Australian habit of lifting the voice at the end of the sentence as if asking a question or seeking your approval/understanding.

'And it was raining, really hard' (on 'hard', the voice goes sharply up as if '?' were there and '... you know what I mean?' were tacked on the end), 'but we had no umbrellas ...' (up again on 'umbrellas' ... 'you know what I mean?').

This verbal tic can be infuriating to the novice but it will insidiously creep into your own voice over time, sure as the sun shines. And when you think about it, it is really quite a friendly habit, this constant seeking of your involvement in the conversation.

Antique Hangovers

Some Australian English is in fact more original and 'pure' than the version spoken in Mother England today. Many Australian words were long ago discarded in England. Australians as a rule betray their innate conservatism by clinging on to old forms and idioms, while at the same time building on top of them by creating new ones. This makes Australian English quite a rich, 'dense' language.

Again, you have to look back to white Australia's roots in 19th-century, Cockney London and Ireland to understand this. Quite apart from the accent, how else can you explain the extraordinary survival of Cockney rhyming slang in everyday Australian speech? It even gets printed in the daily newspapers as a matter of course—like the photo caption I once came across, reading 'Mr So-and-So on the dog and bone'. The photo in question showed Mr So-and-So using the telephone.

I might have passed this by and thought nothing of it, had not a young Aussie friend remarked to me over a coffee, 'So you're all on your Al Capone, then?' when I said my husband was away. That of course translated as 'So you're all on your own, then?'

I must mention here, however, that at least one reputable dictionary lists 'Al Capone' as the rhyming slang for telephone (and not 'dog and bone'), but 'Pat Malone' as the rhyming slang for 'alone', so I am not quite sure where this leaves us. But the examples I have cited have come from my first-hand experience.

Thinking Little
An Australian idiosyncrasy is the strange obsession with reducing any word possible to its diminutive form.

Hence 'postie' for the postman, and even 'U-ie' for a motorist's U-turn. This too is quite a catching disease and the longer you stay in Australia, the more you will find yourself slipping into the habit.

There is a similar group of words which has been shortened with '-o' at the end: 'reffo' for refugee, 'Freo' for the port of Fremantle in Western Australia, 'rego' for car-registration, 'journo' for journalist, 'muso' for musician, and so on.

Together, these two forms of diminutives are thought to number at least 200. This list is sure to be growing by the minute.

Conversation Smoothers
Then of course, there are the famous Australian catch-phrases, 'No worries' and 'She'll be right,' epitomising the nation's fabled plucky optimism and laid-back style. These are by no means clichés and are still in common use, although 'Not a problem' seems to be gaining ground. 'She'll be apples' (from the rhyming slang 'apples and spice' for 'nice'?) belongs to the same family of phrases.

However, it must be said that the trials of economic hard times have of late strained even the most sanguine of Aussies and such phrases increasingly have a hollow ring to them, belying the desperation beneath.

Another, fairly newly-arrived, phrase in this conversation-lubricating category is 'There you go.' This crops up all over the place and if you use it skilfully, it will help you blend into the Australian background nicely. As a shop assistant hands over your change, she may well say pleasantly, 'There you go,' as may a waiter delivering your order.

The Art of Abuse

When it comes to insults, the Australian suddenly springs to life and abandons his laid-backness with a vengeance.

If you should happen to become the butt of his artistry in this department, try to take it all with a smile and a pinch of salt. Do not take it to heart. In Australia, you must always be a sport. Better still, once you have got the hang of things, give back as good as you get—it's expected, and accepted.

Australian English is particularly rich in invective (especially the obscene sexual variety), easily matching close rivals, such as Cantonese, for example. Four-letter swear words are used like punctuations by the man-in-the-street and even by politicians in Parliament. 'Bloody' hardly raises an Australian eyebrow. There is much worse to come.

If you come from a genteel background, it is best you prepare yourself for this and train yourself not to hear it. There will be no avoiding it. (The most painful experience is when your children start picking it up.) Relegate it to wallpaper status, for that is all it really is—wallpaper. Those 'bad' words have lost their violence and their meaning in Australian English, through over-frequent use.

'Bastard' is one word that leads to great misunderstanding. Learn that in Australia, more often than not, it is used affectionately, very rarely as an insult. Only when it is applied to a 'Pommy', an Englishman, is it really meant to hurt. (There are many other terms of racist abuse, but I shall deal with these in another chapter.)

Paradoxically, however, such words as 'F...' are still considered fundamentally taboo in Australia, as elsewhere. It was only in 1985 that the Western Australian police charged the Sydney comedian Rodney Rude with obscenity for using the F... word to excess onstage (once every three minutes, during a 90-minute show).

Western Australia has been one of the last bastions of a once uniformly puritanical Australian culture, yet this case was dismissed in the end with the following rationale, to quote *The West Australian* newspaper of April 22, 1986: 'Used in combination with the word "off", the offending word was vulgar and quite impolite, but well understood and not necessarily obscene. The word's primary meaning was "to copulate" but more often than not it was used simply as a strong expletive, and repeated use had tended to lessen the impact.'

Punchy Politicians

The master of Australian invective without sole recourse to swear words must surely be the former Australian Labor Party (note confused spelling) government's Prime Minister, Paul Keating, although even he has stooped to berating his political opponents in public as 'Boxhead', 'Pig', 'Clown', 'Sleazebag' and so on.

'At least I'm doing this for the history books,' Keating once told an over-investigative journalist. 'You're only doing it for tomorrow's fish and chips.' (A reference to the traditional wrapping for fish and chips, old newspapers.) To a leftwing delegate at the New South Wales state ALP conference in 1982, he remarked, 'You could talk under wet cement.'

The ALP's former Foreign Affairs and Trade Minister, Gareth Evans, has a reputation for foot-in-the-mouthers. Not only did he dismiss a local policeman as 'F...ing useless!' while on an official visit to South Africa in 1991, but he also used the F... word in Federal

Parliament in 1990, the first to do so in 20 years, dutifully recorded by Hansard. But then, Evans was reported by Alan Attwood in *The Australian Magazine* to have said to a friend, 'F... it, I'm not going to stand around being diplomatic and nice to everyone. If people had been less diplomatic about Hitler, we would not have had the f...ing Second World War.'

That just about sums up the standard Australian attitude to excessive politeness: it is anathema in a truly democratic society. Being able to call a spade a bloody spade is a politically important Australian freedom.

As for the Silver Bodgie himself (see Glossary), former Labor Prime Minister Bob Hawke is well known for once turning aside from the heckling of an old-age pensioner to remark *sotto voce*, 'Silly old bugger!' The remark was unfortunately overheard by the entire nation, courtesy of TV and radio.

With leaders like these using lingo like this, the man-in-the-street needs little further encouragement. After an upbringing soaked in English hypocrisy and a young adulthood saturated with Asian evasiveness, I personally have found this trait refreshing, once you get over the initial shock.

In the same vein, Australians have concocted some extraordinary and often ingeniously insulting similes, making hyperbole a typically Australian vehicle. 'Three old ladies dressed like Queen Elizabeth II in floral prints and sensible shoes tell me they think their premier Bob Hawke is as "shady as a rat with a parasol",' reported Singaporean journalist Chai Kim Wah in the Sunday Times of Singapore, November 26, 1989.

The simile is a dynamic living form. Of very recent coinage is one I myself heard: 'Yeah, he's as busy as a bricklayer in Beirut!' Then there is 'He's as camp as a row of circus tents!' referring to a person's gay tendencies. 'This idea hasn't got a snowflake's chance in hell!' is a popular one right now. More on the scatological side is 'That's not worth a fart in a hurricane.'

31

Mis-Speak

Differences in vocabulary can sometimes lead to hilarious misunderstandings, or embarrassing double entendres. Take, for example, the experience of my Malaysian-Eurasian friend, a fresh migrant to Australia. Invited by some new Australian friends to their dinner party, she asked politely if she should bring anything along and was at first puzzled by their response: 'Yes, bring along a plate, will you?' Poor things, she thought, they must be a bit short of crockery, and so she took along practically her entire dinner service, only to discover that a 'plate' referred to a dish of cooked food. This was what is known elsewhere as a 'pot-luck' dinner, where each guest brings a contribution of food, a very common variation on the 'Bring Your Own' or BYO theme in Australian life.

And then there was my other Malaysian friend, a timid new migrant in his early teens. He had made arrangements to meet someone on a particular street and so he was loitering there quite peaceably at the appointed time until he noticed a large sign which said, 'No Standing At Any Time'. Panicked, he proceeded to pace up and down wildly in the belief that so long as he kept moving, he would not be arrested. But this was in fact a traffic sign, which in other countries would probably have read something like 'No Parking' or 'No Waiting'.

The Tender Tea-Trap

The classic in this genre is, of course, the Australian 'Tea'. The worst case scenario is that you, an English or Asian migrant, have invited your Australian friend round for Tea. The Australian will wait around hopefully—and hungrily—for a long time before he or she realises that 'Tea' is just tea, and very little more.

For an Australian, Tea is the full evening meal, known to most other cultures as 'Dinner'. Beware of 'The Tea Trap'—it still catches out many a foreign visitor!

Subcultures as well as communities within multicultural Australia have spawned their own lexicons. The surfing subculture is one example: when they refer to 'a Margaret' in Western Australia, they mean a big wave of the type found around the popular surfing beaches of Margaret River in southwestern Australia.

A Beer is a Beer is a Beer?

Besides the macro-differences between Australian English in general and other 'Englishes', there are also inter-state micro-differences to be considered.

In Tasmania, you can have a Jimmy (a beer) but elsewhere you would probably just ask for a Stubby (a small beer bottle holding 375 millilitres). If in Western Australia, you ask for a Middy measure of beer, you will get seven ounces, whereas in New South Wales, the same order would bring you 10 ounces. In New South Wales, a Schooner will bring you 15 ounces of beer, but in South Australia, only nine ounces. And so on, *ad nauseam* ...

A pint, thank goodness, is just that.

As you can see, Australians take their beer ('grog' is the more authentically Australian word) very seriously indeed, and you will have to, too.

Budgies are Black

Input from ancient Aboriginal cultures, not to mention many newer migrant, minority cultures, has further complicated Australian vocabulary. Experts say the state with the heaviest intake of Aboriginal words is Western Australia—words like 'monaych' for policeman, 'nyunga' for an Aboriginal and 'wongi' for an Aboriginal from the goldfields area around Kalgoorlie. But you are unlikely to hear such words used in the city of Perth itself.

Few non-Australians realise that words as universally adopted as 'budgerigar' and 'kangaroo' are in fact Aboriginal.

33

Spelling Bee Damned?

The language is of course evolving, like any other living language. But that does not seem to be sufficient excuse for the sheer volume of misspellings on show in Australia.

I was charmed by the offer of 'Lovely Cheeries' outside a grocery shop and intrigued by the display of 'Laces and Brades' at a drapery shop. It was fascinating to learn in a leading television and entertainment magazine that the popular TV compere John Mangos has a beautiful 'Frency Penny' tree in his garden, but surely, this must have been a Frangipani?

Semi-literate shop signs and the like could perhaps be excused in the context of a multicultural nation full of 'NESBs' (Non-English Speaking Background persons). But what really is disturbing is the fact that very few official letters escape serious spelling mistakes. In 1996, 30 per cent of Year 9 students (14-year-olds) did not have basic literacy skills.

Add to this, uncertainty throughout the country as to whether to adopt English or American spelling and the whole situation spells, as it were, confusion. Even the ruling party of the 1980s–90s, the ALP, spells itself the Australian Labor Party, rather than using the English 'Labour'.

Joke for Democracy

Language, of course, is the foundation of any nation's sense of humour. And Australia's humour is special indeed. It is considered a sacred cow of sorts.

Significantly, when certain states decided in 1989 to legislate against public incitement of racial hatred, racial jokes were specifically excluded from the list of offences that could be penalised under the new laws. It is an article of faith in Australia that everybody must be able to take a joke. The freedom to pull tails, tweak noses and generally satirise all comers is considered fundamental to democracy.

Probably the most internationally known of Australia's satirists is Barry Humphries, who has dissected Australian society far more cruelly than any outsider.

A great deal of non-satirical Australian humour is outrageous in some way, whether salacious or sacrilegious. There is almost nothing you cannot make fun of, from cripples to Christ on the Cross. Nothing is sacred, except the right to poke fun itself.

Catch shows like *Fast Forward* or comic acts like the *Doug Anthony All-Stars* on TV and experience this for yourself. It is typical of the quirky Australian sense of humour that this trio of daring young men is for no good reason named after a retired former leader of the ultra-conservative National Party, Douglas Anthony.

Australian humour is above all as dry as the country itself, always understated, and if possible, mumbled out of the corner of the mouth. Listen carefully—there are some gems around.

Your Verbal Camouflage

Finally, a word of advice to those trying to acquire Australian camouflage: do not rush in too enthusiastically greeting everyone 'G'day, mate!' This phrase is so quintessentially Australian that if you don't have a 'full-on' accent, to use another Australianism (and if you also look a little strange saying it, like, say, you are Chinese by race), you cannot really pull it off.

A useful greeting, more easily adopted by foreigners than 'G'day,' is 'How're yer going?' (frequently followed by the rhetorical 'Orright?'). On the other hand, the phrase 'No worries' is quickly and effortlessly adopted by most new arrivals, with some success. Also, the casual dropping here and there of single words, such as 'rego', 'dag' or phrases such as 'Good on yer!' (to indicate approval) can be achieved quite naturally.

To help you along the road, here's a selected glossary of the most commonly encountered or the best-known Australian-English words.

GLOSSARY

Akubra The classic broad-brimmed Aussieman's hat, now very chic, once the headgear of rural folk.

Arvo Afternoon. 'See you this arvo.'

Barbie The barbecue pit in your back garden, the centre of all social action during the Australian summer. Barbies are also barbecue parties serving charcoal-cooked meats and salads, always in the open air.

Bathers Bathing costume, swimming costume.

Battler A quintessentially Aussie concept, fronting a philosophy of life. The battler is the little man, the underdog struggling to survive, often in conflict with the top dog.

Beaut Great! Also common is 'Beauty!', pronounced 'Bewdy!'

Bickies Bucks, money. 'I reckon I could earn big bickies on this deal, mate.'

Bludger Usually used in the term 'dole-bludger'. A bludger is anyone who sponges off anyone else, someone who never buys his round of drinks, and in the case of dole-bludging, someone living off the state's unemployment benefits.

Blue A quarrel, a row, or else, a blunder.

Bodgie The Australian equivalent of a Teddy Boy in the 1950s. Former Prime Minister Bob Hawke has been dubbed 'The Silver Bodgie' for looking like a leftover Teddy Boy at times earlier in his political career, complete with loud jackets and sideburns, albeit silvering ones.

Bonzer Like 'cobber' (see below), this is another word which outsiders think is quintessential Strine but it too is obsolete now. It used to mean 'excellent'.

Bucketing To get or 'cop' a bucketing, is to be reviled, strongly criticised. The phrase recalls the pre-flush toilet days when human excreta were collected in buckets; in other words, when you get 'bucketed', you get a bucket of shit poured over you.

Buckley's Chance No chance. Origins of this phrase are obscure, but certainly of early 19th century date and Buckley clearly was a very unlucky man. This is also used more concisely, as 'You've got Buckley's of winning this bet, mate!'

Chook A chicken.

Chunder To vomit, the word deriving from a warning on board ship to those unfortunates happening to stand below the seasick, 'Watch under!'

Clayton's A Clayton's thing is a false or 'bluff' thing, not the real thing. From a non-alcoholic drink of the same name—a drink that's not a drink.

Cobber Fondly believed by many to be one of the most typical Aussie slang words, referring to a friend, this word is in fact just about dead in the Australian dialect.

Cocky Originally, a smallholder farmer from the smallholder's propensity to grow crops, only to have them eaten up by pest cockatoos. Used on cockatoos as well.

Crook Sick or ill, badly done or formed, not right.

Crust Your bread and butter, livelihood. The question 'What does he do for a crust?' is quite common.

Dag Derogatory. A dag (the word being derived from the filthy matted wool at the hind end of a sheep) is someone who's awful in some way, whether badly dressed, pretentious or boring.

Daks/Strides Men's trousers. 'Daks' originates from a brand-name.

Dingbat A weirdo, someone eccentric or deranged.

Dinkum Most famously used in the fuller expression 'Fair dinkum', meaning 'Honest, it's the truth!' It refers to the 'real thing.' 'Dinky-di' is a more intense version of this.

Dob In To inform on someone, to betray, especially a friend, workmate or neighbour. Dobbing in, even to the police for a crime, is not considered admirable behaviour in the Australian value system.

Drongo A hopeless loser, a stupid or clumsy person. After a horse in the 1920s which persistently failed to win a single race.

Drum Information, the latest news, the inside story. 'What's the drum on that takeover proposal, Pete?'

Dunny A legendary item of Australiana, the outdoors W.C. (toilet, lavatory) shed, pretty rarely encountered in cities nowadays, but in the countryside, still, anything goes.

Esky Portable cooling box used to carry food and drink (more importantly, beer) to picnics on the beach or in the park, etc. Derived from the original trade name, 'Eskimo'.

Full Bottle Fully informed, well up in. 'Henry's not full bottle on this issue, so let's call Reggie instead.'

Furphy A rumour or false report. It arose from soldiers' tall-tale telling while sitting around water carts (servicing the latrines) branded with the manufacturer's name, 'Furphy'.

Globe Where other English-speakers might buy a bulb or a light-bulb, Aussies always ask for a 'globe'.

Gong Medal or badge of authority. 'He looked important alright, all covered in gongs, he was.'

Good Oil All the latest news, the gossip, the low-down.

Grog Booze, liquor. Any alcoholic drink, but usually beer.

Guernsey A symbol of acceptance, from a type of sweater, and the team jersey you get on selection for a footy team.

Gutser Come a gutser, meaning to come a cropper, to fail dramatically.

Jackaroo/Jackeroo Usually a young city-slicker working on a sheep or cattle station in the rough outback to get first-hand experience of farming. A jackeroo's life is almost synonymous with toughing it out.

Jammies Pyjamas (Pajamas).

Lakkies Rubber bands (from 'elastics').

Larrikin A rowdy no-gooder, a hooligan, a mischievous youth, a trouble-maker. But also a scallywag with a golden heart.

Lolly/Lollies An abbreviation from 'Lollipop', it means any sweet or candy, especially brightly coloured ones.

Nong A fool or simpleton.

Ocker The ultimate, uncultured Australian boor. He is almost certain to be found wearing shorts and thongs, as the Aussies call what others call flip-flops, Japanese sandals, etc, and clutching a can of beer over a protruding belly. He is also characteristically jingoistic and insular when confronted with other races, creeds or cultures or indeed, any culture at all. Thankfully, his tribe is dwindling very fast.

Pokey Poker machines, or more rarely, a jail.

Poofter A derogatory term for male homosexuals, very commonly used, probably to reaffirm what Australian men see as their central macho identity.

Pooh Shit. 'Oh, the cat's just done a pooh on the carpet,' or 'Oh dear, looks like I'm in the pooh with my boss again!'

Rage This has very recently acquired the meaning of 'to party wildly'. Hence, an all-night rock-video TV programme on Saturdays is titled Rage. You may well be invited to 'go rageing' at the weekend; do not be alarmed, this is probably an invitation to visit a few discos. It may have its origins in a farming term referring to over-excited cattle.

Ratbag An eccentric or stupid person. Gradually coming to have a very general derogatory meaning.

Ringer An outstanding performer. Originally the best shearer in the sheep-shearing shed. But in northern Australia, it usually only refers to a cattle muster.

Ripper Similar to 'beaut', this means 'terrific!' 'What a ripper night we had!'

Roo-bar A large and solid structure made of metal bars attached to the front of Australian cars. Any car driving out of the city needs this fixture to cope with kangaroos bounding into the headlights on country roads at twilight or night. A collision with a kangaroo will otherwise result in far more serious damage to you and your car than to the 'roo itself!

Root A dangerous one for Americans, this one. Americans may use it to mean cheering on their favourite sports team—'I was rooting

The roo-bar to cope with kangaroos on roads. Photo by Siva Choy.

for the Mets'—but in Strine it refers only to sexual intercourse, being the equivalent of 'screw'. You have been warned.

Rort What the Americans and British know as a 'scam'—a fraudulent scheme or stunt.

Sandgropers Natives of Western Australia, because their state is largely desert sand.

Shonky Dubious, fraudulent, charlatan.

Shout Both a noun and a verb. A shout is a round of drinks, for which someone has to pay. 'When my shout came round, I did the honours. But the whole evening, he never shouted one drink!'

Smoko Short for a 'smoke', it has come to mean all features of a break from work, for a smoke, for tea and sandwiches.

Spruik (verb) **Spruiker** (noun) A weird one, this, apparently of unknown origin but used as far back as 1902. It looks South-African-Dutch, doesn't it? It means (verb), to advertise something loudly and vigorously as if selling on a street market and canvassing for customers. 'She used the child's school report to spruik the child's genius all over town.'

Sticky Beak A graphic word for the nosey parker, he or she who sticks his or her nose into things. It can also be used as a verb.

Stubby When not a small beer bottle, a pair of tight, short shorts for men. Rarely an attractive sight.

Swag In the past, the ill-gotten goods carried by a thief or vagabond, but today used of any traveller's quite legitimate bags and baggage. 'Here, you can rest your swag here while you come inside.'

Tart This sounds most offensive to English ears, since in modern English outside of Australia, it would normally refer only to a prostitute. But in Australia, it just refers to any young, and usually pretty, woman. 'Eh, that new tart he's dating is a bit of alright!' It is actually a contraction of the affectionate 'sweetheart'.

Technicolor Yawn Coined by Barry Humphries' comic-strip anti-hero, Barry McKenzie, this lurid phrase refers to a particularly violent bout of throwing-up, usually induced by an excessive intake of alcohol.

Tube A can of beer, another word popularised by the Barry McKenzie comic strip of the 1970s.

Two-up A traditional Australian gambling game based on spinning two coins and betting whether they will fall as two heads or two tails. A two-up gambling den is often referred to as a 'Two-up School', but even Australia's most respectable casinos feature this game, which originated in the pioneer outback.

Wag To skip something, drop out or play truant. 'My daughter's been wagging school for weeks, the head teacher just told me.'

Whinger Anyone who complains too much instead of getting on stoically with being a battler like the rest of Australia. 'Poms'—the British—are supposed by Australians to have developed whingeing into a fine art.

Women's Business Those rituals and secrets within an Aboriginal group that are taboo to men.

Wowser A killjoy, one who lectures, a puritan. The wowsers would like everything to close up on Sundays again.

Yakker Not to be confused with 'yacker' (a talker), this word means 'work'. 'Did a bit of hard yakker in the garden the other day, pulled my back, mate.'

Yard A general term used for the land at the back of your house, whether it is in fact a garden or a paved area.

Youse Probably of Irish origin, substitutes for 'you'. 'Youse blokes is OK,' or 'One of youse, come over here.'

Some Idiomatic Phrases

I'll give it a go; I'll give it a burl.
I'll try, never mind if it doesn't work, but I'm sure it will ... This mindset, while optimistic, can however lead to amateurism when it comes to the more precise technologies.

I suppose it's better than a poke in the eye with a burnt stick.
It's better than nothing. Again, this sums up the dryly humorous Australian approach in ordinary conversation. As *The Bulletin* weekly magazine put it in 1974, this is the Australian way of expressing ecstasy. The answer to a question like 'I've just won the Lotto for a million bucks, whaddya think of that?' could well be 'S'alright ...'

If it was raining palaces, I'd get hit on the head by the dunny door.
I never have any luck.

Don't come the raw prawn with me.
Don't try to bluff me, to put one over me.

Good on yer!
Good for you, well done!

In like Flynn.
To seize an opportunity with enthusiasm, especially a sexual one. It derives from the energetic romantic exploits of the Australian-born (Tasmanian) Hollywood hero of 1930s movies, Errol Flynn.

A cut lunch and a water-bag.
An old bushman's way of saying 'It's a long way.' 'You're going there? Well, it's a cut lunch and a water-bag for sure.'

I'll be in that; I'm up for that.
I'm pretty keen to do that, alright.

Some Common Aboriginal Words

Billabong A waterhole.

Boomerang The curved Aboriginal hunting weapon that returns to its owner after hitting its target, making sophisticated use of aerodynamics.

Corroboree A festive gathering, a get-together, usually with music and dance.

Humpy An Aboriginal bark hut, now any rough hut or shelter.

Walkabout The habit ingrained in Aboriginal culture, of temporary migration from one's home base, for an unplanned period of time and often without a specific goal in mind. Used now of anyone who disappears mysteriously for a while to be alone or to escape something. 'Can't find Bill anywhere, musta gone walkabout.'

Some Common Diminutives

Brickie Bricklayer.

Chrissie Christmas.

Cozzie Swimming costume.

Deli Delicatessen shop or counter.

Divvie Dividend.

Footy, Footie Australian Rules Football.

Pokie Poker machines, in casinos, etc.

Prezzie Present, gift.

Sickie Taking sick leave off work. Often used jokingly, on the understanding that it is just a way of getting off work. 'Your party's on Thursday morning? No worries, I'll just take a sickie and I'll be there.'

Tazzie Tasmania.

Tinny A tin can of beer.

Uni Where others might say 'varsity' (antique British) or 'U', the Aussies say 'Uni' for University.

Selected Rhyming Slang

Bag of Fruit Suit.

Butcher's For Butcher's Hook = Look ('I'll just take a butcher's at the baby for a minute').

Chevy Chase Face. (An interesting potential source of confusion for Americans, this one, as a well-known comic film actor in the USA is also named Chevy Chase.)

Dog and Bone Telephone.

Khyber Pass Arse.

Plates For Plates of Meat = Feet.

Pot For Pot and Pan = Old Man = Dad.

Steak and Kidney Sydney.

Titfer For Tit for Tat = Hat.

Trouble and Strife Wife.

Selected Acronyms

ACT Australian Capital Territory, the territory of the Federal Government, in which is situated the city of Canberra, the seat of Federal Government.

ACTU The Australian Council of Trade Unions, a power in the land.

AJA Australian Journalists' Association.

ALP Australian Labor Party.

ANZAC Australian and New Zealand Army Corps. A word to conjure myths of the Australian warrior with, a word endowed with great sanctity, referring to war heroes and martyrs, particularly during World War I and to some extent, World War II as well.

ASIO Australian Security Intelligence Organisation, Australia's official intelligence outfit (like the British MI5 and American CIA, etc.)

RAAF Royal Australian Airforce.

RAN Royal Australian Navy.

RSI Repetitive Strain Injury, a topic of some controversy recently, as workers have claimed compensation, sick leave, etc. based on this malady. Some doubt whether it exists, but it refers to the damage done by very fast hand and arm work in repetitive patterns, particularly as performed by computer keyboard operators and typists.

RSL Returned Services League, an ex-servicemen's association, synonymous with crusty old conservatives, usually anti-migrant and anti- just about everything about New Australia.

RSPCA Royal Society for the Prevention of Cruelty to Animals.

SBS The Special Broadcasting Service, established in 1977, which runs programme material by, for and about ethnic minorities in Australia. SBS TV has in fact gained acclaim beyond the minority communities for its excellent coverage of foreign news and enlightened programming, including good foreign feature films and documentaries. It features newsreaders and presenters of non-white and non-Anglo Saxon origin, even if they have foreign accents.

TLC Not exclusively Australian, this one, but I have noticed many Asians struggling with it. It's short for 'Tender Loving Care'. When your friend's little Billy has got a bad flu, you might remark, 'Oh, I'm sure he'll get well soon with a bit of TLC from you!'

Chapter Three

A SENSE OF NATION

'Australians are the most morbidly small-minded, petty, nationalistic, chippy, insecure, over-sensitive houseplants ever to find their way out of the greenhouse.'

—Anglo-Australian warfare surfaces in an editorial in England's *The Evening Standard,* reacting to Australian reports of 'Pommy whingers' in 1997.

Australians know how to laugh at themselves, as I have said. But try laughing *at* them as an outsider and you will find the ground rules have suddenly shifted beneath your feet. Such sensitivity is not unusual in young nations—and white Australia's 200 years or so *is* still young in the history of nations.

Get Wise about Gallipoli

I have said that anything is fair game when it comes to Australian humour: from cripples to Christ on the Cross. This is true. But not Gallipoli …

Gallipoli? You will certainly have to get wise about Gallipoli if you wish to penetrate the Australian psyche. Anyway, you only have to stay long enough in Australia to hit the Anzac Day national holiday on April 25 to understand its importance.

No matter how small the Australian town you may chance upon on April 25, you can be sure there will be an Anzac Day parade around the local war memorial, complete with emotional speeches, brass bands and little boys clutching their fathers' hands, both wearing the traditional cocked Digger slouch hat. ('Digger' has been the name for an Aussie soldier since World War I, but nobody seems to know for sure why, possibly because so many Aussies are miners of Australia's considerable mineral resources, including gold.)

Gallipoli was the site of a great battle during World War I, in Turkey. The only thing is, like Dunkirk, France, in World War II, it was a great defeat and retreat, not a great victory.

The British, who still remember the evacuation from the beaches of Dunkirk with pride, and perhaps the Americans, who similarly still remember non-victories like Custer's Last Stand against the Sioux Indians in the 19th century or MacArthur's retreat from the Philippines during World War II, may perhaps empathise with the Australian celebration of failure at Gallipoli.

For others, particularly 'face'-conscious Asians, it may take a little longer to get the hang of things. You may as well hear the whole story now, from me. It will save you some mystification later, when the great April 25 fuss hits you via the newspapers, television and radio. As columnist Max Harris has commented in *The Weekend Australian*: 'Australians regard an honestly won failure as the essence of success. We're a weird mob.'

Anzac Day commemorates the terrible trials of the Anzacs—the Australian and New Zealand Army Corps—in their attempts to scale and control the rugged sea-cliffs at Gallipoli, from the landing date, April 25, 1915, until their withdrawal on December 19 that year. During this time, 8,000 or so Australians (and more than 2,000 New Zealanders, as well as French soldiers and others) were killed, and 19,000 Australians were wounded. Their bravery in the face of hopeless odds won the Australian soldier an enduring reputation thereafter, to this day—one reconfirmed elsewhere, as at the battle for Singapore in 1942.

The real significance of Gallipoli lies not so much in the nobility of the Australians' dogged courage in attempting the almost impossible, nor in their legendary 'mateship' unto death, but rather in the fact that they were fighting for, and obeying orders from, the imperial British government. This despite the fact that Australia had announced its intention to become independent of Great Britain in 1900 and had proclaimed the Commonwealth of Australia in 1901, holding the first federal elections that same year.

The sense of abandonment experienced at Gallipoli—it was all British war leader Winston Churchill's fault—saw the beginning of the end for Australian ties with the 'mother country', Britain. Australian director Peter Weir's epic film of 1981, *Gallipoli*, conveys this well; find a video of it if you can.

Underlying the Gallipoli celebration each year then (including the wheeling out still of octogenarian and nonagenarian survivors), is not anti-Turkish feelings (on the contrary, the fashion nowadays is for survivors of both sides to embrace one another), but strong anti-

British sentiment, and a feeling of 'To hell with all the others.'

The historic animosity for the British felt by the Irish, who formed a large part of Australia's original convict settlers, has reinforced this feeling. (Britons, beware of telling your favourite Irish joke in Australia before you ascertain your host's family origins.) Gallipoli crystallised a sense of nation; hence its sacred-cow status when it comes to acceptable jokes.

The moral of the story: do not poke fun at Gallipoli and, despite his cultural ties with England, do not imagine that the Australian is just an Englishman in disguise. He is his own person. For one thing, he has learned to cope with a country about 24 times the size of the British Isles.

Breaking from Britain

Yet it is only recently that Australia has broken free of the British sphere of influence.

Although the federated Commonwealth of Australia was proclaimed in 1901, only in 1986 did the Australia Act finally sever most ties with Britain by denying Britain the power to make laws for Australia or to exercise any governmental responsibility, and by removing the mechanism of legal appeal to the British Privy Council.

Nonetheless, the Queen of England remains Queen of Australia, represented by the Governor-General since she herself is 20,000 kilometres away. Australia is a member of the British Commonwealth of Nations and there are still some antique clauses squirrelled away in the Australian Constitution: for instance, the Queen of England can still disallow Australian legislation within a year of her Australian Governor-General's having approved it.

For more on this topic, see the section on *The British*, below.

A Jigsaw Nation

Few outsiders realise that Australia was for long no more than a collection of separately autonomous colonies. Nationhood is still a very new thing.

To make matters worse, internal communications and understanding have been hampered both by the geography of a harsh and huge desert terrain, almost 4,000 kilometres from east to west, over 3,000 kilometres north to south, and by economic stupidities such as the airline duopoly which made it cheaper to fly abroad than to air-commute internally, until airfare deregulation in late 1990.

The remnants of that early colonial structure, still expressed in the independence of the six state governments, are only now being broken down. For example, only in 1991 was a decision taken to form national bodies which would standardise legal procedures, electrical power, road systems, and the gauge used on railway lines across the country. But whether this will actually materialise is still in doubt. Inter-state differences have been a great block to economic progress, and to crime-busting too, for many years.

For years until 1991, sausages had differing content regulations in different states, preventing their inter-state sale. Quite often, a single product had to wear different labels and packaging in each different state. There were three definitions of bread; one state demanded that margarine be sold only in cube-shaped packages.

Electricians, plumbers, doctors and lawyers needed licences to work outside their home states. A rail cargo container sent east-west from Sydney to Perth was subject to four changes of locomotive, five safe working systems, six sizes of loading gauge and had to spend 12 hours at sidings for crew changes and inspections.

New moves are now being made to enable the states to raise more of their own revenue by taxation; the Federal Government thus far has raised 80 per cent of all government spending.

HOW AUSSIES SEE SOME OF 'THE OTHERS'

Chapter One dealt with stereotyped images of Australia and Australians. In their attempt to define their own national identity, Australians nurse quite a few stereotypes of their own when it comes to other nationalities, races, creeds and cultures. Understanding these may also help you 'position' yourself better when relating to Australians.

The French

Well, they are not to be trusted and are a reprehensible race by virtue of their nation's espousal of nuclear testing all over the place, and more particularly, on Australia's doorstep. Yet, paradoxically, little is said or remembered of British nuclear tests inside Australia between 1952 and 1958.

The spontaneous response of an Australian audience to the very mention of the French on a nationwide satire-and-entertainment show, *The Big Gig,* not so long ago, was memorable: 'Bastards!' roared the audience spontaneously and with gusto. Similarly, a heading in *The Weekend Australian*, 25–28 September 1993, read simply, 'The Bloody French'.

Some of this Francophobia stems from the famous Australian 'cultural cringe': inferiority when confronted by European sophistication, history, culture and what-have-you. So when an Australian reviles 'the frogs', he is really only getting his own back for being made to feel small when he fails to cope with a French menu.

Francophobia is also yet another legacy of Australia's British heritage and the historical British hostility to the French.

The British

Better known to Australians as Poms or Pommies (believed to be a reference to their convict past in Australia—Prisoner Of Her Majesty or POHM), the British are also more usually referred to as Pommy Bastards or else, Whingeing Poms. To whinge is to gripe, complain or moan. Aussies believe that the Brits specialise in this art, which they are further alleged to have brought to a high level as shop stewards dominating the Australian trade union movement.

The Round House, 1831, Fremantle, Western Australia. Old prison legacy from Britain. Photo by Siva Choy.

Indeed, the New South Wales Anti-Discrimination Board found in 1997 that the largest number of people complaining to it during the previous year were not Asians, but Poms, hogging 22 per cent of the complaints.

Pommies also do not bath enough, says Australian folklore, hence the phrase 'As dry as a Pommy's towel (or bathmat)', apparently first coined by the comedian Barry Humphries' Barry McKenzie character.

Traditional ties have weakened considerably since Britain joined the European Economic Community and gradually dropped in her ranking as one of Australia's most important export markets. Tee-shirts emblazoned with such legends as 'Keep Australia Beautiful—

Shoot a Pom' and 'Grow Your Own Dope—Plant a Pom' have been sighted.

The paradoxical thing about such attitudes, of course, is that the Queen of England is still Queen of Australia and much white Australian culture derives directly from 'Old Blighty', meaning England. However, this may not be true for much longer, for the Republican movement is intensifying in Australia now—the Australian Labor Party resolved at its national conference in 1991 to seek the status of Republic by 2001.

Republicanism is such a hot issue in Australia that in 1991 debating opponents came to blows on national television. It became a central political issue in the 1992–93 general elections, when Labor pinned its colours to the Republican mast, provoking intense national debate and throwing the traditionalist Liberal party into disarray.

The fact that Labor was re-elected in the face of deep recession is in part indicative of the shift in public opinion towards Republicanism. There is, however, ambivalence about the Australian flag showing the British Union Jack: Labor wants to abandon it but some old hands feel it has been a rallying point of pride, particularly during the two world wars. Recent polls have only 35 per cent of adults favouring any change, and of these 24 per cent say 'not now'. One result of the new climate of opinion is that new Australian citizens no longer have to swear allegiance to the British Queen: they can choose between this old oath or the new one which merely declares their loyalty to Australia.

Since the Queen's accession to the throne in 1953, the Morgan Gallup poll found that the percentage of Australians who want to retain Queen Elizabeth of England as Australia's head of state had fallen from 71 per cent to 56 per cent (1991) and is currently believed to stand between 30 per cent to 40 per cent. The presence of large migrant communities who have no ties to Britain certainly has much to do with this.

Like American Texans, Aussies like everything Australian to be biggest. Photo by the author.

Americans

White Australians share many national traits and also historical experiences (such as gold rushes) with the Americans. The two nations are also military allies, together with New Zealand, under the ANZUS security treaty dating from 1952. There are several somewhat mysterious American satellite surveillance and defence installations in Australia's remote heartland. This special relationship however looks a little strained in the context of the US-subsidised wheat sales to China in 1991 which undercut already desperate Australian wheat farmers and exporters.

The two peoples are similarly outgoing, both preferring informality, tending to the brash and loud, and wearing their opinions and emotions on their sleeves. They have both conquered a big country (Australia and the mainland USA, excluding Alaska, are almost the same size), including quite a bit of rough terrain.

White Australians too have their cowboys and, in the Aboriginals, their Indians. It is significant perhaps that one of the many delegations of helpers who have visited Australian aboriginal settlements to advise on coping with social problems like the petrol-sniffing addiction, came from America's Indian reservations, where they share the same problems. The two nations also share the passionate rhetoric of freedom, human rights and democracy.

The two people's languages and their cultures—from drive-in everything and hamburgers to country-and-western music, and of course, television imports—are drawing closer every day. One Australian newspaper columnist recently complained bitterly that somebody had changed the old English word 'torch' to the American 'flashlight' behind his back when he wasn't looking.

In general, there is a feeling of natural affinity. And it must be said, of admiration on the Australian side, despite a regular chorus of complaint against American cultural infiltration. Occasionally, the admiration takes the negative form of 'cultural cringe' (see Chapter One) in relation to American superiority as a world power. For one thing, it is generally agreed, by Australians too, that America saved Australia from a Japanese fate worse than death during World War II.

Everybody, on both sides of the argument, is delighted at the symbolically significant union of quintessential Aussie Paul Hogan (*Crocodile Dundee*) with his American leading lady. On the darker side, some Australians to the left of their Labor leaders look askance at Australia's strong defence and security links with the USA, and at the alleged American (and CIA) penetration of the Australian political process.

For a fascinating exposition of this school of thought, among other things, see London-based Australian journalist John Pilger's devastating and controversial book, *A Secret Country*.

Italians and Greeks

Most jokes about the Italians and Greeks are quite good-humoured. After all, an awful lot of Australians can claim Italian or Greek ancestry (almost 2 per cent of Australians even now were actually born in Italy, and about 1 per cent in Greece), and Melbourne in the state of Victoria is accounted the world's second biggest Greek city. The Italian accent is often caricatured, as in the W.A. Salvage advertisements on Perth television, where 'Luigi' genially instructs the viewer on how to 'Sava-Da-Moni'.

It is generally agreed that any houses sporting neo-colonial porticoes, pillars, columns and the like usually prove to belong to, or to have been designed by, nostalgic Italian-Australians—from my own observation, they really do!

New Zealanders

You might imagine that Australians would feel some affinity with the 'Kiwis' of New Zealand, by virtue of being close neighbours, as well as military allies.

Not so. As far as Aussies are concerned, Kiwis are pinching Australian jobs—their passports allow them free entry to and employment in Australia and there are tens of thousands of them in Australia—and are nearly as responsible for the rise in crime as the Vietnamese. Well, almost.

The Australians further resent the Kiwis' often revealed sense of superiority (they do not share the Australians' convict ancestry) and 'English ways'. There is really little love lost between them.

The Tasmanians

Now, this is an awkward one. Tasmanians (often jocularly referred to as Taswegians) are Australians. But you wouldn't think so from the way most mainlander Australians talk about them.

Tasmania (affectionately known as Tassie, pronounced 'Tazzie') is Australia's smallest state and an island, 240 kilometres off the southeastern corner of the mainland, with a population of less than half a million spread over more than 67,000 square kilometres.

Tasmanians are a standing joke in mainland Australia. The basic premise of every Tasmanian joke is that Tasmanians are hillbillies and country bumpkins (including lonely farmers habituated to questionable sexual practices) afflicted with the mental and physical consequences of extensive inbreeding: hence the many jokes referring to them as having 'two heads', 'pointy-heads' and the like.

But What about Pauline Hanson?

I mention all the above as a prelude to answering the question, 'Are Australians racist?'

When I first wrote this book in the early 1990s, against a backdrop of a Labor-government Australia officially dedicated to multi-culturalism, I answered this question with 'No, they are equally rude about absolutely everybody, of whatever colour or creed.'

I also pointed out that Aboriginal Australians are the ones suffering most from any Australian racism. I asked the reader to examine his or her nation's own glass house. I pointed out that Australia's tradition of free expression opens her up to more bruising public discussions of sensitivities like race than are possible in more restricted societies.

All of this remains true, but in the context of a Liberal government under Prime Minister John Howard replacing Labor's Paul Keating since 1996, a body of opinion previously silent unfortunately has been emboldened to speak up. Its xenophobic, sometimes racist, voice is that of independent Member of Parliament, Queenslander Pauline

Hanson. Not of course, that John Howard has ever actively espoused xenophobia or racism; but many believe he has too passively stood aside from restraining such views, and so indirectly encouraged them.

Pauline Hanson and her camp have expressed strong opposition to Asian immigration, to financial aid and welfare grants to Aboriginals, and to certain forms of foreign investment. While she apparently represents many white Australians-in-the-street—only partially educated, she herself runs a simple fish-and-chips shop—her words have brought far more sophisticated toads out from under their stones. Therein lies the real danger to Australian traditions of fair play and equality that she poses.

But let us get Hanson and her crew in perspective. First, she is not all-Australia, and definitely not representative of officialdom. Many Australians passionately oppose her or think she has 'gone over the top.'

Second, her speeches constitute exactly what many migrants have come to Australia for: freedom of expression—the correct response therefore should be to disagree with her yet defend to the death her democratic right to hold and express her views. But, but... her views *are* bad for Australia's business relations with the important Asia-Pacific region, or for her booming tourism industry.

Third, did Australia explode into racial violence after the Hanson bandwagon got rolling in 1996–1997? No, not at all. So far, it has been words, words, words. And you know that those cannot break bones.

Lastly, try to empathise: Hanson stands for the dying throes of the old 1950s Australia. Imagine the trauma of being jolted awake from a comfortable introspective Anglo-Celtic dream and forced to make yourself a place in the world or worse, in Asia, on pain of economic death. Of suddenly not knowing or understanding your immediate neighbours, newly arrived foreigners. For disturbed people like Pauline Hanson, the rules have been changed with brutal abruptness, the golden age has evaporated, and it all seems terribly unfair—'stop the world, we want to get off!'

But rest assured, the future of Australia is not on Pauline Hanson's side. Relax, do not become hyper-sensitive, and all will be well.

Asians

Before we talk about Australian attitudes to Asians, let us first translate the word 'Asian' into Australian: it means, almost exclusively, Chinese and Vietnamese, and perhaps sometimes Japanese too. It does not usually refer to Indians, for example. In other words, it refers to those of Mongoloid stock. Among racists, it is a euphemism for 'slant-eyes'. This is quite different of course from the meaning the word 'Asian' has acquired in, say, London or Birmingham, UK, where it is used to refer to South Asians.

Australia is striving very hard to make the dream of integration with Asia a reality. Children are learning Chinese, Japanese, Malay and Indonesian at school these days; such studies are already compulsory in the schools of some states.

There are also countless new research and study centres specialising in strengthening Australia's links with Asia.

The country deserves some sympathy and understanding for making the effort in the first place. And multiculturalism should not be one-sided. While Australians 'give it a go' and try to understand myriad alien cultures, surely newly arrived guests should reciprocate?

The White Australia Policy

The White Australia policy dated back to the 1901 Restrictive Immigration Act which kept out non-European immigrants, following an influx of cheap Chinese labour to the Australian goldfields after the 1840s.

Among other things, the policy produced silly situations like the case of twin brothers with mixed parenthood, one looking Indian and the other European. No prizes for guessing which one got in and which one didn't. And many a southern European was rejected for immigration in those days, on the grounds of being a touch too swarthy.

The attitudes of those times spawned a rash of consumer products like Golden Fleece Soap, which said it would 'Keep Australia White'. This policy was not abandoned till 1973. Up to that date, Australians were taught to be afraid of the 'Yellow Peril' from the north, be it Japanese or Indonesian. It takes time to shake off such grim instruction.

Yet, curiously, I must mention here that a Chinese-Australian and Sri-Lankan-Australian friend of mine, both of whom arrived in Western Australia long before 1973, have told me that they were well treated at that time, 'like guests, like a special novelty'. Even today, I can report that a Chinese friend was hosted to a welcome tea-party by his new Aussie neighbours and another Chinese lady regularly exchanges cooked dishes from her kitchen for handyman fixing about her house by her Australian neighbour.

That said, quite a few Australians do believe that the Vietnamese have brought an increase in crime (proportionately, in fact, they generate less than their share of national crime), that other Asians have brought exotic diseases like tuberculosis and hepatitis B, and that migrant Asians are taking Australians' jobs. You will find similar misconceptions about immigrants in almost every country experiencing a sudden influx of them.

Cultural Burps and Misunderstandings

Considering the country's long isolation from Asia under the White Australia policy and considering the rapid social change, if not turmoil, that large-scale Asian immigration has brought about over the past decade or so, it's surprising there is not more overt racism in Australia.

However, let us now 'sensitise' ourselves by looking at some of the things that can trigger Australian hostility.

Like the Chinese man I saw spit upon the marbled pavements of the luxurious Burswood Casino Hotel in Perth, Western Australia.

Like the Vietnamese I saw haggling over a few cents at a simple Australian neighbourhood second-hand sales fair, where nothing was priced much more than A$5. How to explain in a few seconds to the offended Australian vendors the long tradition of bargaining in Southeast Asia? How to explain to the Vietnamese that there was an unspoken gentleman's agreement that such friendly markets were fixed-price?

Like the Chinese students I saw yelling and shouting in their native Mandarin at an Australian university bus-stop, without any regard for how uncomfortable it made the Australian commuters around them feel: 'Are we in Australia, or what?'

Like the Singapore tourists at Perth hotel buffets who piled their plates high with food they couldn't finish, simply to get their money's worth, leaving behind mountains of wasted food.

Or the Asian shoppers who transferred their market customs to their local Australian supermarket, poking their fingers into fruit and vegetables, and test-eating some of them, 'not done' in Australia. The Japanese tourist who poured tomato ketchup over his breakfast cereal didn't go down too well either.

The Mystery of the Vanishing Abalone

Then there is the abalone problem off Western Australian coasts. For decades or more, ordinary Australians have enjoyed their annual abalone harvest, sticking firmly to the rules, or so they claim: take no more than 20 pieces per person per day and leave the small ones alone, to generate future stocks.

But in 1991, the Western Australian state government had to cancel that year's fishing season outright. There was no abalone left and it looked likely there might not be much more in future either. Who dunnit? 'The Vietnamese,' said some Aussies. 'The Chinese,' said others. 'All Asians,' said yet others. 'Not us,' chorused the

61

Asians. It was the big boys, the Australians with the commercial interests.

Obviously, the Western Australian Fisheries Minister at that time, Gordon Hill, thought somebody not English-speaking had done it: among the measures he announced when cancelling the season was a multilingual education programme for fishermen.

And columnist Mike Roennfeldt, writing in *The West Australian* newspaper said: 'Everyone, including the media, has been so terrified of being labelled racists that the obvious truth has been ignored. It seems to me that tippy-toeing around the fact that the whole abalone problem lies directly at the feet of Australians of Asian descent is actually being more racist than facing squarely up to the truth.'

Whatever the rights and wrongs of this case, it is a good example of why some Australians may have reservations about Asians.

A very similar thorn in Australian flesh is the Indonesian 'poaching' of Australia's valuable trochus shell. Between 1989 and 1991, Australian patrol boats arrested 150 Indonesian vessels, mostly from Sulawesi, for fishing inside Australian waters, in a multi-million dollar campaign to stop illegal fishing.

From the Indonesian fishermen's point of view, fishing off Australia, for fish and shellfish, for trochus and for sea-slug (known as *trepang*), is a centuries-old traditional right, which in many cases they had negotiated amicably with the indigenous Aboriginals. Besides, they are poor and desperate enough to just keep on coming.

To top all this off, Australians generally feel that Asian societies are reprehensible for their lack of social and political freedom, in short, for not being like Australia.

The rows with Malaysia over the 1986 hanging in Malaysia of two Australians, Kevin Barlow and Brian Chambers, for carrying drugs (Australia does not have the death penalty for any crime), the ABC TV screening in 1990–91 of a soap opera titled *Embassy* set in a fictional Southeast Asian Muslim country called Ragaan, which just happened to be located between the borders of Thailand and Malaysia, and over

Prime Minister Paul Keating's infamous reference to Malaysian PM Mahathir as a 'recalcitrant', are cases in point.

The series *was* insulting to Malaysia. But the Australian government does not control the country's media, a simple fact which many Asians find very difficult to understand in the context of their own 'guided' media.

The Challenge of the Crescent Moon

Islam is indeed a topic calculated to raise the hairs on the back of many an Australian neck. This reaction stems from a blend of ignorance and blind fear. Australians are not alone in this.

People in Middle Eastern dress, especially women in veils, are too visibly different on Australian streets. Iraqi president Saddam Hussein's Gulf War in 1990–91 hardly helped. It will take great patience and tolerance on both sides if this barrier is to be breached.

It certainly was alarming to hear white Australian residents on the eastern side of Australia reacting to the prospect of a mosque being erected in their neighbourhood. They howled their opposition. Their reason: property values would slump (unfortunately, possible), and 'the kiddies wouldn't be safe to walk home,' as one woman-in-the-street put it to the TV cameras, a revelation of shocking prejudice.

But on the more positive side, when I tuned in to an ABC radio programme on the subject of Iraq, during the Gulf War, while fully expecting to hear more of the same, I was pleasantly surprised. (The topic was whether or not Iraqis and the Arabs in Australia—particularly Australians with Arab ancestry—should be allowed to demonstrate against Australia's anti-Iraq stand, as they had already done.)

Many of those who called into the radio station were themselves migrants to Australia way back, just after World War II—from Britain, from Germany, from Eastern Europe. Of 15 callers, seven said, No, Arabs in Australia should not be allowed to demonstrate against Australian government policy, while a majority of eight said, Yes, absolutely, they must have the same democratic right to protest as other Australians, but they must not be allowed to burn the Australian flag, or commit acts of violence.

Just for the record, there was one caller who declared flatly: 'No I reckon we should not have Arabs in this country. I reckon they are all mad.'

But try telling all this to my Singaporean-Malay and Muslim friend, who is married to an Australian girl of Roman Catholic Italian parentage, Cindy, and lives in Perth (which, like many other Australian cities, is well supplied with Islamic 'halal' butchers). Cindy is now a good Muslim—the couple have found a mosque in Perth to attend every Friday—and she produces fine Malaysian food every year for the Muslim feast of Ramadan, at the end of the fasting month, clad in traditional Malay dress.

Does she ever get teased or harassed about her new religion? 'No, no—not at all,' she smiles gently. End of conversation.

The Japanese

Then there is the Australian unease about the Japanese, who admittedly own huge chunks of their country, most notably in Queensland, where they hold about 93 per cent of all foreign-owned hotel rooms, for example.

This unease is deepened by actual or culturally inherited memories of the Pacific War during World War II, in which Australian soldiers, like many others, suffered bitterly at the hands of the Japanese.

I have already remarked elsewhere that it is a serious impediment to happiness in Australia not to be able to speak English. The Japanese often suffer from this inability. Columnist Ruth Ostrow, writing in *The Weekend Australian*, reported with outrage how a Japanese tourist was made fun of in a Gold Coast hotel bar. He kept ordering Scotch without ice. Each time, it came back with ice. 'No locks, no locks!' he kept yelling. The waitress and staff erupted into giggles every time.

If nothing else, Australia's A$14 billion tourism industry needs Asia. In 1996, Japan supplied 20 per cent of the total four million tourists, with Korea and Malaysia growing rapidly. Estimates in 1996 suggested that by 2005, six out of every 10 visitors to Australia will be from Asia.

The Asian Future

But Australia knows she must come to terms with Asia, as a matter of economic survival if nothing else.

On the other hand, two-thirds of the companies recently surveyed by the Australian Department of Employment, Education and Training were exporting 85 per cent of their sales to English-speaking countries. With the huge single markets of Europe and America-Canada-Mexico looming large on the world stage and likely to turn in on themselves, this hardly seems wise.

And, by 1990, International Monetary Fund figures already showed per capita GNP in countries like Singapore (US$9,620) and Hong Kong (US$8,418) to be edging close to Australia's US$12,590, while Japan had already left Australia behind, with its per capita GNP of US$19,553. There has been much talk in Australia of late about the 'middle-classing' of Asia: a belated recognition of the buying power in Asia's markets.

Besides, within the next 40 years, something like 20 per cent of Australia's population is likely to be of Asian origin. Australia will not only be a part of Asia, as it must be on the basis of geography alone, but Asia will already be a part of Australia.

NATION

National Flag The Australian Blue Ensign (for merchant ships, the Australian Red Ensign). This blue flag has a British Union Jack in the upper left corner, closest to the flagpole, with the seven-pointed Commonwealth star below it; to the right are the five stars of the Southern Cross constellation, identified as 'Crux Australis' as early as 1679, seen only in southern skies such as Australia's. Now that talk of a Republic is active, there is a lobby for a completely new 'Ausflag', possibly using the national colours of green and gold. But the debate is by no means over yet.

National Animal Emblem Kangaroo.

National Flower Emblem The Golden Wattle. Australia boasts about 900 species of this desert-adapted tree or shrub, which belongs to the Mimosa family within the Acacia genus.

National Colours Green and gold.

National Coat of Arms Granted in 1912 by King George V of England, the shield is supported by a kangaroo and an emu amid branches of wattle.

National Anthem Up to 1974, the British national anthem, *God Save The Queen*, was also Australia's, but in 1974 a national poll replaced it with the 19th century song *Advance Australia Fair*. *God Save The Queen* is now only played when the Queen herself or her representative, the Governor-General, is present.

Chapter Four

BEING A MIGRANT

'The lazy country will be the lovely country, the white society will be
the honey-coloured society, and the ugly duckling will become a
honey-coloured swan.'
—Dr Stephen Fitzgerald, Australia's first ambassador to China, as
head of the University of New South Wales Asia Centre,
in *The West Australian*, November 24, 1990.

This chapter is not a detailed guide to the labyrinth of getting permission to migrate to Australia. It just gives a snapshot of what it is like to be a migrant, and what migration has meant to Australia.

Even if I wanted to give you a detailed 'how to do it' guide, I doubt I could. For a start, the rules of the immigration game change fairly often—signposts to change usually are imminent federal elections and economic upheaval. The current recession has put the Labor government under further pressure to restrict immigration on the grounds that it is useless to import more people if you cannot give them jobs. There does seem to be some sense in this argument, if you view it objectively. As a result of economic recession, making Australia less attractive to migrants, and lowering government quotas, immigration levels are now down to about 80,000 a year.

Some analysts sincerely feel that mass immigration, peaking at 172,000 newcomers in 1988, the year when recommendations that the level be fixed at 140,000 per year in future were accepted by the government, takes out of the economy more than it contributes.

There is also the fear of potential social tension, hitherto largely and happily avoided.

The Shifting Sands of Immigration Policy

As an example of the rapid shifts in policy, when I was applying to migrate, in the mid-1980s, it was possible to become a Business Migrant and virtually buy your way into Australia providing you could prove you had A$500,000 capital to invest, a business to run, and enough funds to keep yourself and your family for a set period of time. (I hasten to add that this did not apply to me.) Some 9000 business migrants were admitted to Australia on this basis between 1983 and 1991, bringing in A$1.5 billion. It was also possible to bring in your aged parents once you yourself had settled in Australia for a while, on the grounds of 'family reunion'.

Another category of accepted migrant at that time was the foreign man or woman who intended marriage with an Australian, or even

Sydney's old Queen Victoria Building was restored as a shopping arcade by Asian investment. Photo by Siva Choy.

those who had a *de facto* rather than a *de jure* relationship with an Australian—in other words, whether they were going to get married or not.

By 1991, all three of these programmes had disappeared, largely because of migrants' abuse of the system. The Business Migrant programme was revamped because cunning would-be migrants, many of them Asian, were simply recycling lumps of money from one applicant to the next, and then failing to run a business in Australia. Now business skills and capital are checked carefully. In 1996 alone, business migrants brought in about A$850 million.

At the time of writing, the rule on importing aged parents is that the parent in question must already have half or more of all their children settled in Australia, otherwise, sorry, the door is closed.

As for the migration-for-marriage scheme, naturally that led to so many marriage-of-convenience scams, with Australian girls often being paid handsomely to go through mock marriages with foreign-

Alec Fong Lim, late Mayor of Darwin, a symbol of what the migrant can achieve in Australia.

ers, that it had to be curbed. The sad result is that genuine lovers now have to go through a lot more hoops to prove that their marriage to an Australian is bona fide before they can get residence in Australia.

The Grey Face of Australian Bureaucracy

Sometimes the rules are uncomfortably vague. For example, there has been a great deal of confusion over how long you have to stay in Australia to confirm your permanent residence as a migrant. As a migrant myself, I have never received any official written or verbal instruction on this matter. Here again, you see a fine example of how grey areas develop in Australian policy, purely because Australians have a democratic horror of the tyranny of rigid law: this leaves everyone in the dark.

However, it also means there is flexibility—a smile and a nod could well win the day, whereas in many other countries, rules are rules, and there's no way round them.

It is true, at the time of writing, that if you want to apply for Australian citizenship, you must spend 24 months in Australia, not necessarily consecutively, within your first three-year migrant's visa, or within your first five years in Australia—which is in fact a very generous provision. If you want simple renewal of your three-year migrant residence visa for another 12 months you will need to show 12 months' (non-consecutive) residence in Australia within the first three years. Spouses of Australian citizens will more easily get a five-year renewal.

But it's anyone's guess half the time, and really, the horse's mouth has to be your local Australian High Commission or Embassy. Note that policy changes can be dramatic at times of elections (compulsorily every three years), especially if there is a change of ruling party.

Familiarisation Techniques

Would-be migrants would be well advised to read the Australian press for at least a year before they make their move. I myself subscribed to *The Weekend Australian* for a year before I migrated, and picked up the odd copy of my local *The West Australian* daily whenever I could find one. *The Age* of Melbourne and the *Australian Financial Review,* besides the weekly *The Bulletin,* are also good backgrounders.

It's a good idea too to have visited Australia before you decide to migrate there. This may sound like unnecessary advice, but not if my husband is anything to go by: a Singaporean-Indian, he was determined to migrate there without ever having set foot in the country.

Because he is black, I was just a wee bit nervous and insisted he travel across the country both with and without me first. This he did—and came back singing its praises even more loudly. So we filled in the forms, got all our official documents legally certified in multiplicate (a tedious and expensive business) and settled down to something like an 18-month wait before we got the good news.

71

The Questions Some Migrants Ask

Unquestionably the funniest experience we had in the migration process was the group counselling session at the Australian High Commission in Singapore. Once upon a time, it had been possible to offer individual counselling interviews to accepted migrants, but as numbers rose, this was abandoned in favour of group meetings.

The questions we heard asked by the predominantly Asian-Singaporean migrants at our session boggled the imagination. I take my hat off to the extremely patient immigration officer who had to handle them. She did so in typically Australian dry, wry style.

The session kicked off with 'When I come to Australia, can I bring my servant with me?' No, was the answer, ours is a do-it-yourself society. A shy couple was worried: considering the strict quarantine laws, could they bring into Australia the kangaroo skin which they had bought in Australia on a holiday? 'No worries' was the not unexpected answer to that one.

A strapping young man with no apparent health problems was extremely interested in how soon after landing he could qualify for Medicare (the subsidised medical service), the dole (social welfare payments for the unemployed) and a state pension. One could somehow guess what direction he was going in and I am sure the beleaguered immigration officer privately labelled him a potential bludger on the spot (see the Glossary in Chapter Two).

Agitated beyond belief was a Chinese man who asked whether or not he could regularly import Chinese dried mushrooms to Australia after setting up home there. Life, it seemed, would be meaningless without them. Food-import controls were strict, said the officer, and anyway, Australia grew perfectly good mushrooms of her own. No, no, insisted the Chinese, I mean our black mushrooms, our *Chinese* ones, you know? The implication seemed to be that no Australian mushroom could ever be a match for a Chinese one.

Of course, yours truly, being English, was concerned only whether or not she could import her pet dog. The answer to that one is, only if you want to go through a very long, expensive and potentially traumatic quarantine clearance process. For example, if I had wanted to take my dog from Singapore to Australia, it would have had to be cleared first for six months at an approved centre outside of Asia, like London or Hawaii, after which it would undergo three more months of quarantine in Australia itself. I could not countenance either the expense of the implied airfares and kennelling charges or the emotional trauma to the dog. She stayed put in Singapore.

You Can Take It with You

What *can* you take into Australia when you go? Probably everything you own, although as much as possible should be over 12 months old, and you should have the documentation to prove this.

When my husband and I first landed, we had a typed checklist of the property we were carrying with us (including a large fax machine I had refused to ship, because I needed it immediately for work), complete with every item's value, age and serial number. This was much appreciated by Customs, and speeded clearance considerably.

The rest of the documentation should be handled by your freight-forwarding agent, who will let you know whether or not you are required to be present for a meeting with Customs when your cargo arrives. In our case, we were not.

Some items can be a particular problem: for example wooden objects or cane/bamboo/rattan may be treated as a hazard to Australian agriculture because of the bugs they may hide, and this will mean careful fumigation at the very least. Once again, with such problems, you should check carefully on the latest rules with your nearest Australian government representative office.

But remember, once you have taken up residence in Australia, you will be travelling as an Australian; when you re-enter Australia, your allowance for purchases (such as radios from Singapore and the like) will be restricted to a value of A$400 per head. Anything above that must be declared, with a supporting document proving its sale value.

If you are travelling regularly in and out of Australia with an expensive item of equipment—a lap-top computer, say—we have found it useful to ask Customs to note down the serial number on a Customs form before leaving Australia, so that you can later prove you did not buy it on your trip abroad and are therefore not liable for duty. Customs will often tell you there is no need to worry when you first approach them with this one, but we suggest you insist in case the next Customs officer is less understanding.

In general, when returning to Australia, we have found that honest declaration when in doubt really pays. On the few occasions when we have had to pay duty, we have always found it very reasonable, being usually around 20% of the sale value, above your A$400 allowance.

Toughing It Out

But don't get too smart by arranging for under-invoicing at a fantastic bargain-basement price; Australian Customs officers know very well what are the likely selling prices for most items, whether you are coming from Singapore or from London. Like Customs officers everywhere, they react pretty brutally if they discover you have been trying to take them for a ride.

Be careful too with illicitly-copied computer software: Australia strictly enforces copyright protection laws.

Never, ever try to sneak in food or plant material (that includes cut roses and orchids, Mum's home-made jam and Auntie's fantastic curry powder) without declaring it. It's a very serious offence. You may get it approved if you declare it; or like my friend with the tupperware of unwrapped smelly cheese he didn't want to leave behind in his fridge at home, you might not.

Everyone has had at least one horror story with Australian Immigration/Customs officials. They can be toughies, although they come on initially with brighter smiles and more friendly chat than any of their counterparts worldwide. At least, the men do. So relax. But take my tip: never get in the queue for a woman immigration or Customs officer's desk. I would like to be more sisterly, but for some reason, they are much nastier than the men.

I shall not easily forget one such unsmiling lady at Perth airport who had our entire luggage searched, apparently for drugs, just because we had travelled in and out of Malaysia once too often for her liking. Nor how she thrust her hands triumphantly into the tatty, torn silk lining of my suitcase—at last, a false bottom—flipped suspiciously through the pages of my notebooks, and even had my Indonesian wooden puppets' heads X-rayed for secret compartments.

By comparison, the men are more laid-back, but therefore also fallible. Although emotionally scarred, we survived one of our migrant residence visas being accidentally cancelled at the airport (inspect your passport carefully to see what has been done before you leave the airport)—a frightening discovery made only just before our next flight.

On balance, though, a cool temper combined with a modest and pleasant demeanour will see you through. No showing off, please. One well-heeled Chinese visitor learned his lesson. Asked what he had come to Australia for, he facetiously replied, 'To spend money.' This was not a sensitive remark in the context of the Australian recession and the average Customs officer's salary. Needless to say, they took him apart.

What Use Are Migrants?

Why then, does Australia want migrants? Well, some segments of Australian society in fact do not want them at all. Others, possibly as much as half the population, would prefer them to come from white Europe. But all major political parties currently accept migration as necessary. Australia must have more people than its current 17.7

million, to gain economic strength, to build a bigger internal market. (There is a contrary minority view, however, which holds that immigration may well exceed the unique, desert-bound Australian ecology's natural 'carrying capacity' for a limited number of humans.)

Disagreements tend to focus on how many should be admitted, and what type—European or Asian, skilled or unskilled, English-speaking or not, and so on. In the old days, it was believed that the only way to resist the 'Yellow Peril' from the north was to breed and multiply—'Populate or Perish', the slogan went. Nowadays, the official credo is that, to integrate with the booming economies of Asia, Australia needs Asian immigration.

Immigration doesn't just make money by stimulating the economy; it makes money *per se*. Migrants brought A$4.3 billion into Australia in 1989 alone, making immigration the nation's third biggest earner after tourism and wool at the time.

The same things are said about unwanted immigrants all over the world, no matter which cultures are involved: they contribute to social disorder, they cause rises in crime, they import new diseases, they pinch local jobs ... In Australia, they said it about the Greeks and Italians, even the British, when they first arrived; they say it now about the Vietnamese, Chinese and Japanese—and some of the people saying it today are in fact Italian-Australians, British-Australians and the like, former migrants themselves.

Each generation of immigrants must undergo its own baptism of fire, emerging tempered from the crucible.

A Migrant Nation

Much is said nowadays about Asian migration to Australia. It is sometimes forgotten that between mid-1947 and the end of 1951, Australia took in 170,000 of post-World War II Europe's 12 million displaced people. There is a fascinating account of this programme, written both from the point of view of Immigration officers and migrants in a study titled *Angels and Arrogant Gods,* from the Australian Commonwealth Government Publishing Service.

At first it was 'whites only, please'. Migrant Britons were offered financially-assisted passage to Australia from 1946 to 1982, when the practice was discontinued. Many an Asian and other migrant today arrives by plane with a substantial bank balance (having sold a house back home), a container-load of possessions and university qualifications to boot.

It is humbling to reflect on the fact that those early European migrants often arrived in Australia only after a harrowing journey aboard an overcrowded ship, without a penny in their pockets and committed to a compulsory work contract (usually hard manual labour) with the Australian government in some remote corner of the country, where they were housed in makeshift huts at best.

You had to stay two years before the government would even give you your passport back. But then, where you had come from, you didn't even have food …

Such were the original New Australians. There was no talk about 'multiculturalism' in those days. You were supposed to become Australian, as quickly and as convincingly as possible.

It was not until Gough Whitlam's Labor Party came to power in 1972 that the racist immigration policy was finally laid to rest. In 1976, the first Senior Immigration Officer was appointed to an Asian posting. These changes came just in time to accommodate the Vietnamese boat-people refugees of the 1970s. By 1986, Australia had taken in more than 100,000 Indochinese refugees. The total number of refugees from all sources taken into Australia between 1945 and 1985, however, was a massive 430,000.

Before mass migration programmes began, back in 1947, fewer than one in 10 Australians had been born outside the country. The population then was about seven million. Today, about a quarter of Australians are either first or second-generation immigrants and more than two-thirds are of mixed ethnic origin. Australia is a country of 130 nations. Some Sydney suburbs are 42 per cent of non-English speaking origin. By 2021, the total population should be about 25 million if present migration patterns continue. By the year 2010, say some studies, the Chinese-origin population of Australia alone could exceed one million. But still, in 1996, one-third of new settlers came from Europe and the former Soviet Union.

Multiculturalism—Handle with Care

Beyond simple migration, the Labor government has further espoused multiculturalism within Australia and has put its money where its mouth is.

Multiculturalism is reckoned to cost the Federal and State Governments about A$514 million a year, or about A$30 for each Australian, revealed *The Australian* newspaper in its own 1991 investigation. These costs are incurred in a range of activities, from the Special Broadcasting Service (SBS) catering to minority culture, to ethnic language booklets on everything under the sun and English-as-a-second-language programmes.

This policy worries even some proponents of Asian migration, let alone conservatives concerned with preserving Australia's British heritage. They worry about 'ghetto-ism'.

The recent upheavals in Eastern Europe amply demonstrated the problem, as did the Gulf War of 1990–91: émigré communities of Serbs and Croats in Australia avoided, or attacked, one another in tandem with the factions developing in what was Yugoslavia, while Romanian-Australians denounced the Ceausescu 'moles' in their midst after the Romanian revolutionaries had despatched their former dictator. I even know of a Eurasian group which has fractured along lines demarcated by whether one is of Dutch/English or Portuguese origin.

Many migrants and refugees have, perhaps understandably, imported their domestic political and social problems into Australia.

These nations within a nation have made many uneasy.

This is an ongoing debate, as it is in some other countries too, such as Britain: should migrants be forced or persuaded into cultural integration? For instance, can Muslims be obliged to submit to Australian customs and laws?

America demonstrates that there can be solutions. I myself am confident that Australia too will cope, eventually. 'She'll be right.'

Rubbing Shoulders with the World

As a migrant yourself, you may well find multiculturalism exciting. For the first time, you will find yourself side by side with exotic cultures you never dreamed of encountering before.

How, for instance, could my Sri Lankan engineer friend ever have guessed he would end up marrying a Colombian girl in Australia? Listening to the interplay of this family's three different accents when conversing together in English at their Australian dinner-table is something of a treat: his voice still heavily Indian-inflected, hers distinctly Spanish, and their little girl's, why Australian, of course.

You may have to be more careful than you were before. I have already mentioned how problematic 'Irish jokes' may be in the wrong company. There are other potential social gaffes to avoid: you may find it next to impossible to mix your Serb and Croat friends from Yugoslavia, for example, and it would be most ill-advised to invite an Armenian and a Turk, or a Tamil and a Sinhalese, together for tea.

Yet multiculturalism is a furnace in which hitherto unheard-of new alliances may be forged: I think, for instance, of the Portugal Day hosted by the Portuguese Consul in Perth, which saw peoples of all the former Portuguese colonies come together in song, dance and festivity: from Indonesian Timor, from African Mozambique, from Latin American Brazil, from Goa in India, from Malacca in Malaysia and from Macau off China. And yet they were all Australians too.

Indeed, one's definition of an 'Australian' blurs somewhat when confronted with pedigrees like those of my friends. Former residents of Singapore, they now live in Perth. My girlfriend's mother was born in Shanghai and looks Chinese, but doesn't speak the language. (Her parents were Czech-Japanese on one side, Irish-Chinese on the other.) My girlfriend's father, on the other hand, was a Latvian who had fled his Baltic home-state during the Russian Revolution of 1917, to Shanghai via Siberia; in Shanghai, he had been adopted by a benevolent Iraqi-Jewish opium trader.

This couple got out of China in 1954, using the wife's part-Czech descent as a pretext for exit. And so to Singapore, where my ostensibly Singaporean, now Australian, girlfriend was born to them.

My girlfriend's husband is a mixed Irish-Eurasian from Singapore. Should anyone be surprised that their little girl has turned out fair and freckled of skin, with stunning red hair? I challenge anyone to top this family on the multiculturalism scoreboard.

Multiculturalism and the promotion of ethnic politics has led to ethnic lobbying. Former Malaysian-Chinese Dr Eric Tan, a prominent surgeon and community leader in Perth, has a shrewd idea of future directions. Himself an 'Asian-Australian' for 30 years now, he told me, 'You can expect a trend towards the Chinese community entering Australian politics Australia-wide.'

It seems a Chinese-Australian Prime Minister of Australia may well be on the cards. There is already one Bill O'Chee of Queensland, at 24 the youngest person ever elected to the Australian Senate (for the National Party, straight from the rural heartlands), in 1990, whose grandfather was China-born but Irish-ised his name to 'O'Chee' to fob off Australian racism. Bill's mother is Irish, his father Chinese.

Integration without Tears

You, as a migrant, should at least be sensitive to Australian concerns about multiculturalism. It is natural, and also helpful in the initial stages of migration, to turn to support organisations comprising your former compatriots. In every Australian city, you will find the right club for yourself: Greek, Italian, Polish, Serb, Croat, Tamil, Malayalee, Sri Lankan, Timorese, Eurasian, Singaporean or what-have-you.

But you would do well to make an effort to meet Australians by joining some of their activities too—from your street Neighbourhood Watch (crime-watch) committee, to the local church, the local heritage/history society, or a nature-walking group. Trouble is, you find that many of the 'Australians' around you prove to be migrants too. But even this discovery serves to make you feel more at home, less of an oddity.

Remember that Australia is remarkable for the ease with which you can strike up a conversation with a stranger. Don't be shy, speak up if you want to make friends, whether on the bus or when picking up the children from school along with other parents. This dictum applies especially to naturally conservative Asians.

Remember too that elaborate structures are already in existence to help migrants: consult your local phone directory for contact with bodies like the Ethnic Communities Council or the Multicultural and Ethnic Affairs Commission. Ask them for advice, and the contacts for other migrant assistance centres.

As for general information, if you look up your phone directory listing for Recorded Information Services, or letter 'D' for 'Dial-It', you will be astounded at the range of things you can find out over the phone. Similarly, Australia excels in the prolific production of first-class information leaflets and brochures. A browsing session at your local library, Council and other local government offices, as well as hospitals, and medical and migrant resource centres, will harvest a sheaf of such literature.

Take an active interest in Australian politics and social issues by reading the local press; sample typical Australian activities, such as the local footy (Australian rules football) or cricket matches. Watch television and listen to the radio; make a point of seeing the latest Australian movies and plays, art exhibitions and so on. This will help you converse with Australians on their own ground.

If, by any chance, your English is less than perfect, work on it. The language is crucial to your integration.

Mum's the Word about Home

In the same box comes the problem of the 'Back home, we do it this way …' syndrome. Avoid at all costs making public comparisons, particularly invidious ones, between your motherland and your newly adopted home, Australia. This goes down very badly with Australians. Put yourself in their place and this becomes very easy to understand. Also taboo — and many Asian migrants need to learn this — is talking about money and the cost of things (property, cars) all the time. Listen, Look and Learn—But Keep Quiet.

The Migrant Blues

No matter how gungho you have been initially about making a new life in Australia, there will come those moments when you feel depressed, alienated … You wonder if you have made a mistake. This applies to all—and I include those of Anglo-Saxon background, who may be all the more shocked to discover how 'foreign' Australia can be. How much more, non-European migrants.

In many ways, the respectable, older middle-class migrant may suffer more, and more silently, from culture shock than a refugee. For refugees, there are all sorts of support and aid groups. For simple migrants—once you land, you're on your own, mate. The older you are, the harder it is. You will find that your young children, in contrast, take to it like a duck to water.

You must accept that it usually takes something like two or three years before you feel comfortable, begin to 'fit'. Whatever you do, don't give up before you have given it a go for a couple of years. Believe that it will get better. Statistics show that migrants usually quit within the first three years, but rarely later than that.

It's the little things that get you down.

For those used to lively, noisy city streets and housing estates at night, it can be the lack of people, the silence of the dimly lit streets of suburbia. Residential areas resemble menacing black holes at night: Australians seem to live mostly at the back of the house, turning off all the lights at the front as an economy measure, leaving a faceless and unwelcoming streetscape.

A Singaporean Malay friend in Perth recently bought a plot of land and decided to build his own house on it. When I looked at his plans, I exclaimed, 'But why have you chosen to live so close to a highway?'

'It's the silence,' said he. 'I just can't stand it. I just have to have more noise, else I get lonely.' Some call it peaceful, others lonely.

No more food-stalls or cafés in the street, unlike Singapore, Kuala Lumpur, Athens or Paris. Faced with steep restaurant prices and early closing times, you do more home entertaining than ever before. Not a soul on the streets; and it's not all that safe to walk the streets alone at night, either. And in the winter, well, you wouldn't want to.

Beaten, you retreat behind the four walls of your home like the rest of Australia. Having read the over-active local press for the latest, often horrific, crime stories, you fearfully lock up the house and barricade your bedroom door with chairs for good measure.

Unfortunately, in the setting of Australia's high unemployment rate of around 10 per cent, or more, fear of crime is justified. It was only yesterday that Perth-dwellers still left their doors and windows open all the time, and never locked their cars, but alas, no more. I myself was greeted by a friendly brick through my window before I even moved into my new house. Just a minor burglary attempt, but still …

I got a burglar alarm and paid a monthly fee to connect it to a monitoring station that would call the police if it went off. I would recommend a dog too if you have the time to maintain one, as well as metal grille-reinforcements to windows and doors.

Transportation

If you have never driven before, which was the case with me, thanks to tiny Singapore's excellent public transportation and punitive car costs, those four walls of home quickly become a cosy cage.

The transportation situation is the reverse in huge Australia. One of the keys to happiness in Australia is having a driving licence: don't leave without it. (If you hold one already, you'll probably only need to pass a simple oral test within a few months of arrival in Australia in order to convert it to an Australian licence—but check this with your local police station.)

Mum, your favourite nanny, is no longer just around the corner; your best friend no longer just a phone call away.

More Bummers

For those accustomed to 24-hour shopping—as many Asians are—it takes some getting used to that one must get to the shops by 5.30 p.m. on a weekday. Or to remember that Thursday is late shopping night (in Perth, anyway). Forget Sundays (except for that nice Thai lady's delicatessen shop, and the Asian food centre).

Some migrants, especially Asians, are uncomfortable with the degree of freedom and free speech they find in Australia. They feel bombarded by brutal frankness, harassed by the sight of nudity and sex on television and in the cinema. In a way, they miss the firm framework of stricter rules and the soothing absence of moral choice. They are used to governments making decisions for them, like proxy parents. But suddenly, nobody cares what they do. So they feel uncared for—freedom too can create culture shock.

Another bummer, to use an Australian phrase, is the Australian pace of work, much slower than say, a Singaporean, a Hongkonger or an American might be used to. One former executive with a multi-national corporation, whom I know resigned in frustration from a civil service job, told me, 'I was going crazy, just twiddling my thumbs doing nothing all day. I had finished my work!' Needless to say, she wasn't very popular with her laid-back Aussie colleagues. Another rule—don't show off by working too hard if you want to be loved. Or work hard, but disguise it somehow.

More serious is the discovery on arrival, too late, that your professional qualifications are not valid in Australia. This is a very common problem, so do check carefully what you need to do to requalify for work in Australia, well before you arrive. Otherwise you will join the growing band of doctors, teachers and engineers running take-away food shops or struggling on student study grants.

Awful Things That Could Happen
You learn the hard way about certain basics of Australian life: if you forget to leave the rubbish bin out on the kerb for emptying on the appointed day (usually once a week only), too bad. After the third visit in a week from a door-to-door canvasser for charity, you learn to say 'No,' or ask them to send a letter instead.

You thought that swimming pool in the back garden a great idea, but now you find it costs a bomb to maintain in tip-top condition, the local Council has passed a rule on regular pool inspections (charging you an inspection fee for good measure) and any pools considered too accessible to children (your own or other people's) must be surrounded by an ugly isolation fence that will cost the earth to install.

You are terrified of your first winter after many years of living in the tropics, so you decide to order three tons of firewood in advance. Trouble is, there was no arrangement for when exactly it would be delivered. The wood arrives while you are out. It has been dumped in the back lane outside your garden fence, a good distance from your woodshed. You spend the next three days trudging back and forth with wheelbarrows and baskets to transport it all into the woodshed.

Yes, all this has happened to me.

Children Change

Luckily, however, I am not a parent. Migrant parents get upset when their children show signs of assimilating too well.

Singaporean friends of mine were typically protective Asian parents: they were driving their young son to and from school every day. But the boy soon asserted his new identity, demanding the same independence as his Australian schoolmates, who were all left to cycle to school by themselves. He didn't want to be seen as a sissy by his peers; he was going to be an Australian. The parents agonised for some time over road safety before giving way.

More serious identity problems may surface later. All that a migrant parent can do is be ready for these when they come, and perhaps just try to live with them.

Although such parents invariably will assure you that they migrated 'for the sake of the children', paradoxically they are filled with dread at the thought that their offspring may become loud, boorish and rebellious, or generally fall victim to sex, drugs and rock 'n' roll, as it were. Some kids do indeed react against their own background. That is a natural part of their adjustment process and must be accepted as such. The first symptom of mutation is the child's changing accent.

I witnessed an extreme teenage reaction to Malaysian roots. Gathering together for a home-cooked curry, the adults sat down with gusto to whack the goodies in time-honoured Malaysian fashion: with their fingers. When the family's daughter arrived home with her Australian friends, loud expressions of disgust were heard from her. The adults understandably told her to get lost. From the girl's point of view, she had been shamed before Aussie mates by her parents' primitive table manners, quite unacceptable to an Australian.

Yet I have also seen the Australian children of first-generation migrants cheering for their motherland's soccer team in matches against Australian teams. So you never can tell ...

Australian education in democracy and rights can make a parent's life perilous indeed. My Eurasian lawyer friend from Singapore got his comeuppance when he discovered that his Australian-born teenage daughter had reported him to the local Human Rights and Equal Opportunity Commission for giving her a typical Asian 'tight slap' over some minor cheek the day before. She should have reported him to the local welfare authorities; but the incident did give him some pause for thought about brats' rights as he prepared his defence ...

Admirable environmental education in Australian schools can also produce annoying little home preachers, demanding you buy only dolphin-friendly, ozone-friendly and recycled-paper products.

On the Positive Side

It would be negligent not to warn you of the migrant blues. But there is a brighter side, some of which I hope will emerge in other sections of this book. Among the plus points are the exhilarating experience of freedom, space, and that special bright light that the Australian climate and geography produce. Enlightened attitudes to medicine, to education and to the environment abound. There is an easy friendliness on the streets and the peacefulness of daily life—and real, wild democracy. There is the excitement of a vast, largely wild land.

You may decide you like it all so much that you want to become an Australian citizen. Check on your own country's rules about dual citizenship (allowing it or not allowing it) before you take the plunge.

Having spent 24 non-consecutive months within your first five years in Australia, you are eligible to apply, and the letter confirming your citizenship can come as quickly as a surprising two weeks after you apply. The ceremony at which you receive your Certificate of Australian Citizenship, necessary before you can get an Australian passport (without which you cannot safely leave and re-enter Australia once you are an Australian national), could be a few more weeks. Here is one new citizen's account of the modest ceremony at which he received his citizenship, in Perth, Western Australia:

'We all trooped off to the Mayor's office, me and my two witnesses (you are not allowed more than two). On the seats in this room upstairs was a small package with our name tags on and a leaflet explaining our rights and duties as citizens. Altogether, our group of new citizens numbered 30.

'The Mayor's deputy made a speech and then they called us up in groups of about four or five to recite the oath of allegiance to Queen Elizabeth II (that probably won't go on much longer) and the country. … The Mayor shook our hands and gave us our certs, and also a little badge with the Aussie flag on it for us to wear. Then we posed with the Mayor for a photo if we wished, holding up our certs.

Chapter Five

DREAMTIME AUSTRALIA: THE ABORIGINALS

'There's nothing I would rather be
than to be an Aborigine
and dream of just what
Heaven
must be like
where moth and rust do
not corrupt
when I die I know I'll be
going up
'cos you know that I've
had my hell on earth—
Here I live in
this tin shack
Nothing here worth
coming back to
drunken fights and
awful sights
People drunk most
every night.
On the way to
a Bran Nu Dae
Everybody every body
say ...'

—from Bran Nu Dae, an Aboriginal musical,
written by Jimmy Chi of Broome, Western Australia

89

If I begin simply by saying that this chapter is a minefield for the unfortunate author, you may get part of the picture.

There is no topic more sensitive in Australia—although the Anzacs and Gallipoli come a close second—than the Aboriginals. Approach the subject with caution; as I have said before, better shut up and listen, than put your foot in your mouth.

For a country as dedicated to the pursuit of democracy and human rights—and as critical of South Africa's track record—as Australia is, the 'Aboriginal problem' is a particularly painful Achilles heel. Every Australian, and every visitor, whether migrant or tourist, confronts 'the problem' sooner or later, and deals with it in his or her own way, sometimes with grace, but often with guilty resentment, or angry aggression.

Aboriginal children in Northern Territory outback. Photo by the author.

On the other hand, it is also very easy indeed to live in Australia without getting to know any Aboriginals, even without seeing any, particularly if you live in the larger cities. For many Australians, they remain but shadows on the fringes of life, phantoms that flit through the newspaper headlines.

For Americans conscious of their nation's lamentable track record with their own Indians, for white South Africans and for many others, Australia's problem is a case of *déjà vu*. Wherever we come from, we can probably conjure up other examples in the world which do not necessarily counterpoint only whites and non-whites; many a 'coloured' migrant race too has dominated another, weaker, similarly 'coloured' native race—in Southeast Asia and elsewhere.

What is 'the problem' in Australia? Basically, it is the spectacle of an underclass, which happens to be black, disadvantaged in almost every way, pushed to the fringes of society, so demoralised that it also seems to be bent on committing mass suicide in a variety of ways. And this in the midst of relative, white affluence.

They Came First

The Aboriginals themselves would prefer to be called names from their own languages: Koorie in the east and south (meaning 'Our People'), Nyunga in Western Australia, Yoingu in the Northern Territory, Anangu in central Australia and Nungga in South Australia.

These names, however, have not caught on to any great extent within white Australia, even less so in the world beyond Australia. For this reason, I am using the more conventional 'Aboriginal' in this chapter, with no insinuations attached.

'The First Australians' is the phrase most favoured among Australian liberals nowadays when referring to the original, black Australians, who may have come to Australia from Southeast Asia at least 40,000 years ago. Indeed, the Aboriginals' curly hair, blue-black skins, spread noses and thick lips are reminiscent of the peoples of southern India and Papua New Guinea. My Tamil husband is convinced they are fellow Tamils and prehistoric geography does make this conceivable. He is often approached in the street by Aboriginals as a 'brother'.

The term 'First Australians' serves to remind all Australians, whether migrant or of many generations' standing, that they are all newcomer settlers to some degree, compared with the Aboriginals. If you are a migrant 'new Australian', do not expect Aboriginal Australians to find common cause with you as a fellow minority, not even if you happen to be black.

For the Aboriginals, post-World War II migrant settlement of Australia has simply added to their woes, adding yet more human strata above them, further blurring their claim to real ownership of the country. Immigration has pinned them even more firmly at the bottom of the social pile.

Australia's most famous old-generation Aboriginal politician, lawyer and Martin Luther King-style freedom fighter, Charlie Perkins, Australia's first Aboriginal university graduate in 1965, expressed this feeling when he spoke out roundly condemning Asian immigration in the mid-1980s.

Statistical Phantoms

Aboriginals are thought to have numbered around 300,000–500,000, perhaps even more, when the Europeans arrived in Australia in 1788. The fact that their population had fallen to around 22,000 by 1860, as the European population zoomed above one million, speaks tragic volumes. But nobody really knows the true statistics, because Aboriginals were non-persons in census terms right up to 1967.

When the whites first arrived in Australia, they declared it an 'empty land', *Terra Nullius*, as if it were uninhabited. This was very convenient as it obviated the usual legal need to negotiate any kind of lease with traditional owners; the land could simply be taken. As writer John Pilger has put it in his *A Secret Country*, the Aboriginals were not accounted human but rather 'part of the fauna'.

Now the Aboriginals are known to number in the region of 230,000—the numbers rose from 160,000 to over 227,000 between

1982 and 1987 alone. This startling rise is in part due to a real improvement in their treatment, and to a higher than average birth rate, but partly also to the increasing acceptability of declaring publicly one's aboriginality, even in the case of mixed-bloods. In the bad old days, mixed-bloods—'half-castes' as they were called then—were barred by law from claiming Aboriginal ancestry.

Only in 1967 did a referendum produce a 90.8% popular vote to recognise Aboriginals as Australian citizens (which unfortunately for many of them, also gave them for the first time the legal right to drink alcohol), but their right to vote under exactly the same, compulsory, conditions as other Australians was not enacted until as late as 1984.

Trauma of a Nation

The Europeans brought with them the flu, smallpox, venereal disease and many other ailments previously unknown to the Aboriginals, against which they had no immunity. The infinitely better armed settlers also hunted down the simple hunter-gatherer Aboriginals like animals, sometimes even putting out poisoned meat for them, as if for rabid dogs. They raped Aboriginal women and children. They ignored, despised or actively destroyed Aboriginal culture. This was attempted genocide, an orgy of cruelty.

The most famous incident among a long litany of such happenings was the 'Myall Creek Massacre' of 1838. For this wanton killing of innocent and defenceless Aboriginals, women and children included, seven of the 11 whites accused were hanged. But such justice was unusual.

The still unexorcised shame of this terrible time haunts the national psyche—as well it should, for it is by no means over yet. Although official policies of discrimination are long gone, you will still hear dreadful things said of 'the blackfeller' in white society all over Australia; the deeper you get into the countryside, the worse the things you hear. To far too many white Australians, Aboriginals are still boongs or abo's, the old terms of contempt now taboo in polite urban society. Even my otherwise charming Aussie friend spelled it out for me: 'They're all bludgers (the Aboriginals), that's what they are! Never worked for any land, never bought any land, just inherited it, that's all!'

Blatant cases of discrimination still surface regularly in the press. In 1989, Aboriginal university graduate and youth welfare officer, Julie Marie Tommy, successfully sued a Western Australian pub-hotel for refusing to serve her at its bar. It transpired during the case that the hotel had also set aside separate whites-only and blacks-only bars. Such scenes are repeated endlessly throughout rural Australia today.

The scandal of Aboriginal deaths in police custody has recently erupted into the public mind, with the publication of a Royal Commission enquiry into at least 105 unexplained Aboriginal deaths in police and prison cells during the 1980s. In so many cases, what may have begun as a simple arrest for drunk and disorderly behaviour has ended with sudden death. Fingers have been pointed at the police but in the end, the finger points at all Australians.

For Their Own Good

By the beginning of the 20th century, the best an Aboriginal could expect from life was to be relegated to an Aboriginal reserve and get some sort of a job with the white man. In some states, the Aboriginal was forbidden to consume alcohol, to marry or have sex across the colour line, or to carry a firearm.

The 1930s saw a fully articulated policy of assimilation, with or without Aboriginal consent, for mixed bloods. Out of a sort of twisted benevolence, the white authorities systematically removed Aboriginal children, particularly those of mixed blood, from their mothers 'for their own good', in an attempt to integrate them into white society and obliterate their aboriginality forever. Often, however, they were simply put into domestic servitude, akin to slavery.

The basic idea was to weed, and breed, out Aboriginal genes, leaving the full-blood elders to die off peacefully, thus eliminating the Aboriginal race altogether. This was thought to be the 'kindest' stratagem for dealing with 'the problem'. The descendants of these poor orphans have ever since been searching for their parents and grandparents, not knowing who they themselves really are, nor where they belong. Their story is movingly told by one of their own, a Western Australian mixed-blood Aboriginal psychologist, writer and artist, Sally Morgan, in her excellent journey back to her own roots, *My Place*.

Absorbing the Difference

Today's policy, first set by Gough Whitlam's Labor government in 1972, is to allow Aboriginals self-determination. Slow assimilation of the Aboriginals into modern white society, so that they may share in its benefits, is on offer, in line with the wider goal of building a multicultural Australia. But never forced assimilation. Every effort is made at official levels to encourage Aboriginals to preserve their culture.

Assimilation is no easy matter, for there can be no disputing that Aboriginals are 'different'. And within the community called 'Aboriginal', there are also many differences, some of them originating from tribal barriers, but others delineated more by whether Aboriginals have grown up in towns or the countryside, are mixed or full-bloods. Following are some examples of the most striking differences with white culture.

Travelling the land is a deep instinct with the once nomadic Aboriginals and so their penchant for going 'walkabout'—disappearing without warning, for days, weeks or months—is legend, giving them a reputation for unreliability. The concept of possessions and property is alien to Aboriginal culture, the antithesis of Western materialism; when you are nomadic, you don't carry around too much luggage. They share easily and expect others to do so too, which can sometimes make them seem too free with others' goods.

Even when tribal bands of Aboriginals in their natural state wandered through each other's territory, defined only by a delicate structure of oral precepts, there was never any attempt to 'conquer'

95

one another or 'acquire' the land. So when the whites came, it never dawned on the Aboriginals that they had lost their land, since such a concept was unimaginable. Only when the whites erected fences to keep them out and filled the land with sheep and cattle, depriving them of their hunting grounds, did they begin to react with hostility, but in vain.

Confinement within four walls induces claustrophobia in many Aboriginals, once upon a time used to ranging across some of the vastest open spaces known to humankind. Hence, even when offered a neat little home, they may opt instead to create a rough camp outdoors, in the garden. In the view of unsympathetic whites, this looks like a perverse insistence on creating slums and an innate lack of 'civilisation'.

Diet of Death

The European newcomers were the harbingers of Aboriginal death in many shapes and forms. They brought flour, sugar, alcohol and tobacco, among a host of other goodies which were to destroy the Aboriginals' health. The most visible result for the casual observer is Aboriginal obesity. Mind you, the whites are hardly immune.

Research in the 1980s and 1990s has demonstrated that the Aboriginals' spartan original diet of berries, roots, insects, and occasional fish or wild animals like the goanna lizard or the kangaroo, was far better for them. Hence a trendy new cuisine wave among whites, too, called 'Bush Tucker' now sweeping hip Australia—but more of that in Chapter Ten.

The lamentable state of Aboriginal health today is certainly one more reason for Australia to continue feeling ashamed. Heart disease, diabetes, tuberculosis, even trachoma and malnutrition, you name it, they've got it. Aboriginal life expectancy in the 1980s, at about 55 years, compared poorly with an expectancy of 73 and 79 years for white males and females. This ill-health itself stems from poor diet, poor living environment and often unstable family life. Alcohol abuse, petrol sniffing and domestic violence are rife in Aboriginal families (not that Australian whites do not have their share, but the problem is far more pronounced among Aboriginals).

As many others have put it before me, Aboriginal Australians live a 'Third World' life in the midst of a 'First World' nation. Their out-of-town settlements resemble the worst sort of refugee camps, or the black townships of South Africa.

Rights Restored

Such conditions make it extremely difficult for Aboriginals to take advantage of the many special aid and affirmative-action schemes which now exist to help them enter mainstream Australia. They still have a very steep climb ahead of them, even despite a litany of special rights assigned to them since the 1970s, often much to the chagrin of some less compassionate white Australians.

In gradual steps, different states have, at different times since the mid-1960s, legislated first to turn over Aboriginal reserve lands to the Aboriginals themselves, and then to grant traditional ownership of vacant lands to them on application. Land within towns or already owned by non-Aboriginals is not open to such claims, however. Which means that much of the best land is still withheld from them, of course.

The acknowledged turning point was the Aboriginal Land Rights (Northern Territory) Act of 1976. Of all the states, Queensland and Western Australia have been the slowest movers, with a generally poor record in race relations.

At present, something like 11 per cent of Australia is held by the Aboriginal community in some form or another. Land rights battles continue today, particularly when aboriginal aspirations come into conflict with powerful mining interests. An elaborate bureaucracy of organisations now exists to take care of aboriginal interests, topped by the Aboriginal and Torres Strait Islander Commission, and as more and more Aboriginals gain experience in self-government, one might say there is hope.

The Land-Mother

Land rights are central to Aboriginality. It is hard for outsiders to comprehend the very deep and mystic way in which Aboriginals feel they are bound to the land. This is not the feeling of the white farmer who loves his land through proud possession and control of it. Rather, the Aboriginals feel *they* are owned and controlled by the land. The earth is their 'mother'.

In a far-off 'Dreamtime', believe the Aboriginals, ancestral spirits, beings and other agents of Mother Earth travelled across the land creating people, places, plants and animals. You will hear a lot in Australia about Aboriginal 'sacred sites'. Once a place is declared a sacred site, it becomes extremely problematic to develop it or tamper with it in any way. A pitched battle has been under way for several years now over government development proposals for a riverside site in Perth, formerly a brewery, for exactly this reason. The sacred sites were the halting points where the ancestral beings paused on their journeys across the land. There are many other such cases across the country.

Each Aboriginal's very identity, and position within the tribe or clan, is based on the place where he or she was born, and is linked to an ancestral being, expressed through a plant or an animal. The soil is the source of all life, and the home to which all life returns after death, for recycling into life again. There is no sense of separation from other life-forms. This tunes well with beliefs found in some of the great world religions—Hinduism and Buddhism among them—and American Indian philosophy too.

The Aboriginals lived in complete harmony and balance with the wild land. Their burning-back patterns were an essential part of the ecosystem, regenerating and benefiting many species of plants and animals in an ecology geared for natural fires. They took from the land only what they needed to survive.

Their system of justice was harsh, but effectively meted out by the elders of the tribe—you might be speared in the leg or, much worse,

Ritual spirit poles on Bathurst Island, Northern Territory. Photo by the author.

'sung to death' for transgression of tribal laws. Magic plays an important role in Aboriginal culture. Even white Australians are in some awe of customs like 'pointing the bone'—a form of curse willing an enemy to die—and 'singing', an intensive group incantation, again intended to bring death to the enemy. Stories of victims falling down dead abound.

Kinship and family are central to Aboriginal integrity. Many Southeast Asians and the more traditional Europeans will recognise this group-oriented social structure as similar to their own.

Culture and wisdom were passed on through the community's rich repertoire of oral history, stories and songs—there was no writing—culminating in the formal, and often painful, initiation ceremony for children passing into adulthood. Secret knowledge of sacred things was communicated at this ceremony. To this day, there are many such secrets still carefully kept from the uninitiated.

The Art of Being Aboriginal

One of the most striking things about Aboriginal culture before white settlement was the existence of an estimated 230 distinct Aboriginal languages, with more than 500 dialects. More than half of these languages are now extinct.

While most of these languages, like the Aboriginals themselves, evolved in complete isolation from outside influences, in some areas there was some cross-fertilisation: in the Northern Territory, as well as parts of northwestern Western Australia. For example, ancient trading links with Indonesian fishermen seeking Australia's valuable sea-slugs and trochus shells, led to Indonesian vocabulary entering Aboriginal tongues. In parts of the Northern Territory, for example, the word for 'foreigner' is *belanda*, the Indonesian word for a Dutchman or 'Hollander'.

Aboriginal languages have left their mark on white Australia, in place-names and in everyday words, from 'billabong' to 'kangaroo'. But we can only guess at what opportunities for acquiring extraordinary knowledge have been squandered over the years of white contempt for Aboriginal culture. No research body was set up to study this culture before the establishment in 1961 of the Australian Institute of Aboriginal Studies at Canberra.

Aboriginal culture has since been revealed as vastly more sophisticated than previously understood. On the artistic front in particular, the Aboriginals have contributed to the very definition of 'Australian-ness'.

Aboriginal Australian art, traditionally executed chiefly on the Aboriginals' own bodies, on cave and rock walls, and on strips of bark, has achieved international recognition in recent decades, as Aboriginal artists have learned to transfer it to canvas and transmit it through modern media such as watercolours, oils and acrylic. Especially well known are the dot-mosaic and 'X-ray' styles of painting (depicting animals complete with their skeletal structure and internal organs). The best examples are now, quite rightly, very expensive, and grace the walls of some of the world's premier galleries.

Aboriginal rock painting at Nourlangie, Northern Territory. Photo by the author.

Albert Namatjira was a pioneer Aboriginal artist who scored most of his considerable success before World War II—he died in 1959. But he did it with Western-style watercolour paintings. True Aboriginal art was not to win white acclaim until long after the war. Today, there are many Aboriginal artists of note in Australia keeping tribal traditions alive.

101

Just as creative as the fusion with Western art media has been the recent grafting of Asian techniques like batik—wax-resist textile printing—with Aboriginal motifs, to stunning effect in some areas of the Northern Territory.

The success of Aboriginal art has already helped restore the Aboriginals' pride in themselves and their culture, quite apart from bringing them income.

A Brand New Day on Its Way?

Less well known to the outside world are Aboriginal music and dance, central elements in traditional Aboriginal culture. Here again, Western influences have produced interesting hybrids. Many Aboriginal musicians have shown a talent for pop or country-and-western styles.

Contact between Aboriginal and white Australian musicians has also spawned outstanding white fusion bands such as Gondwanaland (named after the super-continent of some 150 million years ago which, according to Continental Drift Theory, gave birth to Australia about 45 million years ago). Gondwanaland has evolved a quintessentially Australian sound with original compositions featuring instruments as diverse as electronic synthesisers, drums and the Aboriginal didgeridoo, a very long, tube-like wind instrument. The insistent, throbbing drone of the didgeridoo is the sound of Australia itself, an awe-inspiring voice from the desert speaking to the deepest, most mysterious levels of the human soul.

An increasing number of professional Aboriginal dance troupes are now touring little-known Aboriginal dance, until only recently dismissed as primitive, akin to old Red-Indians-whooping-round-campfire stuff. One of Australia's best-known Aboriginal actors and dancers is David Gulpilil. If you saw the first *Crocodile Dundee* film, you will remember Gulpilil as Dundee's Aboriginal friend.

Theatre is another arena now beginning to showcase Aboriginal talents. Actor Ernie Dingo is a well-established example, Western Australian playwright Jack Davis another—Jack Davis in particular has conjured up the bleakness of Aboriginal life in the old days on settlements controlled by whites.

I was privileged not long ago to attend the premiere of Australia's first Aboriginal musical, *Bran Nu Dae* ('A Brand New Day'). The name of its creator was Jimmy Chi, the product of a Chinese father and an Aboriginal mother in the old pearling port of Broome, up in the northwest of Western Australia. There are many other such exotic mixes to be found in the melting pot of Australia.

Bran Nu Dae is a vibrant example of the kind of innovation we can expect from Aboriginal performers in future. Wonderfully raucous, rumbustious and ribald, the play depicts an Aboriginal boy's flight from the city of Perth back to his outback homeland. White society, from the local Roman Catholic archbishop to well-meaning hippies, is satirised mercilessly but in a good-natured sort of way.

The black protest movements of the 1950s and 1960s in the West had their impact on Aboriginal Australia and a new school of writing is now apparent as a result. One of the first and best-known Aboriginal protest writers was Oodgeroo Noonuccal, also known as Kath Walker, a formidable poetess, whose first volume of poetry, *We Are Going*, was published in 1964. Another early success was Aboriginal artist and writer Dick Roughsey, who wrote chiefly for children—works such as *The Giant Devil-Dingo* in 1973 and *The Rainbow Serpent* in 1975.

Sporting Laurels

Aboriginals have also shown exceptional talent in sports. Curiously, the very first Australian cricket team to visit England was a privately-organised all-Aboriginal team, which toured the country in 1868. (However, several of them found England's climate so inhospitable that they had to go home before time; one of them actually died.)

Most sports fans have also heard of Aboriginal tennis player Evonne Goolagong, the 1971 and 1981 Wimbledon women's singles champion. Aboriginal sportsmen have also excelled in football and boxing. Famous Aboriginal boxers include Dave Sands (1940s), bantam-weight Lionel Rose, world champion in his class at the Mexico Olympics of 1968, and Tony Mundine in the 1970s.

Black Politics

Education is the key to Aboriginal advancement, as it is for so many other disadvantaged peoples. The community does already have models to follow: for example, Sir Doug Nicholls, who died in 1988, a pastor, the first Aboriginal to be knighted by the Queen and also the nation's first Aboriginal Governor, of South Australia, 1976–77.

The year 1971 also saw the first Aboriginal Member of Parliament, Neville Bonner—there have been several more since—while 1978 saw Pat O'Shane become Australia's first Aboriginal law graduate and barrister. The first two Aboriginals to be employed by the diplomatic service in the Ministry of Foreign affairs were hired in 1982.

Burnum Burnum, like Charlie Perkins, an Aboriginal lawyer and freedom fighter, is another politically significant figure. His most flamboyant gesture has been to plant the Aboriginal flag on England's white cliffs of Dover, on Australia Day 1988, to claim England for the Aboriginal 'nation'.

Burnum Burnum also masterminded the recovery of the bones of Truganini, the last full-blood Tasmanian Aboriginal, who had died in 1876. Tasmania's Hobart Museum had put them on display up to 1947 against Truganini's express wish that her body be left undisturbed. Her ashes were at last scattered on waters close to her homeland.

Among other activist names you will undoubtedly encounter are Gary Foley, Dr Lois O' Donoghue, Peter Yu (half-Chinese) and Pat Dodson.

The Mabo/Wik Mess

Aboriginal history reached a historic crossroads with the landmark 'Mabo' judgement made by the Australian High Court in June 1992— a judgement named after deceased Aboriginal land-rights negotiator

Eddy Mabo. The High Court ruled that the original colonial designation of Australia as 'Terra Nullius' or 'empty land', was erroneous: the Aboriginals did have valid 'native title' to much of the Australian land.

This has generated hysteria, and more importantly, uncertainty for farmers and would-be minerals exploiters. Is the average suburban backyard secure from Aboriginal land claims? Yes, the Mabo decision stated clearly that no privately-owned land is threatened.

States like resource-rich Western Australia however had concerns because vacant State land certainly was vulnerable to native-title claims and W.A. for one has plenty of that; Premier Richard Court's conservative Liberal state government therefore passed its own legislation to override the High Court judgement. But even if native-title claims do not stand on occupied land, there may now be a case for financial compensation to the original 'traditional owners', the Aboriginals.

A Native Title Tribunal set up after Mabo has been hearing claims. In many cases, all the Aboriginals want to establish is their right of access to properties in connection with visiting 'sacred sites', hunting and fishing, and their right to be consulted on the future disposal of the land. To a large extent, they want not simply access to the wealth that is land, but more the 'Face' of recognition and consultation, to salve the humiliating wounds of their lamentable history—Asians culturally attuned to concepts of 'Face' will perhaps be the first to sympathise with that desire.

But now Australians have an additional ruling to wrestle with: 'The Wik Decision' handed out to the Wik People of Cape York Peninsula, Queensland, in 1996. The High Court in this case ruled that native title can coexist with pastoral (farming) leases and can only be extinguished permanently by a special law, which has not occurred. In other words, the farmers did not have exclusive hold on the land, although it seems their rights have priority when there is a conflict. Any new decision to mine or log such land however must go through a negotiation process with native-title holders first.

In other words, more glorious confusion. This has caused a huge commotion, still ongoing. In reality, nobody wants to face up to the real meaning of reconciliation with the Aboriginals, for at the heart of the process lie the issues of land-ownership and land-use. And land, with its rich resources, lies at the heart of Australia's wealth.

John Howard's Liberal government looks suspiciously likely to move towards extinguishment of native title in all but name, perhaps through strategies like issuing new leases allowing pastoralists to do what they please with their land without reference to Aboriginal native-title holders. As Labor Party Opposition Leader Kim Beazley put it in April 1997 when still, nothing was clear, the Prime Minister seems to have gone into 'furtive ferret mode'.

The big winners in this mess are of course, the lawyers. Native-title claim cases inevitably will go on into the 21st century.

The Treaty at the End of the Rainbow?

There has long been talk of a Treaty of Reconciliation with the Aboriginals. It remains only talk. As journalist John Pilger concludes in *A Secret Country*: 'Until we white Australians give back to black Australians their nationhood, we can never claim our own.'

THE LEISURE ETHIC

'It has been written and said by very incompetent judges of human nature that Australians, by the cultivation of and time devoted to outdoor sports, are degenerating in mental ability. This is, however, not true.'

—Anon, Australian Etiquette, 1885.

Work and Play

Being newly arrived from workaholic Asia, I once made the awful mistake of asking an Australian bank clerk innocently, on a Friday afternoon, 'And will you be open tomorrow morning?'

She stared at me as if I were raving mad and declared firmly, 'Oh no, I should think not! Certainly not!'

Woe indeed is he who attempts to come between the Australian and his or her weekend. Or even he who attempts to push the weekday working clock beyond 5 p.m. Australians put high value on their leisure time.

I have seen it suggested that this attitude is a carry-over from convict days, when work was an imposition on enslaved men. And so the attitude grew that one should never do more than one has to do. Emancipation from the chains of the convict automatically meant freedom not to work if one chose not to.

As Australia's foremost national analyst, writer Donald Horne, has said of his compatriots, 'To some they seem lazy. They are not really lazy but they don't always take their jobs seriously.'

Slowing Down

Once you have learned to calm down your New York, Singapore, Hong Kong or Tokyo pace, you can get used to Australia's slower pace of work, and even like it. After all, there is a lot to be said for being able to spend more quality time with your family over the weekend. And for being able to develop social life, hobbies or further studies in the evenings. And for watching your blood pressure slowly drop, thus prolonging your life.

The Australian 'leisure ethic' (as opposed to the work ethic) cuts two ways. While other people may not always want to work for or with you, it also means you may not have to work so hard yourself.

It seems more than possible that Australians have got this one right, especially when you watch the rest of the developed world struggling with the problem of excess leisure time in this automated, information technology age. Indeed, one of the underlying reasons for apparent 'laziness' in Australia, and for some of the unemployment or under-employment as well, is increasing computerisation and automation, replacing human labour, as is the case in many affluent post-industrial countries today.

Other times besides weekends when you might as well go whistle in the wind as get some action on the work front, are Christmas–New Year, with the wind-down starting fairly early in December, and the Great Exodus at the Easter holiday, in early April. Businessmen, take note.

Appearances Can be Deceptive

Australian workers are deceptive. They look and sound extremely slow and casual. But in the majority of cases, they turn out to be meticulous workers, and nearly always specialists in their field.

You will rarely get that 'I don't know how it works, I only sell the things' style sadly found in many other countries. They really like to discuss their equipment and explain it to you. They will always service it and repair it, unlike the 'escape artists' often encountered elsewhere. If achieving this quality means slowing things down a bit, personally I still prefer it as a work attitude to the 'slam bang thank you ma'am' type of deal which leaves you with not the faintest idea of how to handle whatever it is that has just been delivered.

Perhaps that is one of the reasons the Australian worker costs so much more than others. But remember, costly workers means that you too are rewarded handsomely if you choose a so-called 'menial' or manual occupation—Australia has been called 'a working-man's paradise', although this image has tarnished somewhat with widespread unemployment today.

The cost may be one reason you will get fewer workers on a job than you might see, say, in Asia, where labour costs are low. When my husband and I packed up our goods and chattels in Singapore, our apartment was swarming with at least six men looking very busy indeed, creating much sound and fury. It all looked very impressive.

When our huge 20-foot container arrived at our new home in Perth, there were only two Aussies to unload it. We helped a bit, of course (that is the sort of thing you are quietly expected to do in Australia, anyway), but they would have done fine without us.

Now which of the two teams could be called the more hard-working, more efficient, or more productive, I wonder?

Keep It Friendly, Mate

By 'casual', I mean that Australian workers expect you to be friendly. If you want to develop a productive relationship with an Aussie worker, make sure you offer him a cup of tea and a chat. You will be amazed at how much time (presumably, it's really their boss's time, but that doesn't seem to matter) he has to sit down with you. He will be quite happy to tell you his life story. And that can be quite fascinating sometimes, especially if you are new to the country. I recall one such contractor who told me of his boyhood in the countryside and how farmers used to pay him and his school friends to strangle emu chicks on their way to school, because they were seen as pest birds.

If you come from a country used to a more formal relationship between client and contractor, you would be well advised to adapt to Australia's more chatty mode as quickly as possible. Too much of an 'I'm the boss' or 'I'm paying you, aren't I' type of attitude, or too formal a demeanour could well provoke hostility, or at best, only minimal cooperation. The job might not be done as well.

Tall Poppies

One of the reasons an Australian worker will sometimes look and sound much less competent or professional than in fact he really is, is the ingrained Australian fear of appearing too 'uppity'. This fear often prevents him from competing effectively and from demonstrating his maximum potential.

The Australian does not want to appear too good at what he or she does, lest this in some way offend or put down other people around

Aussies cutting down a 'tall poppy'—faltering tycoon Alan Bond. Illustration from The Australian *of June 28, 1989, courtesy of the artist, Mark Lynch.*

him or her. Worse, to truly excel might put him or her in the category 'Tall Poppy'—and tall poppies exist only to be cut down.

Western societies are quite used to airings of this problem in the context of women's relationships with men: the phenomenon of intelligent women working hard at the 'dumb blonde' masquerade lest they be put on the shelf by insecure men, is well known in feminist circles. But a whole nation working hard to appear dumb?

You better believe it. But then again, you better not believe it—because, as I have said, appearances are deceptive.

Remember, you too must play the game if you are to get on with Australians. If you are working hard, try not to show it or talk about it. If you are successful or intelligent, hide it, or at least actively play it down. If you have money, look as poor as possible.

The Tall Poppy Syndrome in Australia has been described by some observers as 'the psychology of envy'. Eminent academics such as psychologist Professor Norman Feather of Australia's Flinders University in 1989, and historian W.K. Hancock back in 1930, have noted this strong trait in the Australian character.

It is the Tall Poppy Syndrome that most sharply separates Australian psychology from that of the Americans, for whom individualistic achievement in contrast is almost a religion.

Don't Judge This Book by Its Cover

One of the manifestations of the anti-tall poppy school of thought is sloppy dress. This is quite rife in Australia. Viewed benevolently, it looks pleasantly unpretentious, undemanding of others too. But a lot of the time, it just looks, well—sloppy.

In men, it takes the form of shorts for everything—often unpleasantly short and tight ones, too. In women, just poorly coordinated wardrobes. In both sexes, tatty jeans, and above all, the ubiquitous 'thongs', aka Japanese slippers, flip-flops, rubber sandals, etc.

Setting aside the fact that many Australians truly are strapped for

Hotel lounge sign in Darwin suggests how naked Aussies can get. Photo by the author.

cash nowadays, a factor likely to limit one's ability to run a snazzy wardrobe, considering the price of clothing in Australia, the real reason for this lack of attention to personal appearance is the strong desire not to stand out, and above all, never to look at all well off. In short, not to threaten others.

This makes it very easy to dress in Australia, since the trick really is either to un-dress or to down-dress, depending on the time of day. But it makes it very hard to dress up.

It does mean that nobody can be classified by the way they dress. If you come from a country where dress really matters, particularly when negotiating business deals, try to throw your prejudices out of the window when in Australia.

Sickies, Overtime and Wages

Australian work attitudes are in transition right now, as a result of the trauma of high unemployment. It used to be commonplace for younger workers in particular to save on the job, then leave work for a year or two to travel the world, fully confident that they would be able to step straight into a job on their return.

No more. Many avoid taking holidays at all now, in case they return to find their job gone. Others stick to holidays in Australia and keep a watchful eye on the workplace.

For many, the only occupation they will have for some time is regular visits to the Job Centre or the Commonwealth Employment Service office, looking for work, followed by the Department of Social Security to register for unemployment benefits. But among those still at work, certain old habits still die hard. For one thing, the 'sickie' is commonplace. This refers to the institution of declaring yourself sick for the day when in fact you just do not much feel like going to work, or you have set your mind on shopping or picnicking instead. During the 1970s at least, sickies cost Australian industry more than a million Aussie dollars a year in terms of man-hours lost.

Another high cost to the employer is payment for overtime work. Overtime, on top of already high wages (average weekly wage, around A$400 or so), is one of the chief reasons for most Australian shops—except giant chains like Coles and Woolworth's supermarket-stores—not wanting to open for longer hours, or on Sundays, even if they are allowed to do so (which, in some states, such as Western Australia, they are not).

The Dignity of Labour

Australian workers won their basic rights very early, and have defended them vigorously ever since. The eight-hour day was secured by striking stonemasons in 1855, the basic minimum wage in 1907, and the 40-hour week in 1946—working weeks nowadays are closer to 36 hours, or even less in the case of the many industries running on half-time because of the recession. The world's first legislation providing for paid sick leave and paid long-service leave was enacted in the state of New South Wales in 1951.

Australians are particularly hot on matters of industrial safety and health, to a degree that may take some more cavalier outsiders aback.

Without going into the detailed pros and cons, enormous fusses have been made in recent years about allegedly debilitating 'Repetitive Strain Injury' or 'RSI', incurred through repeated restricted movements of the hand and arm in particular—such as those made by high-speed typists and computer-keyboard operators— about workers in contact with asbestos (many of Australia's older homes are insulated and roofed with asbestos), and about the health dangers or otherwise of extended work at Visual Display Units (VDUs) such as computer monitor screens—in 1980, journalists won special cash 'hardship' allowances for operating VDUs, which are still in place.

Service, Civility and Servility

The Australian style of service can be a problem, depending on where you are coming from. Possibly another hangover from the tribulations of a convict past and of the triumphant shaking off of those fetters, is the average Australian's determination never again to bow his head to any man, to serve no one—but to his credit, neither does he particularly wish to be served. Nothing embarrasses and confuses your average Australian, a natural socialist, more than being presented with a servant, as happens to him when travelling in Asia, for example.

Service industries like tourism do have a hard time in Australia. It is not that Australian workers are rude—far from it —but they are offhand, casual and familiar if you compare them with, say, the best available in the European capitals, or in many Asian capitals for that matter. To put it another way, they do not fawn.

Columnist Ruth Ostrow recently complained in *The Weekend Australian* how bad hotel and restaurant service was on Australia's premier tourist strip, the Gold Coast, concluding her diatribe with 'To be unable to serve is a testimony of our ever-present national insecurity complex.'

On the other hand, I surely cannot be the only person who has enjoyed the straight, eye-to-eye equality assumed by all Australian service personnel, and the candour that goes with it: the waiter who warns that you may not enjoy your order as 'it's not so fresh today', why don't you try something else? Anyone flying Qantas, the Australian national airline, will certainly find the service standards set by the inflight personnel, particularly the male stewards, often outclass those on other airlines. If that sounds like a blatant plug, so be it.

One of the glories of the Australian system is that the tip is still considered demeaning by most Australian workers—although admittedly, increasing tourism, migration and the pressures of recession are now all combining to create some cracks in that facade. But traditionally, the tip is seen as the thin end of the wedge towards making excuses for low wages; a man should be paid what he is worth in the form of a decent wage, no more, no less. No tips please, we're Australian.

Everybody Out!

The Australian worker's propensity to strike has become legend, but to be fair, this is indeed a legend, belonging more to a particular period of the 1970s than to the here and now.

Since the Australian Council of Trade Unions (ACTU) signed the so-called 'Accord' (the Prices and Incomes Accord) with the Australian Labor Party in 1983, the problem has muted, with Labor in power since then—in 1991, Bob Hawke was the longest-serving Labor Prime Minister in Australian history.

Wages have since then been determined by a highly structured, centralised and regularly reviewed system of 'awards'. Relations between the labour movement and the Labor Party traditionally have been close, although the unions have become increasingly uncomfortable with right-wing dominance of party policy in recent years. The unions have often shown their muscle over purely political, even foreign-policy issues, for example, against Japanese aggression in China during the 1930s, against Australian involvement in the Vietnam War in 1965, against foreign sailors' working conditions, and against Indonesian action in East Timor in more recent years.

The average number of working days lost in industrial disputes during the 1980s was about 1.5 million a year, much less than the 6.3 million of 1974.

The industry causing the most problems is the mining industry, which accounts for almost half of all working days lost through disputes. It should be noted that this is a troublesome industry in almost every country in the world. Another sticky area is the docks, manned by the tough 'wharfies' or dock workers, still locked into many old-fashioned work practices.

One of the most memorable recent strikes was not staged by what you could exactly call 'the working class': this was the airline pilots' strike of 1989. Although it was defeated by a hang-tough Labor government which refused even to negotiate, this strike for a 29.5 per cent pay rise cost the nation very dear in economic terms, possibly in the region of A$500 million, and all but destroyed a thriving tourist industry. Many Australian pilots laid off during this episode are now to be found flying the airlines of the world, particularly in Asia.

Unfortunately, many of today's strikes, although usually short-lived and focusing more on conditions than on wages, seem to occur in the context of airports—baggage-handlers, refuellers and air traffic-controllers, etc.—which of course gives Australia a very bad name overseas via the tourists suffering the ill effects thereof.

The signs are that the unions now hold far less sway over the political process than when the Labor Party came to power on their backs in 1983, with a former ACTU president, Bob Hawke, as its Prime Minister.

During the decade of the 1980s, Australian labour unions saw their membership drop by 20 per cent, to less than 40 per cent of the workforce. In better times, the Australian rate of union membership, along with New Zealand's, was the highest of any democracy in the world. Recession and unemployment rates of around 11 per cent have accelerated the process of change.

Plans to restructure and rationalise the union movement were announced by the Labor government in 1987. The main objective is to reduce the number of unions from 215 (1987)—only nine of which are truly, numerically, powerful—to about 20 by the end of this century, by means of amalgamating some of the smaller unions.

Handout Heartbreak

Australia is fundamentally a welfare society. But unemployment benefits—'the dole' recently metamorphosed into the 'Job Search' and 'Newstart' allowances—are nowhere near as easy to get nowadays as they used to be, particularly if you are young and strong enough to work. The ongoing restructuring of Australia's economy and labour market is already having real impact on the handout psychology of the dole.

That said, these are extraordinary times in Australia. By July 1991, almost 702,000 people, the majority of them 21–30 year-old males, were receiving the dole.

The problem area now is the 15–18 year-olds out of work who are no longer eligible for the dole. Some observers think the phenomenon of young people on the streets without work or money is contributing to a rising wave of juvenile crime.

Australia's high rates of income tax (for most people, close to 40 per cent) cover not only social security but also include a Medicare levy for the provision of almost-free medical care; your doctor bills the government, or if he bills you, you claim a partial rebate from the government. This perhaps over-generous system, like the unions, is suffering nibbling erosion at present as the government struggles to prevent its costly abuse by the public.

Medicine prescription charges are already high, and a battle has recently been fought between the Labor government's right and left wings over the institution in late 1991 of a A$2.50 'cooperative charge' which doctors are now to charge anyone wishing to consult them for anything (the object being to discourage frivolous visits to the doctor).

But when the moan goes up about decent taxpayers forking out for layabouts on the dole ('dole-bludgers') or for fake 'sickies', as it often does, my thoughts go to two mercy cases I have encountered. One was my girlfriend whose little girl was born four months prematurely, with cerebral palsy which prevented her from walking properly. In the other case, another girlfriend's daughter, aged about eight, was quite suddenly diagnosed with a hole in her heart. Both stories had a happy ending, largely thanks to the welfare system.

After Hours

Australians draw a sharp line between work-time and play-time. And they work hard at play. Their favourite form of play is sport, whether spectator or participatory. Sport—the practice and the theoretical knowledge of it—is your surest and shortest route to the heart of Australians, your safest topic of conversation with the highest and lowest in the land.

Australian politicians scramble to be associated with sporting events and to be seen as such on the TV screen. Prime Minister Bob Hawke himself pops up every so often on telly to offer his views on the current state of football, and so bolster his popularity ratings.

Because so much of the population is concentrated around the coastline, water sports are important—swimming, sailing, surfboarding, windsurfing, water-skiing and rowing, as well as white-water rafting.

But partly because winters are usually short and mild, many other sports can be played almost the whole year round. Cricket, Australian Rules football ('Footy') and horse-racing are three of the most important; with reference to the latter, take note that the Melbourne Cup races (first Tuesday in November) are a national happening of massive significance, albeit a public holiday only in Melbourne itself—do not try to talk to Australians (even overseas) about anything else on this day.

Tennis is popular, thanks to the stunning victories at major championships such as Wimbledon by top-calibre Australian players like Evonne Goolagong Cawley and more recently, Pat Cash.

Golf in Australia is not the preserve of the moneyed elite as it is in so many other societies, but is enjoyed by all, at minimal cost. Fine Australian golfers have emerged regularly, Greg Norman being one of the most recent names to hit the international sports pages.

Australia has had an international sporting presence for almost a century, at first as part of the cricketing British Empire, later as an independent member of the world community—the 1956 Olympics were hosted in Melbourne, with Australian swimmers taking eight of the 14 available gold medals. The annual Formula One Grand Prix motor race has been staged in Adelaide since 1985.

White-water rafting in Tasmania. Photo by John Rance.

Sport has always played an important part in Australia's concept of foreign diplomacy.

Willow and Leather

The Melbourne Cricket Club was established as early as 1838, but cricket was played in Australia much earlier than that. It seems slightly odd that a sport so strongly associated with the British Empire and the British upper classes should have rooted so easily in convict-settled Australia, but the game is indeed a national passion.

If you do not come from a cricket-playing nation, my advice is that you read up on this puzzling game before attempting to relate with Australia.

The first 'Test' match between Australian and English cricketers was won by Australia, at the Melbourne Cricket Ground in 1876.

Thereafter, the Test trophy has always been the 'Ashes', supposedly the ashes of the dead English game at that 1876 match. Test matches were a sensitive topic for Australian sportsmen until quite recently, in 1989, when Allan Border's team won back the Ashes on tour in England—this was the first time the Australians had retrieved the Ashes in England since 1934.

Cricket pundits worldwide are familiar with great Australian cricketing names like Sir Donald Bradman (more than 28,000 runs against England in Test matches 1928–48, and a record of 1,448 runs in one season unbeaten until 1971), Richie Benaud, Ian Chappell, Dennis Lillee, Jeff Thomson, Greg Chappell and Allan Border, to name but a few.

To get by with the sports small-talk that is essential to survival at the Australian dinner table, in the pub or at the neighbourhood barbie (outdoors barbecue party), you will also need to be familiar with two particularly famous cricketing incidents.

The first of these is the 'bodyline' incident in the 1932–33 English tour of Australia, during which English bowlers were believed to have bowled directly to Bradman's body in a deliberately threatening manner. Several Australian batsmen were injured during this tour and Australian feeling against the English cricketers rose to fever pitch.

In the second incident, the boot was on the other foot, with Australia monopolising the infamy. This was the notorious 'under-arm' tactic against New Zealand in 1981. Bowler Trevor Chappell, one of three famous cricketing brothers, was instructed by his captain, coincidentally also his brother Greg, to bowl underarm for the last ball of the limited-over final.

The New Zealand team at that point needed six runs from the last ball to level with Australia in this one-day match, but Chappell's stratagem effectively denied the opposition a tie with Australia—it would be impossible to hit the underarm-delivery ball hard or high enough to get time for runs while the fielders chased it. Australia's reputation for sportsmanship suffered a bashing and underarm bowling was subsequently banned, as underhand and not cricket.

Australian Rules Football

This virtual amalgam of rugby and soccer was invented in Melbourne in 1858. It is a lot rougher than soccer, with plenty of hand-ball, body contact, hand-passing and the like.

The good news does not seem to have spread outside Australia, but domestically, footy is the leading ball game and an authentic item of Australiana which all visitors should experience for themselves. Loyalties focus on local clubs, which compete in a relatively recently established national competition.

The America's Cup

The America's Cup sailing event has been a national obsession ever since Australia won it in the USA, in 1983; Australia has competed for the Cup since 1962.

The victory of the 12-metre yacht Australia II, owned by Western Australian business tycoon Alan Bond and captained by John Bertrand, made Australia the first nation to take the Cup away from America since the inaugural race in 1851. The yacht featured a controversial, revolutionary winged keel designed in Australia by Ben Lexcen (who died in 1988).

The nation went simply bananas in the delirium of this triumph. Much effort is now being expended in the attempt to repeat this victory.

The return event in 1988 brought great prosperity to the host city, Fremantle in Western Australia, as well as to Perth, although unfortunately only very temporarily as it appears with hindsight. Australia failed to retain the Cup, which went initially to New Zealand, to Australia's great chagrin. However, New Zealand was ruled out of

*The America's Cup was a great happening for all
Australians. Photo courtesy of G. Devadas.*

order in court for sailing what was in effect a catamaran, not a yacht,
and the Cup returned to America by default.

All a Bluff?

Strangely enough, despite the strong sporting culture which permeates
the macho-skewed Australian social ethos, statistics show that a large
number of Australians are physically lazy, overweight and unfit. It
seems that only about one-quarter of the population is taking adequate
exercise.

And so it was that in the 1970s, the government launched a
campaign featuring a slovenly, beer-bellied couch potato named
'Norm', who only watched sports on the small screen from his living
room sofa, 'tinnie' in hand. He was berated into more physical activity
with the slogan 'Life, Be In It.' But Norm remains a familiar sight
today.

Chapter Seven

MATESHIP AND MACHISMO

'My mate is always a man. A female may be my sheila, my bird, my charley, my good sort, my hot-drop, my judy or my wife, but she is never "my mate".'

—Donald McLean, in *The Roaring Days*, 1960.

Men and Men, and Men and Women

If all you did was watch television in Australia, you might well come to the conclusion that the country was way ahead of the rest of the world in terms of men deferring to women, equality of rights, pay and opportunity for women, and the whole feminist caboodle.

Every other documentary seems to be about something dreadful done to women and children by men—whether it be wife-battering, rape or incest. The concern demonstrated is so great, surely it must be practised in real daily life too?

Not necessarily. What you are really witnessing in the media is a sort of national self-flagellation in penance for the very real sins of the past and, it must be said, of the ongoing present. It is because things have been so bad that all the documentaries are necessary. In any case, it is by no means certain that the deep concern shown really extends very far outside of the sophisticated circle of television documentary producers and script-writers.

But before we can understand how men relate with women in Australia, we must first understand how they relate with men.

Mateship

So much has been written about this uniquely Australian phenomenon that it is difficult for me to know where to begin.

One of the first things the newcomer to Australia notices is that familiar, friendly form of address, for strangers and friends alike, 'Mate'. 'How are yer, mate?' or 'What can I do for yer, mate?'—these are all common currency. (Note that 'mate' is almost never used between men and women, or among women.)

This, however, is a mere casual greeting, albeit of symbolic significance. True mateship is an abstraction of almost mystical proportions. The term was first used by Australia's pioneer chronicler of the bush, Henry Lawson, who wrote his best material during the 1890s.

Mateship refers to that subtle brotherhood felt by men together, especially when they have had to work or fight together in harsh conditions or against great adversity. Rightly or wrongly, implicit in the concept is the idea that women can never share in this emotion (even if feminists would say that 'sisterhood' was the same thing for them). Indeed, traditionally, Australian discussions of manhood,

125

manliness and mateship have made no reference at all to masculinity in relation to women. Women simply did not come into the picture.

The only problem with this concept in post-pioneer Australia is determining exactly what adversity it is that brings men together in mateship nowadays. One has a sneaking suspicion that 'the enemy' may in fact be women—especially wives—and the suburban stresses of home and family that they are seen to represent.

Mateship Uber Alles

Mateship in Australia—the friendship of men with men—can override all other moralities. For example, the man who would 'dob in' (inform on) his drug-dealer mate to the police, would probably be considered to have committed a greater offence than the drug-dealer himself. Like the 'old-boy' networks believed to dominate business life in England, mateship is a system that works quietly behind the scenes of both business and politics in Australia.

Mateship has its highs and its lows. At its lowest, it can descend to brute displays of masculinity akin to gorillas beating their chests. As social commentator Donald Horne has put it, in such cases, 'Men stand around bars asserting their masculinity with such intensity that you half expect them to unzip their flies.'

On the other hand, Horne also characterises mateship as a noble 'ideology of fraternalism' permeating the nation. It means that Australians believe most other people are good fellows like themselves, 'mates'. Optimists all, they believe in the essential humanity of mankind—*man*kind unfortunately being the operative word.

Men's Men

Hand in hand with mateship goes an almost unreasoning horror of homosexuals, tarred 'poofters' or 'queers' by macho Australia. There is a strong gay counter-culture, true, particularly in the great cities of the East, but mainstream 'matedom' vigorously avoids contact with it or, if forced into contact, bashes it, often literally.

A reading of Robert Hughes' account of the early Australian colony, *The Fatal Shore*, yields convincing evidence that it is precisely because homosexuality was violently and sordidly practised in convict society that Australian men have ever since expended great energy in erasing the memory of those terrifying times.

As a result, Aussie males fear seeming too emotional—too female. Among the many Australian men who have, however, bravely resisted this neurosis has been former Prime Minister Bob Hawke himself, who won a reputation for crying in public. While it is uncertain what this did to his male vote, it must certainly have endeared him to his female voters.

On the other hand, his public admission of marital infidelity must have redressed the balance since it would have endeared him to Australian men ('He's human, just like us'), who probably secretly admired him for it, while it may not have pleased too many women.

But try if you will to square this one with the image of a macho hairy-hunky Australia: Sydney is one of the world's great gay capitals and the annual Sydney Gay and Lesbian Mardi Gras extravaganza has become Australia's highest-earning festival and tourist attraction, spawning many other mini-Mardi Gras in other cities such as Perth. The 1997 event in Sydney saw 500,000 spectators on the streets to watch leather-clad 'Dykes on Bikes,' outrageous spangled queens, anything went. And it generates an A\$40-million revenue for Sydney, at last count. I rest my case.

On cooking, normally considered a woman's task in Australia, it is interesting to note how Australian men will take it on quite naturally when it comes to the great Australian barbecue party. There seems to be an unwritten law that it should be the husband who tends the sizzling meat—a kind of hunter-gatherer nostalgia referring to the caveman past?—while the wife may perhaps be pottering around with salads and the like.

SYDNEY GAY & LESBIAN MARDI GRAS LTD.
A.C.N. 003 973 635

POSITION VACANT

FESTIVAL DIRECTOR SALARY $42,000
(PRO-RATA, EXCLUSIVE OF SUPERANNUATION AND LEAVE LOADING. TWO YEAR CONTRACT)

17.5 HOURS PER WEEK (FLEXIBLE)

READVERTISED – PREVIOUS APPLICANTS NEED NOT REAPPLY

The Festival Director is responsible for selecting the performing and visual arts programs of the Mardi Gras Festival. The Festival Director will oversee the Festival Funding Scheme and the lesbian and gay communities' access to the Festival. In conjunction with the Festival Administrator, the Festival Director will be responsible for overall Festival budgeting. The Festival Director is the Chair of the Festival Advisory Committee. The Festival Director reports to the Executive Officer.

Enquiries: For further information call Richard Perram, Executive Officer 02 557 4332 or fax 02 516 4446. **Closing Date:** Tuesday 18 April 1995.

The Sydney gay and lesbian Mardi Gras is serious business as seen in this ad in The Weekend Australian *of April 8–9, 1995.*

Role-Swapping

A climate of economic decline coupled with unemployment has in a way benefited the man-woman relationship in Australia, with part-time work and even job-sharing an ever more possible option for couples. Hence many more men are now staying at home to be 'house husbands'.

The embodiment of the Australian macho opposition to such developments was Queensland's National Party premier, Sir Joh Bjelke-Petersen, 1968–87, who stood against almost everything 'liberal' from feminism and Aboriginal rights to workers' rights and even evolutionary theory. 'The National Party is a real man's party—there are no quiche-eating, sandal-wearing trendies, and no small "I" Nationals,' Sir Joh once declared.

Such attitudes, once considered stereotypical of the Queenslander, are now in partial retreat, as is the National Party itself, following official investigations of the conduct of Bjelke-Petersen and his associates, which have revealed entrenched corruption in state government processes. (Corruption itself—'helping out a mate'—has often been the consequence of extended mateship.)

Sheilas

The scenes you have probably heard tell of, the parties where the men congregate on one side of the room or garden to discuss footy, the women on the other to discuss cooking, babies, or just possibly nowadays, feminist issues—they do still happen.

There is not much you can do about this, as a woman. You might very well find the women's conversations more interesting anyway. If you do decide to ignore the invisible line dividing the sexes and stick with the men, better be sure you can talk about what they want to talk about, and that might mean footy, cricket, politics or women. Australian men still are not entirely comfortable with women—yet a 1996 global survey found them second sexiest in the world after the French (but level with the British?!!).

It seems best as a woman in Australia wanting to get on with the men to play oneself down a bit. Take note of the thriving Filipina 'mail-order bride' industry in Australia; there must be some reason the Australian male feels safer with what he believes (often wrongly) to be the more subservient, sweeter Asian female.

If you are a man trying to be a hit with Australian females, things look a lot easier for you. You need only display some of the common 'European' courtesies—offering to help carry shopping-bags, opening doors, presenting flowers, etc.—and you will be viewed as totally adorable.

Convict Chattels

Another observer of the Australian female condition, Anne Summers, argued in her outstanding account of Australian myths about women, *Damned Whores and God's Police*, that the colonial experience had produced two Australian stereotypes of women—either as whores imported to service men's sexual needs, or as defenders of public morality, 'God's police'.

It seems certain that whether they were whores or not in their original state, many of the 24,000 women transported to Australia as convicts between 1788 and 1852 were indeed forced to resort to the profession, and if they did not, were raped repeatedly by male convicts anyway. Theirs, together with that of Aboriginal women, was a particularly brutalising experience.

Women convicts were exploited, beaten, enslaved and passed around or sold as mere chattels or objects of convenience. Yet for the most part, their crimes 'back home' had been little more than the pettiest of theft. Thus began the relationship of the sexes in Australia. Some say that this beginning has coloured the quality of the relationship ever since.

Puritanism vs Paganism

Curiously, as with the homosexual past for men, this early trauma for

a while produced a diametrically opposite reaction: a strong tradn.
of puritanism took root in Australia.

For long, the place of women was at home with the children, sex
was a taboo subject and censorship of the arts was the norm in almost
every state—such attitudes linger outside the main cities and in some
states more than others, Western Australia, for example. Sex education did not reach state schools until the 1970s and still has not reached
all schools.

The superficially permissive and sometimes outright pagan society that Australia seems to present to the visiting outsider is in fact
constantly at loggerheads with this older tradition of puritanism, just
as it is in a similarly pioneer society, that of the USA.

The austere moral values of the Roman Catholic Church which
held sway over the descendants of the many original Irish-born
convicts, as well as other Christian groups, have for long held sway
in 'middle-Australia'. In fact, until very recently, as Donald Horne
has pointed out, the average Australian lifestyle was downright
killjoy: bars closed at six, liquor was not served with meals, Sundays
were dead, betting was illegal, books were banned, and so on.

Bearing all the above in mind, it may not be too surprising to learn
that all is not well with the Australian marriage. One in three
marriages was ending in divorce at the close of the 1980s, though this
may also have been an immediate reaction to more relaxed laws in the
shape of the new Family Law Act of 1975.

The phenomenon of single-parent families is widespread, partly
as a result. However, because of legal recognition of the status of *de
facto* spouse—unmarried but in a stable relationship—there are many
couples whose relationships approximate marriage. In New South
Wales and Victoria at least, for example, there have been legal
provisions since 1984 giving separated *de facto* 'wives' and 'husbands' rights to the property jointly accumulated when they formed
a couple, providing they have had a prior property-allocation agree-
ment.

Curiously, these laws seem actually to encourage cohabitation of the sexes in preference to marriage, as do some of the tax laws.

Fair Go for Women

There are exceptions to this generally strained atmosphere, particularly in the larger cities. And there is slow and steady change. Certainly, in all the official and legalistic things that matter, Australia's treatment of women now is more than proper.

This must be one of the very few countries in the world to have a federal post titled 'Sex Discrimination Commissioner'—currently held by a woman, as it so happens, but presumably it would be discriminatory to reserve the job for women.

Australian women have had the right to vote since the 1890s and the first female politician, Edith Cowan (after whom a new Western Australian university has recently been named), was elected in Western Australia in 1921. Australia in fact pipped England to the post with its laws awarding women the vote and the right to stand for Parliament, as early as 1902.

Ironically, it was male trade unionists' fear of cheap female labour that triggered agitation for equal pay during World War II. The equal-pay principle, 'for work of equal value', was confirmed in 1972 but

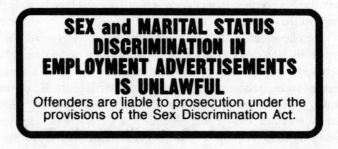

Australians are strong on human rights, as seen in this ad in The West Australian *of December 5, 1989.*

still has not covered the entire female workforce—in fact, on average, women only earn about two-thirds of a male salary for their full-time work.

The 1970s saw many other reforms, such as the introduction of equal-opportunity legislation—classified ads in the media today often carry the banner 'We are an equal-opportunity employer' to underline the point—and a women's minimum wage, in 1974. It was in the decade of the seventies of course that Australian feminism swept the world via Australian author Germaine Greer's controversial book *The Female Eunuch*, published in 1971.

In the 1980s, there has been a boom in feminist discussions, fuelled by the mushrooming of women's studies courses in universities, colleges and even schools, as well as every conceivable feminist art form from women's cinema to women's theatre. Australia is certainly making up for lost time.

Obstacles, Real and Imagined
But many of the protection measures benevolently put in place by the early unionists now precisely stand in women's way: restrictions on what weights women may carry, for example, excluding them from many traditionally male occupations.

Increasingly, of course, automation is making such restrictions redundant anyway. But there are still many spheres of professional work also unbreached by women; the first woman judge was not appointed until the mid-1960s, for example.

Marriage and child-rearing have until very recently routinely meant the end of working life for most Australian women. As late as 1970, women were forced to resign from university service on marriage, and the public service limited the range of jobs they could hold. Things are still made difficult for married women teachers. Married women workers often turn out to be immigrants: about a quarter of the female workforce consists of migrant women, who feel a greater need to get ahead and make money.

As with the Aboriginals, it is not the legal structures that cause problems for female emancipation. Quite the contrary. It is the underlying social climate.

There are still many effectively Men-Only pubs or bars. There may not be any signs saying 'Women, Keep Out'. They wouldn't be necessary anyway. You have only to step inside as a woman to 'feel' the invisible signs. Few women are interested in even trying to stick around.

Australian women apparently are often willing participants in this atmosphere. A cursory perusal of publications like the one most read in Australia (one million copies), the almost 60-year-old *Australian Women's Weekly* magazine (which is a monthly), reveals a predictable diet of English royals, how-to-handle-your-husband/*de facto*/ boyfriend, and pudding recipes, etc.

Hair Talk

An interesting variation on this theme is the Great Australian Coiffure. For example, the average Australian woman-in-the-street has a predictably non-tall poppy hairstyle; usually middle-length and very tousled, the never-been-combed sheepdog look.

What this Australian woman seems to be saying is, 'I'm feminine' (My hair's longish and kind of curly-cute, isn't it?), 'I'm not hard or cold' (Well, look how disorganised my hair is!) and 'I'm not a threat to you' (I can't be too much of a sex-siren or my hair would be longer, wouldn't it?). So, if you are a woman set on touching an Australian man's heart, it might be wise to look a little daffy and tousled. Excessive chic seems to be a turn-off, or at least may never get you beyond the professional colleague stage.

As a man, be warned that although the base of Australian society appears to be sexist in nature, any overt expression of sexism, particularly in conversation, is now a no-no in polite society, if women are present. If they are not, probably anything goes. Neutral words like 'fore-person' (for 'foreman') are commonplace.

Role Models

The unease Australian women sense when struggling to achieve their place in the sun is strange when you consider the number of strong female models already enshrined in Australian history, besides many new ones making their mark right now. The single most powerful model of course was the pioneer woman, who shared with her man the unthinkable deprivations of life in the bush during the 19th century and early 20th century. Only recently have several studies concentrated on her story.

Australian women today have more than their pioneer forebears for role models. There are extraordinary women like Dame Roma Mitchell, for example, the 77-year-old Governor of South Australia, as of 1991. She is the first woman to represent the Queen of England/ Australia in this post, in Australia's 203 years of European settlement.

Dame Roma is used to 'firsts'. In 1962, she was made Australia's first woman Queen's Counsel. Three years later, she became Australia's first woman Supreme Court judge, after which she was appointed the first female Acting Chief Justice.

There are also the former state premiers of Western Australia, Dr Carmen Lawrence (now Federal Minister of Health), and of Victoria, Joan Kirner (now retired from Parliamentary politics), to emulate, both the first women to hold their positions in 1990. Both are acknowledged by their male peers to be impressive, and tough, operators. Both have inherited appalling economic scenarios in their respective states, with which they are both coping more than (wo-)manfully.

Lawrence herself views mateship with fairly benign contempt. She told journalists in 1990, 'They're often extremely competitive and vicious, the so-called "circles of mateship". My observation is that many of the people who take part in these circles of mateship may in fact be grasping for comfort, in what would otherwise be a very hostile world. So I think we shouldn't take that away from them.'

135

Women have excelled in the spheres of life most dear to Australian men: sport and the outdoors. They include remarkable loners like Kay Cottee who in 1987 sailed solo round the world in 189 days, the first woman to do so.

Another remarkable tale is told by Robyn Davidson in her book *Tracks*, recounting her harrowing solo camel journey across 2,700 kilometres (1,700 miles) of desert and scrub between Alice Springs and the Indian Ocean. Treks like Robyn Davidson's are probably just what it takes for women really to touch Australian men. Such experiences almost confer on them the status of honorary mates.

Still, it must be admitted that the trivial, sexsationalist and British Royal Family-adoring tone of some national women's magazines *is* a bit of a worry: take a look at *Women's Weekly* (circulation over one million), *Women's Day* (also over one million) and *New Idea* (954,000) to see what I mean.

Chapter Eight

YOU'RE ON YOUR OWN, MATE

'Democracy does not mean representative government or manhood suffrage, or any other piece of machinery. Democracy is a mental attitude. Democracy means a belief in equality. It is based on the conviction that we are all blokes.'

—Sir Walter Murdoch, prominent Scots-born Western Australian academic, in his *Speaking Personally*, 1930.

Freedom and Democracy

Australia's hunger for freedom is hardly surprising in a nation that began its life in chains.

I am referring to white Australia here. Aboriginal Australians have their own special need for, and definition of, freedom. Their definition is perhaps a more wide-ranging one too, since traditionally, even four walls and material possessions are a sort of prison for them. But the whites owe more of their psyche to Aboriginal beliefs than they realise. In a kind of osmosis between the races, the white Australian has imbibed some of the Aboriginal lust for freedom in the open under the stars.

Between 1788 and 1868, more than 160,000 white men, women and children declared criminals were transported as convicts from England to Australia, then a destination as remote, alien and terrifying as the moon today. No other nation in the world has ever been founded on such an experience.

These were the first white Australians. The bestiality of their lives in their new home is hard to describe and even harder to contemplate. I recommend a careful reading of Robert Hughes' epic account, *The Fatal Shore*. Still, it can be said that the convicts' ejection was in many ways preferable to a term rotting in an English jail. Again, Hughes' book gives a graphic account of exactly how horrible this would have been.

Despite the hardships of their initial landfall, many of the first Australians won their freedom within a short time and set out to make new lives in a new land. The Commander of the First Fleet in 1788, Captain Arthur Phillip, wanted Australia to be a free settlement and tried hard to release convicts onto the land, striving in many ways to relieve the convicts' misery.

But ever since 1788, Australians have consciously or subconsciously been concerned to remove from their lives what Hughes has called 'The Stain' of their convict past, studiously donning a camouflage of almost stultifying respectability for a while. Even in the 19th century, it was ill-mannered to use the term 'convict' in Australia; the euphemism 'government man' was preferred.

It is in this context that one can begin to understand why any imposition of authority, any infringement of personal liberty, no matter how seemingly petty, will arouse Australian passions to a fever pitch.

Don't Classify Me

Thus, it is almost impossible to determine with any certitude any Australian's true identity, so opposed is he to being a digit imprisoned in a computer data-bank, to being categorised in any way.

Until very recently, Australia was one of the very few countries in the world where you could stride into a bank and open up an account in the name of Mickey Mouse or Tom Jones without raising an eyebrow. Nobody checked. However, by the 1990s, banks were getting a little more street-wise and beginning to ask for proof of identity. Nonetheless, this tendency to take you at your word, bordering on naivety at times, does linger on in the everyday social and business life of Australia. It is a direct consequence of every man's respect for the privacy of every other man.

The government strove in vain during the 1980s to introduce the 'Australia Card', an identity card for every Australian, in the hope of controlling social welfare and tax abuses. But the average Australian saw this as the thinly disguised return of the convict's number tag, a sinister infringement of his freedom. No freedom is more treasured in Australia than the right to anonymity. The outcry against the Australia Card was so loud that the government had to abandon its plan (but sneaked it in again by the back door with a compulsory Tax File Number system for all income-earners).

Another form of intrusion on privacy and freedom is the act of asking too many questions. In your efforts to get to know Australians, do not come on too inquisitive—What do you do? Are you married? How many children do you have? Where do you live? etc. are all

139

considered normal questions in many other societies, but not in Australia. Excessive curiosity—'sticky-beaking'—especially at your first meeting, can make the Australian uncomfortable, and may cause him to retreat into a gruffly suspicious shell. Cool it.

Doing Your Own Thing

Freedom can be a lonely privilege. People who are used to more regimented, sheltered lifestyles, where relatives, governments, civic groups, neighbourhood groups, religious groups or whatever all combine to tell you what to do, when and how, often find that they miss this framework in urban Australia. (In the countryside, however, communities are still more intimately meshed.) Such newcomers find the sudden anonymity disorienting. Asians used to paternalistic governments and warmly interactive extended families particularly suffer from this syndrome.

In Australia, people largely leave you alone to get on with your own life, in whatever way you want to lead it. They do not interfere with you, which is pleasant; by the same token, this means you are on your own, mate. All too easily, by extension, it may seem they don't care about you. Yet on the other hand, any direct plea for help, or a greeting in the street, will always be met with a warm response.

Clearly, there are pros and cons to both ways of living. In any case, you can find support groups a-plenty in Australia if you need them. Only in Australia, you have to make the effort to get in contact with them, not wait for them to arrive on your doorstep. Frequently in Australia, if you don't ask, you don't get.

Benign Neglect?

The area where the 'leave things alone' philosophy shows up clearest is in family life and child-rearing. Young Australians are noticeably freer and less disciplined than many other youngsters, offensively so in the eyes of Europeans and Asians particularly.

Here again, the Australian dislike for authority surfaces: parents stand for authority. Former Labor Prime Minister Bob Hawke's biographer, Blanche d'Alpuget, records that Hawke's own family was raised very much in this mould: 'Adult visitors were often shocked by the liberties in speech allowed to the children,' she says. 'Hawke was the obverse of an authoritarian father.'

Liberal parenting, and teaching styles at school too, do produce lively, creative and independent-minded—and opinionated—young people. An Asian migrant friend of mine used to a more dictatorial style of education said that for the first time he could remember, his children considered it a punishment if they were kept away from school, they enjoyed it so much in Australia.

But there are also scary incidents of major vandalism by schoolchildren, displaying that opposition to authority so typical of Australia. In one case in Western Australia, some teenage students simply went to their school at night and set fire to it. There are many other such stories. Dislocation of the family in post-industrial society is hardly a problem unique to Australia. In addition, economic hard times and the growth in single-parent families have made it genuinely difficult for Australian parents to supervise children properly.

Unemployment has exacerbated the potential for the animal energies of young people to spill over into violence. All too often, children are on the streets with nothing to do. Theirs is not a desirable freedom.

At the worst end of this scenario are abandoned children actually living in poverty. There are something like 200,000 children deemed to be living in poverty in Sydney alone, particularly in the western districts. And in 1989, the Human Rights Commission found that about 25,000 Australian children were homeless. Many of them have a drug problem too.

No Leaders Please, We're Australian

Crucial to the Australian concept of freedom of course is democracy. In its simplest form, this is seen as meaning 'Nobody is my boss.'

141

Egalitarianism is another important pillar of the concept. Australians perversely enjoy cutting their leaders down to size to uphold this principle. Typical of the social atmosphere was the incident in 1991 when the then Prime Minister Bob Hawke was shown on television being interviewed in the back of his limousine. Unfortunately, he had neglected to strap up his seat-belt during the interview.

This point was certainly not lost on, nor tolerated by, the viewers, who promptly jammed the television channel switchboard with more than 1,000 complaints—why should Hawke consider himself above the common man when it came to the seat-belt law? (Australia was the first country in the world to make car seat-belts compulsory, in 1971.) Hawke's reaction was wise, and the only one possible in a robust democracy like Australia's: he said he was very sorry and asked the police to treat him like any other citizen. He was duly fined A$100 for his lapse.

In some societies, such public criticism would be unthinkable. But Australians were quite happy to put the matter out of their minds once justice had been done, the leader levelled. Besides, they prefer their leaders to be that way: ordinary men, capable of peccadillos. As Donald Horne has said, 'Australians do not crave great men.' Great men are tall poppy material.

Contempt for politicians and political processes is a reflex emotion for most Australians, especially the younger generation. Respect for authority is very un-Australian.

There is no doubt in the average Australian's mind that politicians are just ordinary blokes like himself who have been 'put up there' with the sole purpose of 'delivering the goods' and serving the people. If at any time they should cease to deliver, begin to behave like masters or, heaven forbid, leaders, they should be summarily removed by the people who put them there. The scandals of corruption in Queensland and of economic mismanagement and influence-peddling in Western Australia in recent times have served only to sharpen such attitudes.

ROAST A POLITICIAN
Hear What Others Say
Then Have Your Gripe
DIAL
0055 11 151

Politicians are fair game in Australia—do not expect respect for authority. There is a dial-it service for almost everything, even badmouthing politicians. From The West Australian *of December 29, 1989.*

The level of rudeness about, and to, politicians on television and in the media, for example, shocks most non-Australians, even the English and the Americans. 'It's a bit like watching soft porn,' said one migrant fresh from respectful Asia.

Fundamentally, it is a healthy attitude. Taken to extremes, it can make government close to impossible at times.

Teamwork Is Australian

Here, pause a while to consider a paradox: the Australian soldier has long been saluted as an excellent fighting man. But isn't good soldiering founded on rigid discipline, hard training, hierarchy and unquestioning submission to officers' instructions? How then does the Australian soldier do it?

The answer is of course that an Australian may be difficult to govern, but he responds better than most to those whom he admires and loves, and who stand beside him, rather than lead from the front. He is a team-worker. 'Mateship' reinforces this.

This principle could be extended to other spheres of life, in work and play. So do not too hastily write off Australian rebelliousness as being destructive to getting things done, nor as anathema to the collective good.

143

Another Way of Getting Things Done

The Australian way of doing things is eccentric and lateral rather than direct, apparently indisciplined, yet both creative and effective. And most important, humane. It is a way that works especially well for artistic endeavours and in the more arcane reaches of science— such as quantum or chaos theory and computer software-generation— which today are by definition anarchistic, as many Aussies are.

Get in Line

Another example of the general philosophy, 'I'm as good as the next man', is the Australian taxi-driver's preference for his passenger to sit in the front seat beside him: he is nobody's chauffeur. This is good behaviour to adopt when in Australia, particularly when you are male. It is not so expected of women passengers.

You should always take your place in the queue, real or meta-phorical, no matter who you are. Beggar or king, you wait your turn in Australia. There should be no privilege, no string-pulling to get ahead of your neighbour.

Well, that is the official Australian ethos, anyway. When prac-tised, it is admirable. But it should be noted that, as the 'WA Inc' investigations in Western Australia have revealed, in reality, there is quite a bit of influence-peddling going on behind the scenes, harm-less 'mateship' though it may seem to its practitioners.

Yet another facet of this stance is the Australian's almost auto-matic sympathy for the underdog, 'the battler'. Similarly, we have already discussed in other chapters his ability to elevate failure into victory. These attitudes are the natural corollary of the anti-tall poppy syndrome.

Dissecting Democracy

How does it all work?

The governmental system is that of a classic parliamentary de-mocracy with full separation of executive and legislative powers, mixed with some elements from the USA. Australia was seen, and saw itself, in the 19th century very much as a repeat of the American experience.

A modification of this basically 'Westminster' system is the existence in Australia of a written Constitution dating from federation in 1901, a rigid instrument which the 'mother country', the UK, of course does not have. The Constitution can be altered only by a referendum.

Australia's Commonwealth Constitution, however, does not cover the area of civil and human rights in the way that the American one does. Chiefly, it outlines only broadly the system of national government and the relationship between the federal Commonwealth and the states. It does not even refer to the right to vote, nor to the exact structure of government and the cabinet. There are proposals to flesh out this Constitution with more detail, and also human rights guarantees.

The Constitution is, however, supplemented by conventions which do spell out details and also control the theoretically extensive powers of the Governor-General. The Governor-General has the power, for instance, to summon and dissolve Parliament, to dismiss ministers, to be commander-in-chief of the armed forces and to appoint judges. Usually, he (or she, one day) will refer to ministers before taking a decision.

There was one celebrated case in 1975 when he did more than that. In 1975, Governor-General Sir John Kerr dismissed the Labor government of Gough Whitlam, after the Senate had blocked supply of funds to the government, throwing the nation into uproar. Thereby hangs a tale ...

Election Fever

Voting at elections is compulsory in Australia for those 18 years old and above. The Aboriginals have had the vote only since 1967.

Popular history has it that Australian democracy was born at the

145

Eureka Stockade riots of 1854, two years before all adult white males were given the vote for the first time, in South Australia (all the states except Tasmania had followed by 1859). The Eureka uprising took place near Ballarat in the state of Victoria, when goldminers barricaded themselves behind a stockade and raised a new Australian flag, demanding the vote and complaining against the severe mining licensing system of the time. The whole affair lasted only 15 minutes before the miners were overrun by troops.

Elections take place every three years. Many observers have pointed out that any Australian government's capacity to implement policy effectively is severely hampered by its need constantly to keep an eye on the popular vote. The vote is not conducted on the first-past-the-post principle. The system is one of preferential voting, with voters listing candidates in order of preference so that votes can be redistributed down the list until one candidate gets a majority vote. This gives minority parties a better chance of making an impact on politics.

Government, Government and More Government

Proportional representation is also adopted in the Senate elections, and in some states. A plethora of authorities, from the State Governments and the Federal Government, to local government, as well as the upper and lower houses of Parliament (the Senate and the House of Representatives respectively), ensures a full-blown democracy.

The national Parliament, at Federal level, is headed by the Queen of England, represented by the Governor-General. (See further comments on this odd situation in Chapter Three, *A Sense of Nation*.) The seat of the Federal Government is at Canberra, in Australian Capital Territory (ACT), which was created in 1911 solely for the purpose of housing government and Parliament. At State level, the Federal structure is more or less replicated, even to the point of separate State constitutions, of 19th century vintage. Each state has its own premier.

Some have called Australia 'over-governed'. The total number of Federal, State and local public servants in 1991 stood at about 1.7 million, for a population of 17 million.

The Fourth Estate

In any democracy, the media are important players, sometimes wild cards. The Australian press certainly ranks as wild, being one of the most aggressive in the world. And Australians are avid newspaper readers, as well as television watchers.

Unfortunately, their choice is somewhat restricted; there is not much light and shade, or depth, to the range of media available in Australia, partly because ownership is concentrated in a few hands. The situation is extremely fluid as I write, but a rough count gives two national dailies, 15 metropolitan dailies and 10 metropolitan weeklies, 39 regional dailies and more than 400 provincial and suburban papers in the country.

As mentioned in Chapter Seven, the *Australian Women's Weekly* (which is a monthly) is probably the most-read magazine in Australia, of about 1600 Australian magazines in all. The *Bulletin*, founded in 1880, is the national news weekly. Somewhat parochial at times, although it does incorporate the US magazine *Newsweek*, it is nonetheless a good barometer of Australian happenings and viewpoints.

The concentration of media ownership certainly runs counter to what should be found in a healthy democracy, although there are laws controlling cross-media ownership, in both television and in print media, for example. Unlimited foreign ownership has been allowed only since 1991, providing no more than 20 per cent of that foreign ownership brings with it voting rights on the board.

So concentrated is media ownership that the only three players worth mentioning now are former Australian-turned-American Rupert Murdoch's News Ltd (which ate up the major Herald and Weekly Times group of Melbourne in 1987, and whose flagship is

147

the national daily, *The Australian*), Kerry Packer's Australian Consolidated Press and the Fairfax group, recently sold to Canadian bidder Conrad Black.

The Small Screen

New laws now limit the extent to which media moguls can corner the broadcasting market; television owners, for example, may not have more than a 5 per cent interest in a daily English-language paper in the same capital city as their television station. Foreign ownership of broadcasting is prohibited.

In 1989, the country had 50 commercial television stations and three remote commercial channels, 140 commercial radio stations and 74 public radio stations, in the private sector.

Democracy flourishes on the radio, with a proliferation of phone-in, 'talk-back' shows. But the most international mindset and highest intellectual quality is probably to be found in a combination of ABC and ABC Radio National. The television equivalent is SBS, the Special Broadcasting Service, besides ABC again. There is heated debate as I write, about the possible introduction of advertising to both ABC and SBS television, till now thankfully both 'commercial virgins'.

Every state, however, also has television channels unique to itself, besides the national 'Big Three': Seven, Nine and Ten, which also tailor content for state audiences.

In an unusual instance of media control, for Australia, the Australian Broadcasting Tribunal has since the 1970s stipulated a quota of home-made drama to be screened on commercial-licensee television. Hence the growth of Australian soap operas like the now world-famous *Neighbours*, saga of the suburbs.

Mind My Space

It is a delicate task to balance freedom against the risk of that very freedom's invading other people's personal space.

Freedom, as I have remarked elsewhere, entails freedom of speech whether you like what the other fellow is saying or not. And democracy is supposed to mean you would die for his right to say it.

Democracy can be inconvenient. It means pressure groups, each lobbying the political process for their own self-interest—the wheat lobby, the wool lobby, the mining lobby, the environmentalist lobby, the feminist lobby, and so on. This tends to slow things down. Decisions take longer to implement. But it cuts both ways: it also means you get to have your say.

Freedom of the Personal Kind

Freedom may also mean that there is a bit more nudity and sex on television than you care for, that someone has the right to open up a sex shop in your neighbourhood shopping centre, that the local pub has a lunchtime 'lingerie' strip show, and that scantily clad young people may be seen on the street kissing and holding hands.

The open display of the human body and relative sexual freedom of Western-style societies like Australia is a particular problem for visitors from Asia and other traditional societies.

A quick scan of the 'Personal' classified advertisement columns in several Australian newspapers will soon reveal the scope of the services available. You can pay to do it in bubble baths, with girls in suspenders, in groups big or small, with or without rubber and leather, to suffer 'discipline', just to watch, or even just to talk about it on the phone. In such a society, the old excuse for not being able to come over—'I'm sorry, I'm tied up right now'—might be only too literally true.

And so onward through the classifieds: Under 'F', a 'French Maid, Ooh La La.' Under 'H,' a 'Hot Housewife' or a 'Hispanic'. Under 'G,' things become decidedly 'Gay'. 'Guy seeks Guy, Chinese or any nationality,' reads one ad. There's 'Lesbian Lucy' too, while one 'Lola' offers to 'dress and make up inquisitive males.' There is some elegant G-for-Gigolo begging under 'G' too: 'Gent,

23. Is there a lady out there who can financially assist one honest young man in dire straits? Genuine ad.'

By no means all these ads are placed by professionals; there are quite a few amateurs, part-timers, one-off thrill-seekers, and those just looking for love and marriage, too.

Look the Other Way

If such things disturb you, it is important to maintain your sense of balance by understanding that most Australians go about their daily lives without a second look at this underworld. They ignore such things, treating them like the wallpaper of life, quite unshocked and often uninterested too. So just take no notice of it—walk on!

Australian attitudes to sex, violence and censorship are in any case ambivalent, reflecting the ongoing tug-of-war between the puritanism of the recent past and a more permissive present already described in Chapter Seven.

In general, the social premise is that non-violent erotica are a useful safety valve for normal human sexual emotions and fantasies. There is an elaborate system of film classification, to indicate films' content to the public: M for Mature, R for Restricted and PG for Parental Guidance, besides G for General and X for Adults-only. X-rated videos, for example, have been banned in most of Australia since 1984, except for the Australian Capital Territory (ACT), i.e. Canberra, and the Northern Territory. Western Australia too is beginning to relax on this one. As a result, the ACT, that sober seat of government, has long been Australia's chief supplier of blue movies through a A$25-million mail-order business, Canberra's fifth largest industry.

You Pays Your Money and You Takes Your Choice

Freedom is a highly valued and generally very available commodity in Australia. The individual is expected to use maturity and judgement when shopping in this supermarket of choice. It's all up to you.

Chapter Nine

THE GREAT AUSTRALIAN DREAM

'The night was dark and stormy
The dunny light grew dim,
I heard a crash, and then a splash,
Good God, he's fallen in!'

—Childhood ditty retailed to the author by Beth Kennedy, a native of Albany in Western Australia. The outdoors toilet in old Australian homes, still to be found in the countryside, is at the centre of countless jokes and tall tales.

Homes and Gardens

A detached house set on at least a quarter-acre garden, with about six rooms, is central to the Australian definition of happiness. 'The first suburban nation', Donald Horne has called his own country, in his seminal psycho-analysis of Australia, *The Lucky Country*, of 1964, a classic to which all subsequent studies owe a debt, including this one.

Certainly, an Australian's home is his castle. A home of your own is the Great Australian Dream.

Impossible Dream?

Unfortunately, that dream has been punctured over the decade of the 1980s, as house purchase prices and bank-loan interest rates soared in tandem, with the latter heading towards 20 per cent or more at their worst (though closer to 14 per cent by 1991).

This sorry turn of affairs has left many young couples unable to contemplate buying their first home, and many older mortgagees unable to keep up their payments. To Australians, this upset has seemed akin to an infringement of their human rights. All across the nation, resentment hangs in the air like smoke over a barbie; the government struggles to meet its people's expectations of affordable homeownership. If you have been able comfortably to buy your Australian house outright, do not flaunt the fact.

Still, something like 70 per cent of Australians are homeowners or mortgagees, a pretty high rate in world terms. Public housing has become the mark of virtual welfare cases—broken families or families otherwise in crisis, the unemployed, refugees and so on—and the housing provided, albeit low-cost, is often only minimally maintained.

Land Hunger

The quarter-acre fixation is also being re-examined, by thoughtful town-planners in particular. How much longer can Australian cities

The homes of the wealthy overlook Sydney Harbour's north side. Photo by Siva Choy.

spread outwards in massive suburban sprawls, as can already be seen in Melbourne and Sydney and as is happening apace in Perth?

Not only does the Australian homeowner expect to own a fair amount of land, but he also expects literally to sit on it. Apartment living, even medium-rise, is only just beginning to occur as an option to most Australians, and the vast majority abhor high-rise homes. One of the most striking characteristics of the Australian city is its low skyline, except perhaps in the very heart of the central business district, where skyscrapers are considered reasonably appropriate for work—but not for home.

I personally find this a much more human way of living. With the population so small in such a huge land, one can sympathise with the Australian's instinctive insouciance about using up land. However, it must be admitted that a widely spread population makes the planning, administration and servicing of cities very difficult indeed. The provision of sewerage, roads, transport and a host of other infrastructure and services becomes a costly problem. Suburban sprawl is not acceptable either to environmentalists eager to protect wild Australia.

It seems most likely then that residential areas within a certain radius of Australian city centres will no longer be able to corner quarter-acre blocks for each housing unit in the future. Noises in this direction have already been made by various city authorities; 'high-density housing', a phrase which would have caused an uproar only a couple of decades ago, is now an Australian planner's buzz-word. An influx of Asian and American investors, more used to apartment-block living, has also fuelled the building of high-rise residential blocks (not that 'high-rise' is necessarily synonymous with 'high-density', however).

The Great Australian Dream is steadily receding to the outer suburbs and the outback countryside itself. But you can rely on the Australian homeowner to fight this 'reform' all the way. He feels as strongly about holding land as some Americans do about the right to own a gun, or the English about the importance of pet dogs.

The Australian Style

The vast majority of Australian homes are single-storey, what are known as 'bungalows' in some parts of Asia, and each home is gloriously individual. It is still extremely unusual in Australia, I am glad to say, to be confronted with serried ranks of exactly identical estate homes looking as though they came out of the same plaster mould, off a factory conveyor belt, of the sort now common in many other parts of the world.

Very much in vogue, at a price, are historic, or even imitation, 'Federation' homes, harking back to a colonial architectural style popular at the turn of the century: these charming buildings usually feature porches and verandahs supported by pillars and elaborately lacy wrought-iron work, among other things. Other recognisably Australian housing styles are the neo-classical and Spanish designs of

Mediterranean origin, 'weatherboard' wooden cottages, and the 'Queenslander', a largely timbered tropical exotic set high above ground level, usually with open verandahs.

The 'Greenie' movement is taking some designs closer to Nature, so timber and stone, or mixtures of the two, can also be seen. A most attractive, but not cheap, 'back to Nature' option is rammed earth, very popular in southern Western Australia, which produces a marvellously smooth caramel-brown surface. It's a strong material and naturally well insulated. Cheaper are baked mud-bricks, but it's an exhausting labour of love to construct a home of these.

On the Ground

One of Australia's greatest attractions is surely the fact that it is still possible to acquire large chunks of wild land, and also to own a home on the ground for a reasonable price. Many a homeowner buys his land and then designs and builds his own house. A whole industry is geared to helping him do this, once planning permissions have been cleared with the authorities. There are catalogues of ready-made doors, windows, roofing, tiling, you name it.

Usually, you call in a professional to lay the foundations at least. After that, you could build it stick by stick yourself if you really wish. But most people use professional builders under their personal supervision.

When buying land, you need to have good advice and to be aware of all sorts of pitfalls. You may well find that you are not allowed to keep your land vacant of a building for more than a set period of time, say, about two years. There may also be requirements that you fence the land, which could be expensive, and there will certainly be strict rules about maintaining fire-breaks and burning back the land every so often.

You could also find that although you own the land, you do not own the soil beneath it, as the government may have reserved mining rights. This could put you in a sticky position if gold or iron ore is found beneath your house. In the countryside, be sure of your water sources, and understand thoroughly the local fire risks.

As in any other country, you need to study planning programmes for the area where you are buying: will your beautiful wilderness be a new town in a few years' time?

These are but a handful of the most common problems with land ownership. Tread carefully. For all these and other important considerations, such as taxation, please do refer to a professional consultant.

Shopping Around

Any day, the newspapers are chock-a-block with house-sale ads. In Perth, I found that it was an accepted Sunday leisure activity to tour the various homes up for sale and open for viewing, sometimes just for fun, sometimes to update one's understanding of the market. These are not display homes, but real people's homes up for sale—the owners just have to go out for the day while a pack of strangers tramp through their home.

Most Australian home sales are done through a real estate agent, followed by a 'settlement agent' who actually sees all the various, final payments through. The agent will be sitting around in the house open for viewing (complete with all the occupants' furnishings). While Australian agents are no more honest than any others, I have found them pleasantly un-pushy, in that they rarely speak unless spoken to.

Here's the drum, as the Australians say, the latest on property, at the time of writing, in late 1991 ...

Taking Perth in Western Australia as an example (but don't ever forget, there are enormous differences, state by state, among Australia's property markets; generally speaking, the East, especially Sydney, is always the most expensive area), residential properties have seen a 30 to 40 per cent decline in value since peaking at the highest ever level in May 1989.

As Mr William F. Shire, Director of Australian Business &

Property Services in Perth, says, 'Prior to this boom period, an average four-bedroom, two-bathroom brick-and-tile house could be bought for approximately A$72,000. This property today cannot be purchased for less than A$120,000.' Obviously, this implies a substantial overall gain to the pre-boom buyer, even after the recent decline.

Another Australian, Mr Peter M. Brown, Associate Professor at the National University of Singapore's School of Building and Estate Management, who is hung about with qualifications much like a Christmas tree with lights (including being a Fellow of the Australian and New Zealand Institutes of Valuers), apparently has got the Australian real estate cycle all figured out. It follows an eight-year boom-bust pattern. There have been property price peaks in 1973, 1981 and 1989. Even with my rudimentary maths, I deduce therefore, that the next peak will come in 1997.

Buy Now

William Shire further spells it out: 'Weak but sustained recovery is likely to commence in late 1991, gathering pace 1992/1993.'

Since yet another Australian real-estate expert, Mr Jeff Litte, Associate Director of Knight Frank Cheong Hock Chye & Baillieu, said that the market had already bottomed, in mid-1991, 'although it may bounce along at the bottom for a while longer', it does seem that now, not later, is the right time to buy property in Australia—even give or take a bit on real estate agents' natural desire to activate markets, since they gain whether you are buying or selling.

Of course, you cannot invest in Australian real estate without the say-so of Australia's Foreign Investment Review Board. If you are not a migrant with Permanent Residence, there is no way you will be allowed to buy an established residential building, although at the time of writing, you can buy a brand new home before it is completed, and you can also buy vacant land on which to build a house within 12 months of purchase.

Financing, whether in Australian dollars or foreign currency, is best obtained from Australian banks with representation in your region or country, say some Australian bankers operating branches overseas. Again, however, note that they have a clear self-interest in saying this. Tempting though the lower interest rates in some countries may be (lower than the 13 to 14 per cent likely in Australia), beware of loans taken outside Australia, as they may attract a 10 per cent Australian withholding tax.

What kind of Australian house is a good buy then, in capital gains terms when you sell? (There is no capital gains tax for the sale of a 'first home' or principal home.)

Here the experts recommend purchases of brick-and-tile (brick walls, tiled roofs) homes in the A$150,000–200,000 bracket, and careful attention to location—not more than 15 kilometres from the city centre, with easy access to the nearest freeway, to schools, shops, parks and bus routes, and so on.

'Brick-and-tile' as opposed to what, you may ask?

Many older Australian homes are built of 'weatherboard'—overlapping timber planks—or of 'fibro', compressed-wood fibreboard, or even metals like zinc or anodised aluminium. In the case of metals, particularly, there will probably be an asbestos insulation layer under the metal cladding. In many old buildings, roofs are either of zinc or other metals, or also of asbestos. The weatherboard styles often have a pretty, old-fashioned and traditionally Australian look about them, but brick-and-tile immediately confers greater prestige, something you have to consider in terms of resale value.

There is also a psychological problem with asbestos owing to a prolonged health scare about asbestosis in Australia. Loose asbestos fibres certainly are not great for your health and intensive exposure to asbestos, in the industrial, manufacturing context, has been proven dangerous. But there really is not much hard evidence about how dangerous it is just to live in a house with asbestos insulation. However, in view of fairly hysterical public perceptions in Australia at the moment, asbestos is probably something a home buyer should worry about, again in terms of resale value if nothing else.

Also prestigious are fenced or walled gardens, although a pleasantly free and open, trusting feeling is visible in the suburban Australian landscape, thanks to the many unfenced gardens. The wealthier the area, however, the more money will have been spent to purchase privacy behind creeper-laden walls. But these are sure insignia of the tall poppy.

Handyman Mania

Because the home is such an important possession, Australians spend an awful lot of time 'doing things around the house' (when not tinkering with the car). In fact, they are forever renovating, rebuilding or extending.

If you want to be a real Australian, you should always have at least one room of your house in total chaos when visitors call on you: 'Oh, we're just renovating the lounge/bathroom/kitchen.' The wreckage of broken timber, drilling dust and stripped wallpaper should be strewn over the floor. The man of the house should be glimpsed, paint-roller, electric saw or wallpaper-steamer in hand, slaving away in his filthy dungarees, or, more likely, shorts.

Alternatively, the whole house, including the tea-set crockery, could be coated in a fine film of red wood dust—'We only just finished hand-polishing the wood floors.' Or there could be a curious odour—'The pest men just came to spray for termites.' All these constitute a perfectly normal state of affairs in any Australian home at any one time.

D.I.Y. is Dinky-Di

If you are in any doubt about my telling the truth in this matter, just take a look at the Yellow Pages phone-book for any city in Australia and see how many 'D.I.Y.' (Do It Yourself) centres you can count.

I guarantee they will take up several pages.

A dinkum Aussie lifestyle—constantly renovating your home. Photo courtesy of Christine Moulet.

D.I.Y. is a massive industry in Australia, partly because the cost of labour makes hiring contractors prohibitive, but also because it is the approved, macho way of 'doing things around the house'. A visit to any major D.I.Y. emporia reveals vast warehouses stacked with every conceivable thingamajig to do every conceivable practical thing from building your own greenhouse to mending a leaky tap. My husband says it's Heaven; others have more mixed feelings.

Most Australian homes have a workshed in the garden, crammed full of tools for this and that, paint tins and so on. And garden tools. Sadly, it must be said, sometimes it is difficult to appreciate what has been achieved by all this toil, when gazing at the ill-matching but all equally awful wallpaper and carpets in many Australian homes.

On the other hand, there is a certain vitality in Australian home decor. Often, in younger and more educated households, the furnishings will reflect the new multicultural society in which Australians now live, as well as a consciousness of Asian neighbours—Italian touches, Aboriginal artefacts, vases bought in Singapore, batik paintings from Indonesia and so on.

The Gardening Syndrome

The garden is the other Australian obsession, very much part of the British heritage. Older Australians (39 per cent of gardeners anyway) illustrate the origins of this heritage beautifully, as they lovingly tend look-alike English country-cottage gardens full of roses, chrysanthemums and dahlias, with verdant lawns tediously kept alive by a water-sprinkler system using bore water from beneath the soil.

Australian grass, such as it is (you will soon become familiar with the menace of everything from buffalo-grass to couch-grass, among various kinds of undesirable grass), is not meant to be green and lush, particularly in the summer. The natural state of an Australian lawn is dry, brown and sparse—come and see mine in Perth any time!

Such English-style gardens are of course quite ridiculous in a largely arid ecology. The 'soils' in Perth, for example, consist almost entirely of sand.

Among the foreign plants which do seem to do well in Australia are those which come from a very similar setting, in South Africa. Thankfully, recent decades have seen the growth of a 'Native Gardens' movement (about 23 per cent of styles chosen) which encourages the cultivation of indigenous Australian species. These 'natives'

Kangaroo's Paw. Picture courtesy of the Western Australia Tourism Commission.

include the Eucalypts, the Acacias (Wattles), the flowering Grevilleas, Banksias, Kangaroo's Paws and so on. They are much more sensible choices than roses or since they demand less attention and waste less water: native plants are geared to manage with very little water.

This great change signifies that at last, the white Australian is coming to terms with his real environment, the Australian ecology, and breaking away from the English motherland of the past.

Putting on a Front

Whatever the character of their gardens, you will see them on weekends, all the gardeners, toiling long and hard at weeding, digging, pruning, mulching (soils are often so dry and light, they need help from woodchips, newspaper and the like) and mowing the lawns.

Businesses providing services such as 'garden bags' delivered empty and collected full of garden rubbish at regular intervals, are thriving. So are lawn-cutting and tree-pruning services, for the lazy.

Interestingly, it is always the *front* garden above all that is so lovingly tended. Traditionally, the back garden, once referred to only as the 'backyard', is a much messier, more utilitarian place, where the washing is hung out, the workshed used for handyman activities, a vegetable patch might be cultivated for cheap, fresh food and the dogs and cats are kept.

The front garden is the image the householder wishes to present to the world; the Australian cares about what his neighbours, and passers-by, might think of him, in terms of middle-class decency.

The Family Dog

Australians have inherited the British love of pets, particularly dogs. Take a look at any public park over the weekend and see how many dogs you can spot being walked; you are bound to see an amazing number, and variety.

If you are settling into Australia and want a dog, you should take a look at typically Australian dogs, most of them stemming from sheep or cattle-mustering breeds. Breeds include the Blue-heeler and the Kelpie. The smooth-haired Kelpie is a cattle-dog that derives from the border collie.

Also typically Australian are the Australian Silky, a long-haired toy dog, and the Kangaroo Dog, a greyhound-Scottish deerhound cross once used to fight off kangaroos and dingos (wild dogs).

Front-Room Formality

A strange thing about the Australian suburbs is the deathly quiet, and darkness, of the streets at night. This is partly because the seasonal weather does not always encourage people to be out on the streets, as you might expect in Mediterranean or tropical Asian settings, and partly because the level of urban crime (or at least the *perception* of the level) does not encourage it either.

But it is also because the front room is never in use and therefore never lit up. 'The front room', also known as the lounge-room, plays much the same role as the parlour did—and still does in some North-country parts—in England. It is a starched, tidy, formal room for

163

'serious' socialising only—a visit from the local priest perhaps, the police, the family lawyers, the doctor, or prospective in-laws. It is not really meant to be lived in.

The underlying idea of course is that most visitors are a) unexpected and b) unwelcome, so they should be contained at the front of the house and got rid of from there. Australians are paradoxical in that, although they are very friendly on the surface, they in fact have a highly developed concept of privacy.

Real life takes place at the back of the house, in and around the kitchen, in the larger 'family room' (also known as the games room or sometimes the rumpus room), and in the summer, on the patio or verandah, and in the 'yard'—which is probably actually a garden—around the barbie (barbecue pit) and perhaps also in and around the swimming pool.

Kitchens are often open-design, allowing for maximum social interaction. A great deal of social life takes place in the kitchen. It is rare to be invited to a sit-down dinner in a separate dining room. More likely, you will find yourself milling around the kitchen talking to the lady of the house cooking at the stove, snacking from a mobile buffet, or standing in the garden around the barbie pit.

Loo Lore

Another odd thing about Australian houses from the non-Australian point of view is the bathroom-loo (john, W.C., toilet, lavatory) disposition. Only the newer houses will have more than one loo. Older and rural homes might even have the loo in a separate shed in the yard—the 'dunny' of Aussie folklore. Writing in *The West Australian* in 1993, Pam Casellas remarked, 'We grew up with good bladders, us country kids, because we were too scared to venture out to the lav in the middle of the night.'

Very few homes have loos in the bathroom itself (the place where you shower or bath)—they are usually separate. So do not ask for the 'bathroom' nor to 'wash your hands', if what you really want is to relieve yourself, as you will probably find yourself facing only a hand-basin and a towel-rail. You will have to be more specific and ask either for the 'toilet' or the 'loo'.

I am pleased to say that the more sophisticated homes are improving on this lamentable situation by installing more than one loo, and also incorporating loos with the shower-room in some rare instances. Despite the British tradition of taking a bath in a tub, or 'long bath' as some call it, most Australians opt for showers in preference, by the way.

Other Rooms

Bedrooms and the master bathroom, if there is one, are designed to be out of the way of visitors and it is expected that they should be treated as strictly private areas.

The Barbie

Some have called this 'the high altar' in the ritual of outdoor living. The outdoors area of the home is very clearly a male domain, controlled by the man of the house. As we have seen in Chapter Seven, the hunter-male cooks the 'primitive' meal of raw meat burned on charcoal. Visiting females should not attempt to interfere. Outdoors settings are the ideal environment for the naturally sociable and easy-going Australian to mingle without formality.

Incidentally, you will hardly ever see the word 'barbecue' spelled properly. It appears everywhere, in advertisements, party invitations and so on, as 'BBQ', 'Bar BQ', and 'Bar-b-que'.

The barbie party is the Australian's safe route to nostalgia about life in the bush, brewing tea in a billy over a campfire. The same macho psychology pushes suburban Australians to wear cattledriver 'cowboy' hats, display huge 'roo bars' on the front of their cars (for fending off kangaroos crossing the roads) or to purchase impressive four-wheel drive ('4WD') vehicles, meant for heavy bush-driving, when in fact they hardly ever go bush.

Visiting

There is certainly more visiting without a prior appointment in Australia than there would be in England. All the same, you have to be careful about your timing.

A very pained Asian friend complained to me once about how he could feel the atmosphere tense up if he called on his friends shortly before 'Tea' (the evening meal, or dinner, in Australia). They would sit chatting very politely, but clearly waiting for him to leave, indeed *dying* for him to leave as time wore on.

In Asia of course, and many Mediterranean countries too, the problem simply would not arise: the family would naturally invite their friend to share the evening meal with them. But this kind of familiarity does not come easily to Australians, so do not expect it; instead, leave at the unspoken but appointed time. Neither is it as automatic to Australians to offer visitors a drink on arrival as it is in some cultures, particularly Asian cultures.

If you come from a society where home-help or servants are easily available, pause to remember that this is not the norm in Australia. It would therefore be a good idea to offer to help clear the table and to wash up. The offer may be refused, but it will certainly be appreciated.

TROUBLESHOOTING CHECKLIST

Here is a random and by no means exhaustive checklist of potential problem areas.

Swimming Pool

'Just what I always dreamed of, my own backyard pool!' you may sigh as you move into your new Australian home. All pool-owners quickly learn how costly it is to maintain a pool in proper condition.

You will be forever measuring the chlorine level, the pH level, the alkaline-acid ratio, tipping in great sacks of salt (for salt-water chlorinators), repairing pumps and filters, and so on.

Pool maintenance is a serious matter in the scorching Australian summer—the hotter it gets, the more likely a badly maintained pool may breed bacteria, the sort that cause meningitis in children, for example. The chemicals necessary to maintain balance in your pool are costly. So budget carefully before rushing for one.

Take note too of our salutary lesson when we accidentally emptied our pool. We had turned the pump onto 'Backwash' to clean out the filter, which entails draining some water out of the pool. We then went to bed and forgot about it. Next morning, hey presto, no pool!

We decided this was a blessing in disguise since the swimming season had just ended and winter was on its way, and thought nothing further of it until someone wiser remarked that he hoped our pool was not fibreglass. Yes it was, we told him.

In that case, said he, better get it filled straightaway, as the sides would probably buckle under the pressure of soil subsidence around the pool during heavy winter rains. Sure enough, when we anxiously inspected our pool, there was a distinct bulge on one side. That meant hosing in about 30,000 litres of water as quickly as possible—and the consequent water bill.

Wooden Houses

Termites, or white ants as they are more commonly called in Australia, are a problem, but so are the chemicals used to spray against them. Spraying once may be necessary, particularly if your home is weatherboard and has wooden floors, as many of the older homes do. But do not listen to the pest-control companies who want to persuade you to treat your home every year—chemicals usually have an effective life of at least three or four years, and could be toxic if they leech into your garden soil, where you might have a vegetable patch ('vegie' patch as the Aussies call it), for example.

Do some research before making this decision, sample a mixture of views, from those of your neighbours to consumer advice bureaux to 'Green' conservationist groups.

Trees

For those who have previously lived in city apartments, it may be quite marvellous to find you have trees in your Australian garden, perhaps fruit trees as well. But be aware that all trees, and especially fruit trees, need special care.

Some species, such as the paperbarks (Melaleucas) may have acid foliage which renders all the soil beneath their canopy bald of grass.

The Blackboy of Western Australia. Photo by the author.

Some may be poisonous to children. Others (like lemon trees) may detest exposure to strong winds. Some unique Australian ones, like the Blackboy, may need to be set on fire every so often, not to mention the huge area they need for their extensive root system.

Once again, you may have to make the difficult decision whether to use chemical fertilisers and insecticides—fruit flies are among the pests attacking stone fruit like nectarines and apricots, for example. Check out your local gardening societies, including the organic ones, and ask their advice—I discovered from an organic gardener that you could hang fruit tree branches with tins full of water mixed with the salty Australian yeast-and-vegetable bread-spread, Vegemite, to act as natural fly traps. But you have to change them every week ...

Creepy-Crawlies

Spiders stand out in this category, with some 2000 species identified in Australia. Some Australian spiders commonly found in the garden and the house are a lot more dangerous than anything you are likely to have experienced before.

In the eastern states, there is the Funnel-web, named after the silken tube it builds at its burrow entrance, one of the world's deadliest spiders—the antidote must be administered almost immediately after the bite to be effective.

In the west, there is the Red-back (related to the Black Widow), a small glossy black spider with a red patch on its abdomen, brightest in females, which are also the more dangerous—again, an antivenin is available, however. The Red-back loves to hide in places like the top of fences, inside letter boxes and on the handles of gardening tools among other places. This spider's bite has been known to kill.

Flies

Your image of elegant luncheon parties on your patio on sunny Sunday afternoons could be marred by a common Australian pest, the fly. There are about 7000 species in the country.

In rural areas, the flies are notorious for their persistence, and their tendency to sit anywhere moist, including your nose, eyes, ears and mouth. Hence the famous 'Australian salute', the constant rhythmic flicking of the hand across the face to keep the flies away. You will find this gesture comes very naturally indeed.

Houses are suitably equipped with extra mesh-and-metal fly-screen doors besides the usual doors, as well as window fly-screens. If you want to enjoy peace in your own home, and if you want to stay popular with your Australian hosts, remember always to close the fly-screens, leaving the normal doors and windows open for good ventilation during the summer.

Burglary

House-breaking is definitely on the increase in Australia, as unemployment forces more young people onto the streets. If you are alert and careful, you should be able to protect yourself. A dog is a good idea. So is a burglar alarm.

The sort of alarm system that links up to a monitoring system connected to the nearest police station is probably best; a loud alarm bell might possibly scare a would-be burglar off, but it wouldn't necessarily get help to you quickly without such a monitoring system. Alarms that use sensor beams to detect movement across rooms are quite effective. Make sure you have a 'panic button' activating the alarm and a working telephone near your bed for emergencies.

Leave lights on and radios or televisions playing when you go out. (Cent-conscious Australians never leave lights on, though.) Lighting systems that switch on in response to movement are also a good idea, to light up the front drive when you drive your car back home, or to light up the garden suddenly, if an intruder climbs over the back fence.

Lock up properly at night and when you go out. Fix metal-grille screens on windows and make sure fly-screens are also reinforced with metal. Never answer the front door without ensuring the second, fly-screen, door is locked; as an extra precaution, use a peephole to view who is calling before opening either door.

Get a house-sitter rather than leave the house empty when you go on holidays. Note that in car-oriented Australia, a car in the driveway usually indicates someone is at home, while absence of a car means everybody is out and it may be OK to break in—one of many good reasons to own a car.

Charity Canvassers

The newcomer is at first intrigued, later astounded, and finally infuriated by the number of people who come to the front door collecting for charities. This is a great Australian nuisance.

Many of these people are professional, paid collectors and while many may need the job, it is very difficult to sort out who is genuine and who may be just operating a neat little scam. The best tactic is probably to ask them to write to you instead, so you can decide at your leisure whether you want to donate, how much and to which charities.

Fire

You must always be aware of the very great danger that fires pose in Australia, especially during the summer, when everything is tinder-dry. Keep an eye on the daily television announcements for the level of Fire Hazard and obey instructions on whether or not it is safe to light fires (including barbecues), at home, in the park, or camping in the countryside. Check with your local city council on rules (legally enforced) about firebreaks on your land.

You may always have dreamed of a country home surrounded by tall trees, but think hard before you act on your dream—10 terrifying days of walls of fire and fireballs hurtling through the skies in January 1994 reached right into the suburbs of Sydney, let alone the country, leaping from tree to tree. Thousands of volunteer fire-fighters demonstrated Australia's gutsy civil spirit, but countless homes were lost.

How to protect yourself if it happens? First, leave the area, abandon your house, *but early*, never at the last moment, that will be too late—when the flames are upon you, it's marginally better to stay put than to run. Out there in the fire-storm itself, you could die of radiation or smoke inhalation. (Equally, even the swimming pool may not be a safe retreat if you have your head above water breathing the smoke, or if the water heats up.) Preventive measures include making firebreaks, clearing gutters of leaves, plugging all holes, including downpipes, and sealing windows, hosing down your property and the land to drenching point, not just before the fire comes, but for days before. And of course, get rid of all inflammable items such as tins of paint or firewood and heating oil supplies.

Rubbish Disposal
We had come from tropical Asia and so were quite taken aback at first to discover that refuse collection did not take place daily. If you forget to wheel your bin out onto your front kerb on the designated night for emptying the next day, too bad—you wait for another week.

Mail Boxes
Your 'postie' (postman) will probably cycle past at great speed on the pavement at the front of your house. The idea is that you should have a mail box out on the pavement at the front of the house so he can drop the letters in as he passes. He will not expect to get off his bike and walk up to your front door to deliver.

Heating
If you are not used to winter, remember that the idyllic Australian summers in the garden do not go on forever and you will need to keep warm, eventually. The most economical and environmentally acceptable way of doing so is to wear good woollen clothes and sleep under a heavy feather 'doona' as the Australians call the duvet or continental quilt.

Take note of our backbreaking experience when wood suppliers delivered three tons of firewood outside our gate, in the public back lane, while we were out. We had to cart the whole lot into the woodshed—this took us three days! Photo by the author.

The winters are generally not very severe—in Perth, for example, night temperatures rarely fall below 10 degrees Centigrade—although Melbourne and Tasmania are another story in this respect.

Depending on where you are in Australia, you may feel you need heating, particularly to provide hot water. The 'sunburnt country', Australia, is the ideal country for solar heating and many homes already have it. You should certainly consider installing it if you have a new house without it, or are building your own home. It's a cheap and very efficient option.

There is enormous romance, of course, in a flickering log fire of a cold winter night. But you should consider what you are burning: Australia's native forests—such as the jarrah trees of the southwest—are precious environmental resources, which should not really be allowed to go up in smoke.

However, you can ask for 'mill ends'—the waste chips and blocks left over from processing at furniture and plywood factories—which

173

are cheaper and somewhat more environmentally acceptable. 'Mallee roots' are another choice, although they too are part of the unique Australian ecology, being eucalypts.

A better path might be to use kerosene oil, a fuel resource with which Australia is richly stocked, as with liquid petroleum gas (LPG) for cooking and so on. But of course, every heating fuel comes with some environmental cost or other.

Cooling

The Australian summer will take some newcomers aback, reaching temperatures of 40 degrees Centigrade and above at its height. It is a dry heat, but the sun comes at you out of a dazzling clear blue sky.

We installed an evaporative air-cooling system in our home, much nicer than conventional airconditioning, and vastly cheaper to run. One attraction with this system is that you actually have to leave windows and doors open to make it work well, instead of being hermetically sealed into the house, as you are with airconditioning. Air passes over recycling running water which cools it.

We manage to reduce 40-degree temperatures to 30 degrees or lower with this system (and 30 degrees down to 20), which is comfortable for us considering we came from tropical Asia. Another advantage is the fact that such systems tend to add moisture, humidifying the extraordinarily dry atmosphere during the Australian summer.

Antique Furniture

If you have brought precious antique wooden furniture to Australia, beware of the dry summers I have mentioned. Most timbers will eventually crack and split as a result. The safest policy is to give your furniture an annual oil rubdown (linseed oil is one option).

A Few Real Estate Jargon Terms

When you scan the Australian classified ads for house-sales, there may well be some abbreviations which are a mystery to you. Following are a few examples—for the rest, consult an Australian friend or real estate agent.

Dbt Double brick-and-tile, a better quality, better insulated version of simple brick-and-tile.

Bgp Below-ground pool. A much better sort of swimming pool than the above-ground sort, this is a properly sunken pool.

Blt in robes Built-in wardrobes.

Brick veneer Simulated brick facing for houses, used as a disguise over inner walls of other materials such as asbestos or aluminium.

Harbour glimpses Common in Sydney, this half-promise means that if you stand on a stool, or if you are about eight feet tall, you can, by squinting through the bathroom window, spot a small part of the spectacular harbour view.

Retic This refers to 'reticulation', the system of below-ground piping which pumps bore water up through automatic sprinklers to tend your garden. When buying a home, it's best to ensure this is already in place as it could be expensive to lay.

Chapter Ten

TUCKER

'We're happy little Vegemites, as bright as bright can be,
We all enjoy our Vegemite for breakfast, lunch and tea.
Our Mummy says we're growing stronger every single week.'

—Ditty of the 1950s.

Nothing divides opinion quite like food—'tucker' is the Aussie word
for it. Different strokes for different folks … And perhaps in no other
area have Australians changed more radically or more rapidly than in
the kitchen, over the past decade. Postwar migration, first the Italians

and Greeks (go to Melbourne for their cuisine), followed by the Lebanese and other Middle-Easterners, then latterly of the Chinese, Indians and Vietnamese, has transformed Australian eating and cooking habits.

Overall, Australian cuisine has traditionally followed in the lamentable footsteps of its English counterpart. Despite England being my own birthplace, I really hesitate to call it a 'cuisine' at all.

Time was, 'food' in Australia meant a roast joint of beef or lamb— or cheaper meat items such as tripe, offal ('fry') or salt-meat—with potatoes and over-boiled greens (they thought them safer this way in the old days), followed by a treacly pudding with custard. Dairy foods were also important staples.

The Australian, his country being a beef and lamb-producer, consumed meat in prodigious quantities and, like the English, was often overweight. During the 1980s, annual per capita beef and veal consumption alone, for example, stood at about 39 kilograms per head. This gastronomic 'culture' still survives in Australia outside of the major cities and in suburban heartlands—French and Chinese gourmets, you have been warned—but the cosmopolitan minority is expanding its influence steadily.

In the 1990s, we have seen the rise of what is known as 'Modern Australian' cuisine, an eclectic and innovative style drawing on multiculturalism, which is fast acquiring a unique Australian identity. You can get everything from lemongrass to couscous in Aussie markets nowadays, and chefs are going to town with some of the world's freshest, purest ingredients.

As an example of the style, cited in *The Weekend Australian* paper, 1997, from the Paramount restaurant in Sydney, try Duck Pie with Shitake Mushroom Sauce and Ginger Glaze—'Everyone iden- tifies with a pie—the term is Australian, the taste is Chinese, the appearance is French,' says chef Chris Manfield. Nowadays you are quite likely to encounter prawns, kangaroo and papaya in the same dish. It's an enormously exciting new scene, and, combined with the

'Bush Tucker' movement (see later in this chapter), it's anyone's guess where it will ultimately go.

To get a feel for the finer points of traditional Australian cooking, do consult Shirley Constantine's excellent *Traditional Australian Cooking*, which is more than just a cookbook; it's a readable social history too. There are some good basic recipes, too, in Margaret Nicholson's *The Little Aussie Fact Book*.

The Asian Invasion

Wandering around historic Fremantle, Perth's twin port-town, not long ago, I spotted an odd item on a traditional Aussie fish-and-chips shop blackboard menu, reading, DIM SIM. 'Wozzat, mite?' I enquired amiably of the proprietor in my newly acquired super-casual Aussie vernacular.

' 'Ere 'tis, luv,' replied he, indicating a squat little item somewhat like a half-spring roll, a pastry case stuffed with vegies and minced meat of some sort. It was priced at about 60 US cents.

'Nao fanks, mite,' quoth I, quailing, recalling with nostalgia the infinite variety that the classic Cantonese Chinese snacks-buffet, *dim sum*, usually offers. (*Dim sum* or *dian xin* is a range of small steamed and fried snacks eaten for lunch or breakfast from mobile buffet trolleys.)

But this was just another example of Asian migrants' subtle subversion of Australian cuisine. Or, to look at it another way, it was an example of Asian cuisine absorbed and mutated within Australian cuisine. Tough to tell who is dominating whom when it comes to 'Dim Sim', Australian-style.

No Need to Bring Your Own

Anyone who's ever flown into Perth airport on one of those ghastly flights that get in at almost 3 a.m. will be familiar with the sight of Asian visitors and returning residents arguing their way past Customs officials with bags of spices and unattractive-looking dried foods, from squid to waxed duck.

Australia understandably has to police imported food and agricultural items sternly to protect its own agriculture against foreign pests and diseases still foreign to its own continental island environment. But I don't know why these would-be gastronomic smugglers persist in running the gauntlet of Customs when Australia is fast producing the goods for them on the spot.

Take my own Perth suburb, for example. Within 10 minutes' drive in any direction are two 'Oriental' provisions stores stocking everything from Chinese *wok* (frying pans) and chilli powder to fresh Indian *roti canai* (bread; Sundays only) and crisp Indian-style *samosa* snacks, and two 'international food centres' featuring stalls offering Indian and Chinese favourites—besides the Italian, Lebanese and Greek dishes which have long been Australian standards.

At one of these centres, white faces are in a distinct minority, the southern-Chinese Hokkien dialect of Singapore and Malaysia is spoken, several characters are to be seen slopping about in thongs (flip-flop rubber sandals), shorts and singlets, and the *char kway teow* (a sort of fried fettucine) could comfortably compete with the Chinese original back home in Malaysia.

It's not just the food centres that have gone Asian, either. Any Australian city restaurant area will feature at least a Cantonese and a Peking-style Chinese restaurant, a Lebanese falafels-and-kebabs café, a Malaysian *satay* (barbecued kebabs) joint, an Indonesian *nasi goreng* (fried rice) restaurant, a Thai seafood spot, besides a Vietnamese restaurant and an Indian curry house.

Unfortunately, you have to shop around quite energetically to identify the ones serving the real thing, because many Asian restaurateurs have adversely tailored their cuisine to Australian taste.

Even the fish-and-chip shops have mutated. Increasingly now, these typically Australian establishments are being taken over by

179

Eating habits have changed with Asian immigration. Photo by Siva Choy.

Asian migrants. Few of them offer only good old fish and chips lathered in batter and salt and served in brown-paper packets (more traditionally, they should be newspaper). Nowadays they also serve *calamari*, or batter-fried squid, a borrowing from Greece, Chinese-style spring rolls, Indian *samosa* (pastry triangles stuffed with meat and vegetable), and other alien imports.

By the way, if by some chance you have never experienced the great British working-class tradition of batter-fried fish and potato chips served up in paper packets, liberally doused in salt, pepper and vinegar, you must go through with it at least once in Australia. After years in Asia, visits to the Australian fish-and-chip shops brought back my childhood and student years in northern England, scoffing the sizzling, calorific stuff from newspaper as I walked along cold wintry streets at night. Very nostalgic.

Asian D.I.Y. in the Kitchen

Some pioneers have been busying themselves for many years to make all this come about. One such is Charmaine Solomon, nee Poulier, one of Australia's best-known Asian residents, a Sri Lankan-born 'burgher' or Eurasian by origin. She has lived in Australia for 30 years. If you are an Asian migrant to Australia, afraid you will no longer be able to eat your traditional food, either because you will no longer have a servant to do it for you, or because you fear Australia will not have the ingredients, take heart from Charmaine Solomon's work.

Mrs Solomon is known for her 16 marvellous cookbooks, almost every one of them an ambassador for Asian food to Australians. Her goal has always been to prove that good Asian cooking can come out of a Western-style kitchen, and she has amply succeeded. Her books are vital to the task of preserving Asian heritage among second or third-generation Australian-Asians. Charmaine is most widely re-nowned for her ground-breaking third book, back in 1976, *The Complete Asian Cookbook*.

In this book, too, it is revealed, for instance, that Australians refer to snow-peas but Americans talk about sugar-peas or mange-tout, while green and red peppers may be described as capsicums, sweet peppers or bell peppers, depending on where you are. *The Complete Asian Cookbook* also lists Australia-based suppliers of Asian ingre-dients and foodstuffs. Here again is a sign of the times; in 1976, Charmaine could list only one shop stocking Chinese goods in Perth, and none selling Indonesian, Malaysian, Indian or Sri Lankan goods. They are all over Perth now. What isn't in the shops is growing in people's gardens—all the Asian herbs, *lengkuas*, *pandan*, *daun kesom*, *serai*, the lot. They got past Customs somehow.

Cutlery

There is one very odd thing about Australian eating habits, especially when it comes to consuming Asian food. I can understand a general reluctance to tackle eating instruments as esoteric as chopsticks, or as alien as one's own pinkies (connoisseurs of Indian and Malay food, however, always prefer to use their hands, as the natives do).

But it does seem really benighted to try to eat fried rice with a *knife and fork*, as most Australians do. The less uptight Australians do at least relax with just a fork. But why, oh why, is there a hidden taboo against eating it with a *spoon* and fork, as sensible Southeast Asians themselves do nowadays?

Apparently, for Australians, it is somehow not nice to use spoons for anything other than soups or desserts, but nobody has ever explained to me why this is so. Even long-term Asian residents in Australia have given it up as a losing battle and are to be seen stabbing away with forks instead. Logically then, the American custom of cutting food into small pieces and then picking it up with a fork should be quite acceptable in Australia.

Mine and Yours

For Asians in particular, the 'my dish' syndrome evinced by Australians will seem quite remarkable. Each diner has his own plate of food in a typical Western-style Australian meal. If a Western-style meal is served at home, care should be taken that food is available in multiples of the number of guests (six carrots for three guests, for example, i.e. two each), as the guests are likely to feel more comfortable if they can actually count how many pieces they are 'supposed' to take for themselves. It is all very precise.

This kind of thing can occur even at Asian restaurants in Australia, where some Australians will order for themselves one plate of noodles or one plate of fried rice, rather than ordering several dishes to put in the centre of the table to share, as Asians would. Call it individualism, selfishness or meanness if you like, but you will have to go with the flow.

Allied with this situation is the 'my drink' phenomenon. In Asian societies, the bottle of whisky, brandy or whatever will be plonked on the table for everyone to help themselves as they wish. In Western societies like Australia, the host will ask you whether you want a drink, serve you a carefully measured measure and wait until you seem to need another one before asking if you do, and then refilling your glass. Appalling as this may seem to some Asians, again, just learn to live with it.

Quick Fix

Unfortunately, one of the less welcome postwar food imports has been 'fast food'. Australians eat far too many 'takeaway' meals, from fish-and-chip cafés as well as from 'Chinese takeaways'—estimated at four to five times a week—and the national expenditure on fast foods of all kinds is about A\$1.5 billion a year. In 1994, it was revealed that more than 8 per cent of the Australian family food budget goes on snack or 'junk' foods, making Australia the world's fourth most enthusiastic consumer of such 'food'. Perhaps not surprisingly, 38 per cent of Aussie adults were also then classified as obese or overweight.

However, a vocal health-food lobby is fighting back. And a 1996 survey found that Australians had a guiltier conscience about what they ate than any other nationality.

The Australian Shopping Basket

One convenient aspect of running a home in Australia is that it is still possible to get quite a few delivery services to your door—the milkman (the 'milko') still exists, for example. The phone directory reveals a host of 'Dial-a-Meal' services.

Australians do the bulk of their shopping in supermarkets and at the many fresh fruit-and-veg markets, especially the wholesale growers' markets, very much in the American style: they load up their big cars with a week's supplies, wheeling the laden supermarket trolleys out to the car across the huge carpark, and store many things in deep-freezers. (The trolleys, by the way, are often obtainable only through a coin-slot machine which consumes, say, a 20-cent deposit, refundable when you return the trolley).

Don't forget, the shops will close around 5.30 p.m., and on Saturday afternoons and Sundays. There is usually one night a week declared 'late shopping night'—Thursdays in Perth, for instance.

The average Australian family's diet includes essentials like eggs, milk, meat and vegetables; Polony sausage (a European infiltration); pizza; pasta; spaghetti (the latter two are listed separately) and tomato paste—the Italian influence. Anglo-Saxon favourites like custard powder and pickled onions are still there. And, oh dear, baked beans.

Consumption figures from the Australian Bureau of Statistics show that Australians were upping their vegie intake, although they certainly hadn't abandoned meat. Their average consumption of meat and meat products rose by 1.6 kg to 85 kg per person, with more pork and 'offal' consumed than before. During the year under study, the average Australian munched through 579.4 kg of food and drank 1.1 kg of tea, 2 kg of coffee, 87.2 litres of aerated water, 111.6 litres of beer and 18.8 litres of wine.

Trial by Yeast

The shopping list would not be Australian if it lacked one particular item—I refer of course to 'Vegemite'.

Vegemite is the trade name devised back in the 1920s for a bread spread which describes itself as 'concentrated yeast extract'. It is the Australian equivalent of Britain's Marmite but different. Indeed, Vegemite was created specifically to compete with Marmite. It was launched in 1923 as 'Parwill' but then changed its name to Vegemite.

Vegemite offers the same kind of test for whether you have integrated with mainstream Australia as that posed by warm beer in

Britain or the durian fruit in Southeast Asia. This dark brown goo usually comes in a small glass jar with distinctive yellow and red labelling and packaging. The strongest impression left by its taste is, well—salt. With yeasty undertones, naturally.

Vegemite is considered quintessentially Australian. If you don't like it or don't eat it, your Australian-ness is open to question. But take heart, some Australians don't.

The ingredients are listed on the packaging as: yeast extract, mineral salt (508, 509), malt extract, natural colour (150), vegetable extract, and the vitamins thiamine, riboflavin and niacin. The numbers are the official food additive codes. The label further points out that five grams of Vegemite gives you half your daily allowance of Vitamin B1, riboflavin and niacin. Go for it.

The Meat Pie

Least attractive of all is the unofficial 'national dish', the Great Australian Meat Pie—meat and vegetables in a pastry shell. A particularly dreadful version of this is the 'Adelaide floater' which features the said pie, with peas, awash in a gooey gravy soup.

As columnist Buzz Kennedy has said in *The Weekend Australian*, 'Meat pies are not meant to be healthy. They are meant to be squidgy and dribbling with gravy thickened with white flour and eaten in great chomps.'

All part of the Australian gastronomic experience, but definitely an 'acquired taste'.

Other Australiana

There are many other Australian endemics when it comes to food. Take 'puftaloons', for example, increasingly rare nowadays. ('I haven't seen a puftaloon for 40 years,' complained one reader recently in a Western Australian newspaper, 'but I suppose that my body, nowadays conditioned to forever seeking low-cholesterol tucker, would not allow me anywhere near one.')

The Great Australian Meat Pie, photo by Richard Simpson, courtesy of Daily News, *Western Australia. This photo was first used to publicise the opening of 'The Jolly Pieman' store in Mirrabooka, Western Australia.*

This is a fried dough-scone, which rises high and fluffy during the frying. Puftaloons have been recorded as far back as 1853—some older Americans may recognise them as 'puff-ballooners'. They were used to fill families up when times were hard and meat was short.

While most puftaloon recipes are simple, using just self-raising flour, butter and salt, mixed with milk or water, there are variations incorporating egg, a dash of tomato sauce, chopped onion and mince-meat. In the old days of pre-cholesterol-scare innocence, you would have fried the puftaloons in 'dripping'—fat dripped from cooking meats like lamb or beef, for long Australia's favourite cooking oil. Like waffles, you are supposed to smother puftaloons in treacle or honey before eating them fresh and golden brown from the frying pan.

Still household names today are Arnott's Biscuits, Jaffa cakes, and Minties, the mint sweets wrapped in green and white paper with red writing on it. Chewiness, say Aussie aficionados, is the factor that elevates the Mintie above the 'Pommy' Minto or Polo Mint. A traditional Australian children's party game is 'Mintie Hunt', where a trail of clues laid outdoors leads to the treasure-trove of Minties.

Among the snacks you will find at venues such as the fish-and-chips shop, are sure to be 'Chiko Rolls'—crisp-fried semi-cylindrical pastries stuffed with corn, potato and gravy, nearly as Australian as Vegemite. Similarly Australian are Anzac Biscuits, made of rolled oats, syrup and coconut, named after the Aussie soldier boys who gratefully received them at the Gallipoli warfront in parcels from home during World War I.

Food traditions dating back to the days of the bushman are Billy Tea—tea brewed in a metal can of boiling water over a campfire—and another camp-food, Damper, a heavy unleavened wheat bread baked in hot ashes, which could 'damp' your hunger.

Fruit

Most fruit grown in Australia today has foreign origins. What some of you may know as a 'papaya' is a 'paw-paw' in Australia and along with bananas, pineapples, avocados and mangos, is common in the tropical regions of the north, mainly in Queensland. Citrus fruit and apples are the most abundantly produced—apples from Tasmania are particularly famous and the Granny Smith apple variety was first developed from a Tasmanian seed.

There are some spectacular stone-fruit to be had in season—

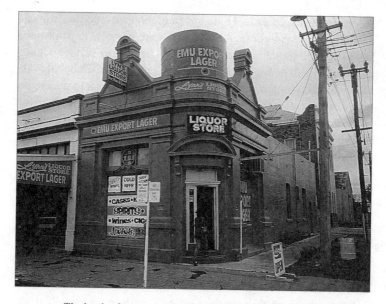

The bottle-shop, an Aussie institution. Photo by Siva Choy.

nectarines, peaches and apricots among them. And there are also home-grown berries such as strawberries and raspberries.

Dining Out

The single most alien aspect of Australian dining and wining is the BYO phenomenon. The acronym stands for Bring Your Own (Booze/ Grog). Few restaurants are licensed to sell liquor, but most will let you bring your own. You will have a pretty miserable time if you forget this custom, only to find yourself without wine to go with your special dinner. So the routine preliminary to dining out is nearly always to visit the bottle-shop first. This custom is in fact a blessing in disguise, since you get a wider choice of wines, no restaurateur's mark-up on prices, and no corkage charge either.

Australian restaurants usually close fairly early (in traditional homes, 'Tea', i.e. dinner, is eaten as early as 6 p.m.). Tipping is rarely necessary. Water is just as rarely offered unless specifically requested.

You will find Australian portions extremely generous. The nation eats heartily, mostly scorning the inadequacies of 'nouvelle cuisine' with all those fancy white spaces on the plate. Some of the best-value meals are those to be found in pubs, sometimes stand-up style at the bar counter. Counter lunches are especially good.

Shouts and Splits

The custom of 'shouting' rounds of drink in the 'pub' (anything from a bar to a hotel is a 'pub' in Australia), taking turns, is entrenched and woe is he (less often she) who forgets it. Remember that Australians are not too well off nowadays, so pull your financial weight at the bar. On the other hand, they are proud as well, so offering to pay more than your share of shouts could also be taken amiss.

Pride really comes to the fore when the bill for a restaurant meal is delivered. The Australian is pathologically opposed to carrying a whole dinner tab, and equally opposed to letting anybody else carry it for him. If you are a man dating a woman, be warned that there is a distinct suggestion you may be angling to bed her pretty soon if you go so far as to pay for her meal. Play safe and offer to 'go Dutch', as the English saying has it—that is, unless you are trying to tell her something.

Asians, and some southern Europeans too, find this particularly difficult to cope with; they are used to immense shows of generosity, hosting whole dinner parties, on the quiet understanding of course, that the others will owe them a debt in turn when the time comes, some time later.

But it is precisely the unspoken indebtedness that the fiercely independent Aussie dislikes about this system. An Australian married to an Asian woman had encountered this embarrassment many times

The pub bar is important to social life. Photo by the author.

and he explained it to me thus: 'We feel our independence has been compromised when somebody pays the whole bill. It's kind of throwing your weight around, showing your power. And when they do that, you haven't any choice in the matter; the next time around, you will have to do it, but you haven't any choice about it.'

So when in doubt, always split the bill.

Traditional Fare

Conventional or traditional Australian cuisine divides into two streams: classic Continental European cum cordon bleu, and good old Australian tucker.

It is possible still to eat quality European food in Australia, however, sometimes in the most surprising places: like the exquisite

French meal I enjoyed at the 1885 Inn and Restaurant in the Margaret River wine country of southwestern Western Australia, for example, the best I think I have had outside of France itself.

Old Favourites

In an attempt to characterise Australian food as compared with any other, one newspaper writer came up with the word 'gutsy'. We have already discussed some of the more hardcore dishes in the genre.

Setting aside the old 'meat and two vegs' formula, however, the strongest item on any truly Australian menu would have to be seafood and fish dishes. Prawns and 'Yabbies', or small freshwater crayfish, are delicious. The Barramundi fish, the John Dory and the Dhu fish are among many great Australian epicurean experiences. Mudcrabs are well worth the effort, oysters world-famous.

More puzzling may be the mention of 'Bugs' on the menu. These are a small seafood item, allied to crayfish, some from tropical Moreton Bay, others from the southern Balmain region.

A tolerable introduction to traditional Anglo-Saxon fare is probably the Yorkshire Pudding. At its crispy, piping-hot best, this is a delicious batter pudding consisting of egg, milk and flour baked in dripping served as an accompaniment to the main dish. Another tasty standard is Steak and Kidney Pudding.

The salad is growing in popularity and variety on Australian menus and Australia's abundant fresh vegetables and fruit make it an ideal option. Asians not used to so much raw food may find it all a bit alarming, but it is indisputably healthy. By the way, you will find it extremely difficult to avoid beetroot, that violently purple vegetable. Australians love it (I loathe it).

Outdoor barbecues are a favoured setting for most Australian food, as we have already learned. The ultimate Aussie, Paul Hogan (*Crocodile Dundee*) made his catch-phrase 'Toss A Prawn On The Barbie' ring around the world, contributing to his country's 2.25 million tourist haul in the bicentennial year of 1988.

And Now for Afters

Australian desserts, cakes and puddings—'afters'—are quite unique. Perhaps the best known are the Pavlova dessert and the Lamington cake. Both of these are delicious.

The Pavlova, it is claimed, was created at Fremantle's Esplanade Hotel in Western Australia, for the prima ballerina Anna Pavlova, when she toured Australia in 1935. It's a mouth-melting froth of meringue, whipped cream and fresh fruit.

Lamingtons, probably a Queensland invention in the early 1900s and named after 19th century Queensland governor, Baron Lamington, are small sponge blocks layered with raspberry jam, covered with thin chocolate icing, like a skin, and then rolled in desiccated coconut.

Other more traditional English puddings personally make me cry, remembering my schoolhood in austere postwar northern England, made miserable in gastronomic terms by the effort of desperately trying to shovel down monumental stodge like Suet Pudding, Golden Syrup Dumplings, Bread and Butter Pudding, or Steamed Jam Pudding, afloat in dreaded yukky-yellow custard ...

Christmas

No matter if the sun is high in a bright blue sky and the temperature well over 40 degrees Centigrade, Australians will still have their Christmas Day lunch very much in the traditional English mode, complete with turkey, stuffing and 'Christmas pud' (more archaically known as 'Plum Duff').

There are some concessions to Australia's 'reversed' seasons. Ice-cream cake does sometimes replace or supplement the Christmas pudding, for example. (They say that in the 19th century gold-rush days, miners would put gold nuggets in the Christmas pudding instead of the traditional sixpence coins.)

Suggested menus in the daily press sometimes even propose a curry as a way of getting rid of Christmas leftovers. Curry in most

Australian households has always been used as more of a disguise for leftovers than considered as an art in itself.

About Tea

'They can't even make a decent cup of tea over here,' a disgruntled migrant Sikh once told me in Perth. He leaned over the table with confidential mien, 'I mean, it's like dishwater!' He snorted his contempt, pausing only to swill down some of his own dubious brew of sugar water laced with coffee.

Such criticism would shock Australians if they heard it. They reckon they know about tea. After all, they take after their English forefathers when it comes to tea: they are addicts. They are the fifth largest per capita tea-drinkers in the world, brewing up 18 million kilos of the precious leaves every year—that's a A$165 million market, largely for imported teas.

Indians like my Sikh friend, of course, are used to a stiff brew of fine tea-dust cooked up for some considerable time, with the milk and sugar, as well as some spices, already in the drink. Whereas the Australian will add the milk and sugar in the cup, whether before or after pouring the briefly-brewed tea.

Once again, do not forget that an invitation to 'tea' is in fact an invitation to the evening meal, a tradition deriving from old-fashioned North-country England.

Bush Tucker

When the first whites arrived in Australia, they took no notice at all of whatever it was the Aboriginals were eating, nor did they even attempt to farm the land for the first five years or so. They simply imported all their food. At times, they well nigh starved on account of this stupidity, or worse, almost killed themselves.

Once, seeing that the Aboriginals ate the roasted seeds of the *Azamia cycad* (an ancient, primitive palm-like tree), the white settlers did likewise. But because they had not observed carefully enough, they died from the potent poisons contained in the seeds. The Aboriginals had learned how to soak and prepare the seeds for consumption, removing toxins, for many weeks prior to cooking.

Over the past decade, there has been a growing realisation that the Aboriginals knew, still know in some cases, how to live off the land, and that this 'bush tucker' can be quite good for the health. It was certainly better for Aboriginal health than the whites' imported flour, sugar and alcohol. Take a food like Billygoat Plums. They have the highest concentration of Vitamin C of any food in the world, as much in a single plum as in a dozen oranges.

Needless to say, knowledge of bush tucker could be the key to survival if you were unfortunate enough to get lost in the outback.

It is estimated that there may be 30,000 types of bush tucker. Perhaps only about 30 or 40 of them have been introduced to urban Australia so far. The first moves are now being made towards mass production and processing of some of these traditional foods, which already appear on the menus of chic restaurants in the eastern states. If you visit an Australian bookshop, you will surely encounter perhaps half a dozen or more major books on bush tucker.

This back-to-nature movement got an immense kick-start from a television series in 1990 titled *Bush Tucker Man* and hosted by Les Hiddens, an army major who is an expert on edible plants from the survival-skills point of view.

Buffalo, kangaroo (raised on farms, not taken from the wild, they say), camel and crocodile hardly qualify as bush tucker any more, so commonplace have they become. Camel meat is turning up in the Australian meat pie. Crocodile, like kangaroo, is considered a particularly healthy meat, being low in fat and cholesterol, with a chicken-like texture and a flavour much like veal.

Aboriginal women have traditionally been the gatherers of tubers and roots, such as yams and ground orchids, in particular, hence the woven or wooden collecting trays, 'coolamons', and 'dillybags' they often carry around with them.

There are grass seeds and ferns which can be eaten, also many fruits and berries. The blue-black Davidson's Plum of the rainforest makes a delicious, sourish jam, for example.

Aboriginals in their natural state also eat wildlife, of course, such as the goanna, a monitor lizard, reputed to be pleasantly edible, if a little gamey, and the fatty muttonbird (short-tailed shearwater) of the southeastern coast. Goanna is another example of healthy lean meat available in the bush.

In some areas, Aboriginals also nibble on live green ants—the green comes from chlorophyll in the plants eaten by the ants and the ants as a result have an attractively tangy taste, rather like lemon juice. One imagines it would take an awful lot of these to make any nutritional impact or to affect energy levels, however.

Gourmet Grubs

And then there is the witchetty grub. The Aboriginals' consumption of these fat maggot-like creatures, live and raw, has acquired a horrid fascination for outsiders, thanks to Aussie tour guides' propensity for macho demonstrations.

Witchetty grubs are in fact insect larvae, usually of wood-boring moths. You do not have to eat them raw (when they taste creamy and squashy—you bite off their heads first); they can be cooked in hot ashes, which renders them something like underdone pork crackling. I have tried both the ants and the grubs myself. Just for the experience.

The grubs, no doubt a fair source of protein, are now appearing on the smartest of menus. At the time of writing, they are available from gourmet supermarkets in tinned soup form (from Bush Tucker Supplies, run by environmentalist Vic Cherikoff—Tel: 61-02-816 3381 in Sydney, with branches in Adelaide and Melbourne). Chef Diane Holuigue recently told *The Australian Magazine* how she served this up to a Florida dinner party in the USA, 'fluffed into cappucino-like consistency and dredged with wattle seed'.

The rest of Diane's Australiana menu included crocodile macadamia brochettes with bush tomato chutney; prawns fried in coconut with curried mayonnaise; quail and emu ham salad, among other more conventional items, such as Australian lamb. (Macadamia nuts, by the way, are another fine Australian native food, unfortunately known to some people abroad as 'Hawaiian nuts', since they were first commercially grown on Hawaii, but originally came from Queensland.)

Another of Diane's efforts produced baby wattle seed blini topped with cress, smoked emu, handmade agnolotti filled with yabbie mousseline, and baby Barramundi fish wrapped in the bark of the paperbark tree (the wrapping, she says, imparts a 'delicate earthy taste' to the food), served with Kakadu plum sauce.

The list of exotica is seemingly endless: the quandong and boab fruits, lilli-pilli berries, warragal greens, bunya nuts, the bogong moth, black nightshade, lemon-aspen lemoncurd and wattle seed everything ...

A great treat awaits the world when bush tucker at last hits international gourmet circles, as it surely will one day.

Grog

We spent a lot of time tramping supermarkets puzzling over where on earth the beer and wine could be, before we cottoned on to the Australian system which has separate 'bottle-shops' (what the British call 'the off-licence') to sell alcohol. If you're feeling lazy, there are plenty of drive-in bottle-shops, allowing you to order and collect through your car window.

Traditionally, Australia has been a beer-drinking nation; the Northern Territory capital, Darwin, is believed to be the world's top-ranking city for beer-drinking and the nation as a whole ranks third in the world, just behind the Germans and Belgians, level with the Czechs.

There is a host of beers to choose from, brewed by five major companies: Foster's lager from Victoria is best known abroad, but there are many others, such as Castlemaine's XXXX (Four-ex) from Queensland, VB (Victoria Bitter), Carlton, and Western Australia's Swan Lager and Redback (named after the spider), among others — and the very latest cold-filtered beers, such as Carlton Cold, or Tooheys' Hahn Ice.

Americans should be warned that the alcohol content in Australian beers is far higher than what they are used to—it is higher than in most British beers too. Some pubs offer in-house brews with extremely high levels (try a Fremantle 'Dog-Bolter'). And of course, Australian beer is always drunk ice-cold, hence the importance of the 'esky' thermos box on trips to the beach or into the bush.

Alcohol always has been an Australian social problem. One estimate reckons that close to 6,000 Australian deaths every year are alcohol-related, including 30 per cent of the 3,000 road-accident deaths every year. While drunk driving unfortunately still is a major hazard on Australian roads, especially at night and during weekends or holidays—one that the novice driver in Australia should be made keenly aware of—it is also a serious offence which can lose you your licence. There are random checks on the roads.

Many Australian pubs feature a 'do-it-yourself' breathalyser affixed to the wall, which will tell you whether you are over your limit or not; permitted alcohol limits vary from state to state. It is the custom in all responsible groups of friends, or among husbands and wives, to decide before going out for the night who will remain sober and within the alcohol limits in order to be the driver when the time comes to go home.

A variety of low-alcohol 'light' beers is now available to help moderate drinkers stay within the rules. If you are a woman, remember that female physiology is such that it takes fewer drinks to push your alcohol readings up than for a man.

The Grapevine

The availability, affordability and high quality of Australian wines are among many good reasons for living in Australia. Most people outside of Australia have no conception of just how good these wines can be; many of the best labels and vintages are rarely seen on supermarket shelves overseas, although the world is all too familiar with the cardboard-cask wines produced in Australia.

This is probably because domestic consumption is so high, at about 22 litres of wine per head every year, the highest figure for any English-speaking country. Wine exports account for only about 3 per cent of production; there are freight-cost problems, not to mention the matter of European, especially French, competition.

Nonetheless, the wine industry is worth over US$1 billion a year to Australia. A clear indication of the quality is the fact that about 13 per cent of the Australian industry is now in the hands of French investors (names like Bollinger and Veuve Cliquot), with the Japanese also emerging as important players just recently.

Although the big names—Wyndham Estate, Wolf Blass, Seppelt, Hardy Bros, Penfolds, Orlando, Lindemans and the like—dominate the market, there are also regional stars like Western Australia's Leeuwin Estate in Margaret River, besides many small independent 'boutique' vineyards, challenging the would-be connoisseur with one-off gems. I myself have much enjoyed bottles from the less well-known Evans and Tate, and Cullen's vineyards, in Western Australia.

Australian wines, largely for obvious legal reasons, are named after the grape variety used, e.g. Shiraz, rather than a European counterpart based on location, such as Bordeaux.

Red Red Wine

What to try? First, be aware that the only wine that Australian vineyards do not seem to be very good at is champagne (which they are not allowed by the French to call champagne, rather than sparkling wine); Australia is still a big importer of the original, French, champagne.

A distinctive feature of Australian wines is experimentation with blends of grapes. They are often fruity and soft, easier for novices to enjoy than some French wines. As a very crude guideline, you will probably like Hunter Valley reds (New South Wales) as well as Coonawarra reds (South Australia), Barossa Valley German-style whites (South Australia) as well as Cabernet Sauvignon or Merlot from Margaret River (Western Australia) and Chardonnay whites from almost anywhere.

Pinot Noir refers to the red grape of Burgundy, best from the cooler areas of Victoria state. Shiraz, also known as Hermitage, is another attractive red, particularly when matured in American oak barrels.

I found it a real joy after avoiding red wine for years while living in the tropics (it sends you to sleep in the heat of the afternoon and/or gives you a headache, is too expensive, travels badly and tastes so-so), to sample good red wine once again in an Australian winter. Note, however, that the days are gone when you could pick up a prize wine for as little as A$5 a bottle in Australia. Prices have risen in recent years. You need to pay closer to A$15 nowadays, or more, but you can often get real gold when you do so.

— Chapter Eleven —

EARNING A CRUST

'Why do business with a country where "She'll be right" means she'll be wrong and the delivery will be late as well?

'Why bother to believe a country whose national catch-cry "No worries" really translates into "We've stuffed it up again"?'

—Journalist John Hamilton, in Western Australia's *Daily News*, December 27, 1989.

It has never been altogether clear whether or not Australians really *want* to make money.

To take one example from everyday life, I once bought some black olives at a supermarket delicatessen counter in Australia. After the woman serving had weighed and priced them, she then said, 'Would you like some of the juice-stuff they're in as well?' Why not, said I. 'Oh yes, I always ask that *after* I've weighed them,' the woman told me, 'because you'd be surprised how much the juice adds to the weight, and to the price.' So I got my 'olives-juice' free, as an extra.

I marvelled at this. A shopkeeper almost anywhere else would have weighed the whole lot and charged for it all. After all, if you want juice, you should pay for it, right?

Not necessarily in Australia—part of the country's charm, but also of its economic downfall.

In another incident, a shopkeeper who was regularly selling out of a particularly popular fruit juice blend told his customers he doubted he would be stocking it much more. Why not? 'Oh, I don't really like it, myself,' he explained. Any self-respecting Asian businessman would have filled his store wall to wall with the stuff.

When I enquired about the cost of hiring a computer from a company specialising in such hire, the reply came that it would be A$20 a day, or A$600 a month, which of course amounted to the same thing. Yet normal business practice would surely be to entice the customer into a longer hire period by charging *less* per day for a longer-term contract. This would benefit both the hire-firm and the customer. This simple way of making more money apparently had not occurred to the rather literal management of this particular company.

Another endearing feature of this syndrome is the Australian shopkeeper's willingness to send you up the road to his competitors, where, he blithely tells you, they will have just what you are looking for and maybe cheaper, too.

Clearly, the desire to make money, or at least, to make profit, is consciously or subconsciously considered an evil reserved for tall poppies.

Just Dig It Up

Australia has been able to afford such complacency in the past because it is so rich in natural resources—bauxite, iron ore, zinc, uranium, oil, gas, coal, lead and gold among them. For a long time, Australia has been 'The Lucky Country'. All you had to do to stay wealthy was go dig something else up. Linkage with England provided a ready market for Australian wool, lamb, beef and wheat. And a past pattern of government protectionism further sheltered Australian business from the real world.

Among the realities are the very small size of the Australian domestic market and the high freight costs of reaching all-Australia—

Western Australian gold mine. Photo by Siva Choy.

the 'tyranny of distance'. A recent report pointed out that Heinz UK could export canned baked beans to Perth more cheaply than its Australian counterpart could get them to the Western Australian capital from its plant in the Victorian capital of Melbourne.

Australian businessmen have found it hard to keep up with a fast-changing world—the increasing self-sufficiency of the European Community (including Australia's traditional business partner, England), for example, the impact of synthetics, as well as increased cotton production, on wool, and competition from almost every direction, especially from low-cost Asia.

There is little doubt about the quality of Australian products. The Achilles heel of Australian business has always been marketing.

The fatal combination of almost unbridled consumerist materialism in the prosperous 1950s and 1960s (often based on credit), and complacency about primary produce and protected industries, sowed the seeds of Australia's miseries in the 1980s and beyond.

A Cautionary Tale

Take wool as a case study of how things can go wrong. It was once said that the Australian economy rode on the back of wool.

In 1990–91, the 70,000 'woolgrowers' of the Australian wool industry, which supplied something like 70 per cent of the world's wool, learned a hard lesson: their market crashed, leaving them with debts of A\$2.6 billion in hand, 4.5 million bales of wool stockpiled and about 20 million of their 166 million sheep shot, because suddenly they were not even worth the food they were eating.

As Jacqueline Huie of the Australian Graduate School of Management at the University of New South Wales told *The Australian* in 1991, 'If you take your eyes off what your customers want, it is at your peril. We took our eyes off our wool customers and as a result it came as a complete surprise when in two years our major customers, the USSR and China, changed and bought next to nothing. Meanwhile, nobody told the farmers. They kept on producing. Can you imagine losing the majority of your customers in two years, doubling your production and not being able to predict any part of it? Even if we didn't know about market research, what about industrial spying?' This has a lot to do with the Australian's basically trusting, naive nature; he does not expect to be deceived or let down. In business, all too often, he can be a sitting duck.

Australia has also made the classic mistake of failing to upgrade into value-added products, rather than just exporting raw primary commodities and produce, and this too has played a role in the wool disaster. In the old days, raw wool went out to England and returned to Australia as a made-up garment; nowadays, Australian iron ore goes to Japan and returns in a made-in-Japan car. This has been bad for the balance of payments.

Not surprisingly, the previous system of a minimum 'floor price' for wool was scrapped in February 1991. The floor-price system had sheltered the industry from abrupt price fluctuations. It meant that the Australian Wool Corporation had been buying back unsold wool in the confident belief that any difficulties for the industry were only temporary. After all, as late as 1989, wool was still Australia's biggest export-earner, nudging wheat.

The State of the Economy

The nation's trade balance is in deficit, to the tune of just over A$1 billion in the early 1990s. Attempts to curb import demand had brought it down from A$3.4 billion in 1981, however.

Total foreign debt is around A$114 billion, putting Australia in almost the same debtor-nation basket as Mexico or Brazil. Most of this debt has been incurred by private-sector borrowing, not by the public sector—at one point in 1990, it was estimated that Western Australian tycoon Alan Bond's empire alone was responsible for about 10 per cent of the national debt. However, agricultural exports are still doing well in Asia and the export of services in areas like telecommunications and technology is a national strongpoint.

Unemployment, as we have seen, is running close to 11 per cent. On the other hand, inflation is at its lowest for almost a quarter of a century, at about 3.4 per cent—wage rises were below 12 per cent during 1991.

A major issue for the Australian economy is the delicate balancing act that must be performed between making money and being 'green'. The environmentalist lobby is extremely powerful and influences some business decisions; more of this in another chapter. One estimate in 1991 suggested that about A$9 billion worth of projects were at risk because of environmentalist or Aboriginal vetoes. The key to this problem hopefully lies in the refinement of the 'Sustainable Development' concept now under way.

Wheelers and Dealers

Australia's businessmen are feeling pretty sorry for themselves right now, however. Quite apart from all the economic pressure they are under, a whole breed of smart-guys among them has recently got its comeuppance after a decade of heady euphoria during the 1980s.

Names like Alan Bond (English-born former sign-painter), Christopher Skase (Qintex group of companies), John Elliott (Elders-IXL), and others were all powers in the land, and national heroes—yesterday.

Today, most of these multimillionaires are ruined or discredited, or both, with debts in the billions of Australian dollars. The 1987 stockmarket crash left them emperors with no clothes but the debts on which their empires were founded. Their main tactic had been to use the tax deductibility of the interest payable on their borrowings, which they had used to acquire companies—and to make money by selling off their appreciated assets later. It was, as *The Australian* remarked, 'a stark reminder that money needs to be earned'.

The survivors—media magnates Kerry Packer and Rupert Murdoch (hiding his Australian birth under an American passport), Robert Holmes à Court (who died recently, leaving his widow Janet in charge), are not without their problems, either.

In falling, these men have taken with them grassroots morale. As long as they were 'up there', ordinary Australians thought they had a chance too, anybody could do it. Instead, Australians have been treated to the spectacle of a series of revelations about the conduct of their governments in tandem with such businessmen, most spectacularly in Western Australia (the 'WA Inc.' and Rothwell's merchant bank scandal), in Queensland and in Victoria.

In Western Australia and in Victoria, the problem was governments fancying themselves as businessmen, taking on what should have been entrepreneurial projects in partnership with businessmen, while in Queensland, it was corruption and dirty tricks generally. Eminent Queenslanders have appeared in court, right up to the level of the former premier, Sir Joh Bjelke-Petersen. In 1991, after an 89-day trial, the former state police commissioner, Sir Terence Lewis, was found guilty of 15 bribery counts between 1978 and 1987 in connection with a protection racket shielding gambling and prostitution rings.

Surviving investors have taken fright at Australia's economic decline and withdrawn from the scene. British businessman Lord Alistair McAlpine, for example, has virtually pulled out of his very substantial property investments in Western Australia, committed under his now debt-ridden Australian City Properties.

When doing business in Australia, you need to be aware of the scars left by all this bad news.

Australian business circles now are sobered, conservative and cautious, very wary of risk or any form of debt. Their main concern is to re-establish their credentials in the international financial community, where the very mention of Australia's businessmen now conjures up visions of fly-by-night bandits, and to deal in solid things, rather than paper.

Boom-Bust

Up to the 1990s, the Australian economy, including subdivisions like the property market, characteristically displayed a strongly cyclical boom-bust pattern.

It is still not clear whether this pattern is really over, as some economists believe and as the since deposed Treasurer, John Kerin, hopes, in his search for slower and steadier development. It does seem likely that boom-bust variations will be less extreme in future. But they are unlikely to disappear altogether.

Part of the national psychology which has contributed to this cycle is the Australian gambling instinct, which easily matches that of those other well-known punters, the Chinese. The gambling obsession stems both from Irish traditions in Australia's colonial beginnings and from the boredom of life in the remote countryside back in the old days: for a bit of excitement, the Australian would bet on anything that moved, and still does.

The government derives considerable tax revenue from this national weakness. Cash-hungry Western Australia alone got about A$28 million out of Perth's (50 per cent Japanese-owned) Burswood Casino during 1990, for example. Foreign ownership of casinos is limited by law to only 50 per cent.

Australians are legally permitted to gamble on horses, dogs, numbers games such as Lotto and the football Pools, as well as on slot-machines or 'one-armed bandits' ('pokies') in some states. You place your gee-gee, doggie or other sporting bet through the government's local TAB (Totalisator Agency Board) office.

In 1989–90, Australian gamblers staked A$11 billion on various forms of horse and dog-racing, out of a total gambling pot of A$27 billion. You will be accepted as one of the boys alright if you join the game.

Casino Culture

Residual puritanism delayed the introduction of (legal) casinos until the first was opened in 1973, in the Tasmanian capital of Hobart. Today they exist in all states except New South Wales and Victoria, numbering eight in all; two new ones are scheduled to open in Sydney, New South Wales, in 1994, creating 7,000 new jobs and raising A$40 million in revenue by the State Government's own count. By 1994, there will be a total of 450 gaming tables in the country.

Beyond this, another five casinos are planned—two in Melbourne, and one each in Canberra, Brisbane and Cairns. There will even be one on Australia's remotest territory, Christmas Island, strategically placed only one hour's flight from the Indonesian capital of Jakarta, which is only a hop away from Singapore; there are no legal casinos in these two countries, but a lot of avid gamblers.

One casino game you probably will encounter for the first time when in Australia is the old outback game of 'Two-Up'. It is based on spinning two coins and betting whether they will fall as two heads or two tails. The simple zinc Two-Up sheds still stand on the fringes of goldrush towns like Kalgoorlie, reminding us of how basic recreational facilities were in pioneer days.

The casinos are crammed full with 'ordinary Australians'. The atmosphere is rarely as classy as at the French counterparts, for example, although there will be private gaming rooms for very special customers, of course.

The Burswood casino at Perth sees 8,000 people a day through its doors. Recession has in many ways induced more people to gamble, out of pure desperation. The big gamblers—'the high rollers'—and often the big winners too, are usually Asians, especially the Chinese of Southeast Asia. (Hence you can get some very high-quality Asian meals in Australia's casinos.)

Turning to the Neighbours

The 1970s and 1980s have seen Australia thrown willy-nilly into the arms of Japan and Southeast Asia as she wakes up to the fact that she is not and cannot be part of Western Europe. This has been enormously wounding, psychologically, to older Australians, who remember the Pacific War against the Japanese, but the majority of Australians understand there is no other route to take to the future. Donald Horne has said simply that this is Australia's destiny, like it or not.

More and more, Australian business is being run by non-Australians, especially the Japanese, who have massive property and tourism resort investments, particularly in Queensland. On average, foreign ownership of three-to-five star hotels in the key tourism areas of the Gold Coast, Cairns and the Sunshine Coast is around 25 per cent. The percentage rises closer to 50 per cent if you exclude lower-ranking hotels, or above 60 per cent if you take other types of accommodation like condominiums and motels into account.

Japan is now the largest foreign investor in Australia, with an investment flow of A$6.8 billion in 1989–90. But Australia, like many others, is still waiting for Japan to open up to imports of Australian agricultural products.

The list of new deals seemed endless as the 1980s came to a close and Singaporeans, Hongkongers and Japanese moved in to pick up bargains. Even my suburban neighbourhood newspaper shop has just been taken over by an Indian from Zimbabwe.

The Australian government is doing everything within its power to create a climate where its people, particularly its young people, will feel their country is part of Asia. Their target is for about 40 per cent of the top 100 Australian companies to have senior executives fluent in an Asian language or at least familiar with Asian cultures, by 1995–2000. However, right now there are still many Australian businessmen who look first to the USA when considering where to invest. In the late 1980s, Asia took about half of Australia's exports, but Australian investment in Southeast Asia fell significantly, while growing enormously in the USA.

Talk of doing more business with Asia dominates Australian public deliberations. The good intentions are clear. There are conferences, trade delegations, fact-finding tours, training courses and language classes. But, as the English weekly *The Economist* remarked in 1989, 'The trouble is that Australians have not worked out exactly what to do with all this talk about Asia, beyond having politicians flying around the region.'

To be fair, such deep change is difficult to effect overnight. Australia's initiative in groups like the APEC (Asia Pacific Economic Cooperation) group, the Asia-Pacific based Cairns Group negotiating with the European Community over trade tariffs, and in stimulating economic links with Vietnam are pointers to the future.

Culturally, though, there are problems. Australia's free press has caused waves for Australian business with its relentless criticism of human rights violations, corruption or other perceived malpractices in neighbouring countries, notably Indonesia and Malaysia. Despite the Australian government's careful distancing act, dissociating itself from such incidents, much damage has been done.

In theory, there is no reason why Australia should not become part of Asia in economic terms; but the 'culture gap' will be very hard to close, even with all those Asian culture-graduates coming out of the Australian universities.

That MFP Thing

You will hear a lot about the 'MFP' proposal in Australia. It is an exciting proposal but it has become mired in political controversy.

'MFP' stands for a rather ugly word, 'Multi-Function Polis'. The idea is to build in Australia the ultimate 'intelligent city', a futuristic metropolis which will showcase high-tech living based on information technology and what-have-you. And the idea has come from Japan. Wherein lies the problem.

Japan is to co-fund and develop the project with Australia.

Australian reactions have ranged from intrigued curiosity, through incomprehension to hysterical charges of a Japanese invasion of Australian sovereign territory.

The proposed site for the MFP, at present, is Adelaide, capital of South Australia. The new city is expected to be 15 years in the building, and to cost a total of about A$2.6 billion, to be funded 40 per cent by foreign investment, 19 per cent by the public sector, and 41 per cent by Australia's private sector. It will have capacity for 100,000 people. When fully established, it is believed the MFP could add A$2.3 billion to Australia's Gross Domestic Product.

Turning Things Upside Down

Australia is now going through an economic revolution every bit as turbulent as a war. Sacred cows of all kinds are being sent crashing to the ground, or at least being chipped away at—the welfare state, the power of the unions, protectionism, state enterprise ...

Much of the action, ironically, has occurred under the auspices of an increasingly right-of-centre Labor government, in power since 1983 (next election, 1993), perhaps because Labor was the party most likely to be able to persuade the average Australian worker to go along with it. As the 1980s turned into the 1990s, Australia briefly overheated, then began to enter 'the recession we had to have' to prevent Australia from becoming a 'banana republic', to use two of former Treasurer and recently appointed Prime Minister Paul Keating's phrases. Small wonder the unpopular Keating earned for himself the sobriquet 'The Grim Reaper'.

Keating has been such a powerful influence on the economy during the 1980s that you would need to know more about him even if he had not grabbed Prime Minister Bob Hawke's job in December 1991. The Liberal opposition is now taking great delight in getting the new tag of 'Mr Recession' to stick to Prime Minister Keating, seen by many as the architect of Australia's current woes.

The character of the man gives you some idea of the unique type of men that get into Australian politics. He displays all the basic qualifications for being a leader of the Australians: a healthy ego, macho pugnacity, and individualism bordering on eccentricity. Keating's only problem has been that his policies have hurt by hitting the wallet. Most important of all, in terms of winning Australian esteem, he is not in the strictest term of the word, an expert; he is not an academic, he is a self-taught economist.

He is also known for having been the manager of a blues band called The Ramrods in his youth (but now he's a classical music buff), for exquisitely tailored and expensive suits, and for collecting antiques, particularly clocks.

Put simply, the Australian government's philosophy has been to reduce demand and inflation, and with it imports, as well as inflation, for the sake of a trimmer economy, even at the cost of jobs and homeownership.

There has been little alternative: if the current account deficit had been left to follow the trend set in the 1980s, Australia might have collapsed and lost control over its own destiny following an International Monetary Fund intervention—become a 'banana republic'.

'Life is Not Meant to be Easy'

So said the former Liberal prime minister Malcolm Fraser in 1971. Most Australians remember, and quote, this phrase ruefully nowadays.

Among the results of the Hawke-Keating economic policies have been sky-high interest rates and by 1991, an unemployment rate well over 10 per cent. Business in particular, farming included, has been hard hit by the high interest rates. Bankruptcies are legion. More than two million Australians are estimated to be living on or below the poverty line, with homeless street-children a major scandal in the larger cities.

Financial deregulation was put in place from 1983 with the Australian dollar floating and falling rapidly in value. Protective import tariffs in key industries like motor vehicles, textiles and footwear are being removed. More businesses will go under, and with them, jobs. Hard-argued productivity agreements are being signed with the notoriously recalcitrant and old-fashioned dockworkers' unions. A putatively socialist government has served notice of privatisation for major state enterprises such as telecommunications and airlines.

The long-term prospects look better for business, but grim for the man-in-the-street. As the economy rationalises and trims off fat, some jobs are hardly likely to come back, even after recovery from the recession—the first signs of which could be glimpsed at the end of 1991. To its credit, the Labor government has realised that the key to the future is re-training and skills upgrading, for which programmes are being put in place.

Poverty Think

You can see recession psychology at work in everyday life. I had never heard of 'lay-bys' until I went to Australia. A sure sign of a cash-strapped people, they are extended hire-purchase arrangements, interest-free, privately contracted between shopkeeper and customer.

So if you fancy a mechanical doll for your little daughter's Christmas present, you can go into the shop in September and ask for a 'lay-by'. The doll will be kept aside for you and you will go into the shop every month to pay off a fixed sum, until you have paid for it and can take it home.

Then there are the busy, informal neighbourhood swap and second-hand markets, usually at weekends, where the elderly and desperate selling their family heirlooms for a song are sprinkled among the younger traders simply out to make a buck. Welfare organisations like the Salvation Army are reporting an entirely new phenomenon: the middle-class unemployed from the mortgage belt seeking help, even food.

Informal groups are springing up, both in the suburbs and the countryside, using barter of services and goods instead of money. At this level, the cash economy has disappeared. Instead people are saying 'You babysit for me this Friday and I'll mow your lawn on Sunday,' or 'I'm a trained secretary, so I'll type out your letters; you're a trained electrician, so after that you can fix my light switch.'

Australia is still comparatively rich, but getting poorer by the minute. It is as well to remember this when dealing with Australians—remember that they may be hiding real distress, never assume they have money.

Scientific Excellence

Australia has sworn to transform its national slogan from 'The Lucky Country' to 'The Clever Country'. It is already well set on that path. Australian achievements in science and technology are well documented, among the best known being in computer software, telecommunications, medicine and biotechnology.

Migrants tend to pack an enormous amount of electrical gadgetry when they move house to Australia, in the belief that they won't be able to get as good or as cheap electronics in Australia. They should pause to check this one out first, however, as often the Australian technology (and design) is superior, and the price either similar or only marginally higher.

Like other countries before her, however, Australia is still making the mistake of failing to link academic research properly with the private sector for implementation. Two important bodies involved in the promotion of research and development are the CSIRO or Australian Commonwealth Scientific and Industrial Research Organisation, which dates back to 1926, and the new Australian Research Council, set up in 1988. If it were not for CSIRO's work on giving wool new properties such as being shrink-proof and capable of permanent pressing, the Australian wool industry would have collapsed much earlier, in the 1950s, when synthetics first began to gain popularity. But the CSIRO is now being forced to seek linkage with, and funding from, the private sector by the Federal Government's decision to slash its own funding for the organisation.

It is generally agreed that, if Australia is to reduce her dependence on primary products, her businessmen must do much more to support the country's undoubted talent for areas such as biotechnology and information technology.

The Taxman Cometh

If I really knew all the ins and outs of Australian tax, I doubt I would be writing this book. I would be sitting back and enjoying my enormous wealth. Because everybody in Australia wants to understand the Australian tax system. Few do.

Coping with Australia's byzantine tax regulations is a national industry. The situation is very 'grey' indeed and it is entirely possible to get totally contradictory counsel from different accountants and tax consultants, as well as from the Australian Taxation Office itself. There has been a single taxation policy operated at the Federal level since 1942, although recent talk of moves towards a looser 'new federalism' raises the spectre of this being undone one day; taxation could be moved over to the State Governments, at least partially.

Here are just a few simplified pointers which seem to be more or less indisputable at the time of writing. Get yourself an advisor, and keep every piece of documentary evidence of every one of your financial transactions that you can obtain.

Tax File Numbers If you are a tax resident (and it can be interesting defining exactly when this is—as Arthur Andersen, a consultancy expert, says, 'There is no clear-cut answer as to when a person becomes or ceases to be a tax resident'), you are required by law to apply for a tax file number. The onus is on you to do so.

Tax file numbers are taking the place of identity cards in the control of individuals. Banks often require to know your tax file number, and social security benefits are not available unless you can give one. In several instances, including the receipt of interest earnings, if you do not provide a tax file number, tax will automatically be levied on the payment at the highest marginal tax rate.

Tax Residency As mentioned above, the situation is not very clear. However, a person present in Australia for more than 183 days in a tax year may be considered a tax resident. A person who usually lives in Australia may be considered a tax resident irrespective of the time he or she actually spends there. Permanent Resident status obviously could be another factor defining the tax resident.

The Tax Year Australia's tax year runs from July 1 to June 30 the following year, not on a calendar year basis.

Residents If you are a tax resident, Australia taxes you on your worldwide income, regardless of whether it derives from, or is remitted to, Australia, unless it has already been taxed in the source country.

Overseas Employment A tax resident who has worked in a foreign country for a continuous period of 91 days or more will be fully exempted from Australian tax, providing he has been taxed in the other country. This exemption applies only to money derived from employment, however.

Non-Residents If you are a non-resident, you will be taxed only on assessable Australian-sourced income.

Overseas Income Income earned by Australian companies resident in low-tax countries will be attributed to their parent companies and taxed on an accrual basis, except in a list of 61 'comparable-tax countries'. But if the comparable-tax country taxes at a low, concessional rate, accrual tax will still apply.

Capital Gains There is no capital gains tax on profits from the sale of your first/main home ('principal residence') in Australia, even if you have been overseas for some time (providing you have not used it to earn rental income during your absence). If you have been renting it out, the capital gains tax exemption applies only for a maximum period of six years' absence from the country. Generally speaking, there are no taxes on capital or wealth per se.

Lump It There is a 'lump sum' tax in Australia which applies to domestic superannuation funds, virtual pension funds, when they are paid out on retirement, and which will probably apply to a new migrant's savings or pension fund if he or she takes them into Australia.

Documentation Australia has only recently relaxed somewhat its formerly very strict 'substantiation' requirements, meaning the tax authorities may wish to see every single original receipt and document to prove expenses incurred. But this is still at the authorities' discretion and it is wise to play safe by keeping absolutely everything, as well as a diary of unreceipted expenses, and a record of items like the mileage done in your car for business purposes.

Expenses The Australian government tightened up considerably on 'business lunch' type entertainment expenses and many other fringe benefits or perks in the 1980s. Generally, they are not considered as expenses for tax purposes any more.

How You Pay Pay your tax in Australia by PAYE, Pay As You Earn, through fixed deductions from your monthly salary. Businesses can remit their employees' payments quarterly, to cut down administrative hassle. Generally speaking, it is more common for the authorities to take tax in advance and rebate later than the other way round; this is a problem for new small businesses setting up.

Raids The tax authorities are in the habit of instituting rigorously severe audits on taxpayers' accounts at random and without much warning. Many live in terror of such audits and there are horror stories of virtual tax raids on private homes. During 1991–92, it was expected that a total of 100,000 taxpayers would be selected for such an audit. This is when you really need all that substantiation documentation.

I know of one person who somehow suspected he would be visited by the taxman in this way. He had all his possessions and assets removed from the house by lorry and greeted the taxman with a tale of woe, saying he had been clean-sweep burgled the night before. This is not something to emulate, of course, but it does indicate the drastic nature of such tax dramas.

Bank Confidentiality One of the world's most easy-going banking systems has changed radically in recent years. Note that all transactions in your bank account of A$10,000 or over have to be reported by your banker, including all international telegraphic money transfers of this amount, measures which are intended to combat tax evasion and organised crime.

Consumption Tax There is no equivalent of Britain's VAT (Value Added Tax) sales tax in Australia—yet. The Liberal Party made such a tax part of its platform for the elections in 1993, but this was a major reason for their defeat at that time.

Rates These are local government taxes, which will vary according to the property you own and the services you enjoy. When buying a house, it is well to check on the level of rates being levied by your future local Council, since some can be quite high.

To quote Jeff Mann, president of Taxation Institute of Australia, in 1991, 'What is fundamentally clear is that the operation of the tax laws is becoming increasingly complex at a time when the stated objective of the Australian Taxation Office is "tax simplification".'

Your Partner in Business

The Australian businessman is strangely schizoid: superficially pally but really quite cagey, seemingly mild and undriven but in fact capable of unbridled aggression, apparently egalitarian and incorrupt

Courtesy of Kookaburra Productions, Queensland.

but actually a lot more 'flexible' than that would imply, casual and relaxed on the surface but deep down, quite tense.

The best way to break the ice is to share a beer together at the pub, to talk about sport, or to meet at a barbie party and talk about anything but work.

The fundamentally anti-intellectual stance of the average Australian sometimes affects business too. People get things done in a makeshift, nonchalant 'She'll be right' fashion, without reference to any real expertise, whether published or in the person of a flesh-and-blood expert.

Be prepared too for the familiarity of official and business letters from complete strangers addressing you as 'Dear Bill' or 'Dear Susan', etc. Australia has never liked honorific titles of any kind and now it seems, even 'Mr', 'Mrs', 'Ms' and 'Miss' have been cast aside forever. It's all part of the egalitarian ethos, although one does doubt that these people would write to their Prime Minister in quite the same tone. I could be wrong, though. This is Australia.

In any case, you will have been very lucky indeed to get any kind of letter. Australians are notoriously reluctant to answer letters. Like the Americans, they respond better to phone calls, and also to faxes.

Chapter Twelve

THE EARTH MOTHER

'One seems to ride for ever and to come to nothing, and to relinquish at last the very idea of an object. Nevertheless, it was very pleasant. Of all the places that I was ever in this place seemed to be the fittest for contemplation.'

—British novelist Anthony Trollope, in his documentary 'Australia and New Zealand', 1873.

The Land of Australia

No matter how urban or suburban the Australian is, the land of Australia lies in his or her subconscious, whether as a sensation of joy, reverence, or fear.

Nobody can live in Australia without being affected by the land, the landscape and the extraordinary ecosystem it nourishes. In his own strange way, the Australian white is linked with the land, just like the Australian Aboriginal. The land is his mother too. Only he does not articulate this half-sensed emotion as clearly in his culture as do the Aboriginals.

You see this subconscious leitmotif reflected in the landscape paintings (except for the very early colonial ones, which rather desperately rendered Australian scenery much like English pastures and oak forests), the cinema and the great literature of white Australia. There is hardly an Australian film that does not linger on the land, long and lyrical.

Seen from the outside, particularly from the white, Western point of view, Australia's is a uniquely harsh, intimidatingly vast and seemingly empty environment, hostile to human life. But the Aboriginal would not agree.

The Basic Facts of the Land

First, let us get to grips with the immensity of Australia. It is about the size of the USA if you exclude Alaska; 24 times the size of the British Isles. In absolute figures, it is 7.7 million square km in area. The mainland distance east-west is 3,983 km, north-south, 3,138 km. The Western Australian capital of Perth and the Northern Territory capital of Darwin are closer to Asia than to any other Australian city.

A continent in its own right, Australia lies across the Tropic of Capricorn in the southern hemisphere, sandwiched between the Indian and Pacific oceans. Antarctica is just 2,000 kilometres to the south. 'Australia' derives from the Latin *Australis*, meaning 'southern land'. Much is made of the Southern Cross constellation of stars as a nationalistic symbol, which features on the Australian flag.

This is the driest continent on Planet Earth, with recorded temperatures of up to 53 degrees Centigrade in places. Men still die in Australia's deserts. A year's reading of the newspapers is sure to yield a clutch of such incidents, even today. There are sad place names dotted over the continent recalling the trials of early explorers—names like Lake Disappointment for a dry lake. Australia still remembers with respect the ill-fated Burke and Wills expedition of 1860, which attempted to cross the continent from south to north; Burke and Wills died of starvation during a terrifying journey.

But there are great variations in climate and landscape, from the lush tropical north with its end-year monsoonal 'wet', rainforests and mangrove swamps, to the chilly temperate forests of the south and the ski slopes of New South Wales and Victoria.

Rocks and Ranges

Australia was once part of a prehistoric super-continent named Gondwanaland that first started to fracture about 150 million years ago. Out of its parts were formed Australia, Antarctica, South America, Africa, India, Madagascar and New Zealand. Australia broke off from Gondwanaland about 45 million years ago. This makes Australia a very old continent indeed, with a geological history dating to the Pre-Cambrian period of 600 million years ago; the landforms of Europe and the USA, in contrast, evolved only up to 65 million years ago.

It is largely a flat continent, with major exceptions like the Great Dividing Range of the east, running from north Queensland down into Victoria in the south, which includes tablelands, alps, plateaux and mountains—the famous Atherton Tableland of Queensland, the Blue Mountains of New South Wales and the Grampians of Victoria, for example. Australia's highest peak is Mount Kosciusko in the Snowy Mountains of New South Wales, at 2,230 metres.

There are some very strange and dramatic excrescences on the otherwise flat Australian vistas, the most famous of these being the

The outdoor life, never far away; here, just outside Canberra. Photo courtesy of Suzie Daroesman.

335-metre tall Ayers Rock monolith, rising straight out of a central plain. The vivid red Olgas, rock monoliths described by an early explorer as 'monstrous pink haystacks', are in the Northern Territory, in the same Uluru National Park as Ayers Rock.

Others include the Pinnacles, about 200 kilometres north of Perth in Western Australia—platoons of natural limestone obelisks standing up to two metres high—and the ancient sandstone formations of the Bungle Bungle range in the remote Kimberley region of northwest Western Australia, rising 450 metres above the grasslands.

The Countryside

Close to 90 per cent of Australians live in capital cities or towns. Few live or even work in rural or outback regions such as the arid, dusty 'Red Centre' around the famous outback town of Alice Springs.

It is still possible to capture the old romance: cattle-drover 'cowboys' silhouetted through a shimmering veil of dust, marshalling

223

great rivers of cattle over treeless bush, one-street towns and two-house stations stuck on lonely plains, the occasional cry of 'Coo-ee!', the old Aboriginal bush cry connecting humans separated by great distance.

But rural Australia is bleeding. The young are leaving for the pleasures of the city. Those who stay are battling high interest rates and the loss of overseas markets for their produce, in addition to regular natural disasters like drought, fire, floods and, in the far north, cyclones.

Doctor in the Air

Life in outback Australia stimulated the establishment of the world's most impressive aerial medical service, better known as The Royal Flying Doctor Service. An Australian-born Presbyterian missionary, John Flynn—'Flynn of the Inland' they called him—was the founder in 1928 of this voluntary organisation funded by government grants and other contributions. The service uses a sophisticated radio network to link outback stations with its hospitals and planes.

Children in these remote areas do their schooling over 'Schools of the Air', using the Flying Doctor's two-way radios. In times of emergency, such as floods or fires, the service helps to drop supplies, and also mounts search and rescue operations.

Fire!

The Australian ecology is built to burn. The Aboriginals have always known this and have used fire as an instrument for controlling and benefiting their environment. Fire disasters are a regular occurrence in the hot summers. The 'Black Thursday' of 1851 in Victoria, the 1939 'Black Friday' fires in Victoria and the 'Ash Wednesday' fires of 1983 in South Australia and Victoria, were terrible examples, with 70 lives lost in the last-mentioned of these.

The worst fires often occur at times of drought. The extremely high temperatures reached in the Australian summer combine explosively with native plants like the oil-bearing eucalypts, which act much like petroleum thrown on the flames. Hot winds from the north do the rest. But fire seems also to stimulate new plant growth.

In recent years, the finger has often been pointed at arsonists, as much as at Nature. Needless to say, setting fires in the summer when the fire-risk has been declared high, is a criminal offence. This means neither a simple campfire nor even the home barbecue fire is safe, if the fire-risk is high enough. Australia has developed a magnificent network of volunteers as well as professionals to combat fire.

The Flora

The 'flagship' plants of Australian botany are of course the eucalypts, a genus classified within the Myrtle family, especially the smoother-barked versions known popularly as 'Gums'.

Eucalypts have a tall and spindly look, with foliage sparsely dispersed along scarecrow branches, that is quite distinctive. They also give off a very special resinous aroma that says 'Australia' as soon as it reaches the nose on a summer's breeze. Or, as with the Lemon-scented or Peppermint versions, their leaves may yield a wonderful perfume when crushed between the fingers.

There are also the Stringybark eucalypts of the east, with their rough barks, and the largely tropical Ironbarks. The giant Karri forests of southwest Western Australia are the second tallest in the world after the California redwoods. The Jarrah, from the same region as the Karri, has a fine red-grained timber often found as polished flooring in older Western Australian homes.

One of the loveliest sights of the Perth summer is the flowering of countless Jacaranda trees (actually South American imports way back when), clouds of lavender-blue.

My husband got quite excited one December day in Perth, telling me, 'Look, we've got our very own Christmas tree, on the front verge!' It was a Bottle-brush, ablaze with tall red flower 'candles', yet another myrtle.

The author in bushland, a gum in the background. Photo by Siva Choy.

In the same Myrtle family again—there are 1,300 species of myrtle in Australia—are the Paperbarks, sometimes referred to in Australia by their genus name, Melaleuca, and quite often identified by their peeling, papery bark. Other familiar myrtles are the Teatrees, which fall within the Leptospermum genus, including the Lemon-scented Teatree.

A famous national symbol, of course, is the Wattle, in the genus Acacia, part of the Mimosa family, with its familiar golden blossoms. There are 900 species of wattle in Australia.

Every Western Australian spring, about October–November, tourists and residents alike are presented with the most spectacular display of exotic wildflowers in the countryside and in the bush. It is literally a case of the desert blooming, in profusion.

Roos and Devils

Australia's long isolation from the rest of the world has contributed to the evolution of some extraordinary life-forms unique to the continent. The existence of the ancient supercontinent of Gondwana-land can be traced from the fact that there are some related species to be found in New Guinea and in South America.

The best-known oddities in Australia are of course those egg-laying, nipple-less mammals, the monotremes—just three of them, being the Duck-billed Platypus and two species of Echidna, also known as Spiny Anteaters—and the pouched marsupials, with the Kangaroo the best-known example.

A less well-known feature of some marsupials is the fact that they have bifurcated penises, nobody knows why. One Aussie zoo director experimenting with the breeding of endangered marsupials said to me, 'Well, maybe we have double the chance of success!'

There are 19 marsupial families, encompassing not only kanga-roos and wallabies, but also arboreal animals like the Koala (*not* 'koala bear', please, a misnomer) and possums, various mice and rats, wombats and 'native cats' (which look more like mongooses than cats). Half of Australia's 250 species of mammals are marsupials.

The Wombat is a wondrous beast, stocky and powerfully built, like a small bear, weighing in at about 40 kilograms. Somewhat less cuddly is the Tasmanian Devil, a smallish black-and-white carnivorous marsupial endemic to Tasmania, which makes the most appalling screeching and grumbling noises, feeds on almost anything, including carrion, and is equipped with jaws that could reduce the thickest bone to shredded-wheat consistency.

Some of the kangaroo-type marsupials have marvellous names, like the Potoroo, the Wallaroo, the Quokka (found only on Western Australia's Rottnest Island, off Perth) and the Pademelon.

Cute at a wildlife park, but the Tasmanian devil's jaws can crunch bone. Photo by the author.

Possums you may get to know better than you would prefer. Although essentially harmless, they are the bane of many a householder's life since it is their habit to hole up in ceiling and roof spaces of ordinary homes, even in the city, scrabbling around and making an awful racket at night.

Here is a brace of trivia, just for interest: the platypus may look cute, but in fact, the male has a nasty pair of poisonous spurs on his ankles, and the name 'koala' is Aboriginal for 'He who does not drink'—the koala gets most of its moisture from the leaves it chews, although actually, it does very occasionally drink liquids. Belying their looks, koalas are not particularly cute, being bad-tempered and sullen, slow-moving animals most of the time.

All native animals are protected under federal law in Australia. However, killing of wild kangaroos, populations of which are thriving and multiplying, is licensed for 'culling' purposes from time to time. Farmers in particular treat these great macropods as vermin, because they compete with domestic livestock for grass fodder. The issue of kangaroo harvesting is charged with emotion in Australia.

Emus and Galahs

There are 700 species of birds in Australia. When the first white settlers arrived in 1788, one of them, surgeon Arthur Bowes Smyth, remarked that as his ship hove into what was to be Sydney Harbour: 'The singing of the various birds among the trees, and the flights of the numerous parraquets, lorrequets, cockatoos, and maccaws, made all around appear like an enchantment.'

Here again, you see the traces of Gondwanaland, with the Australian Emu closely related to other flightless birds like the South African ostrich and New Zealand's kiwi, for example.

Other unique avifauna include the Black Swan. This reverse-image bird, seen in northern hemispheric terms, has caused awful trouble for the Japanese, since their word for swan can only refer to a white bird.

Of course, of all the Australian birds, the 'laughing' Kookaburra is perhaps the most widely known. It is quite a cheeky bird. The few times I have been out to use the public barbecue pits in Perth's King's Park, there have always been a couple of these quite large and handsome birds sitting beside me on my log seat, hinting that they would like to be offered a few slivers of meat, please.

Very Australian too are the 50 species of parrot, from the brightly coloured Rosella and exotically multi-hued Rainbow Lorikeet (my friend Arshak in Sydney calls these lorikeets down to his garden, to feed in psychedelic flocks perched all over his body), to the green Parakeet and the familiar Cockatoo.

There are more cockatoos, however, than just the white-bodied sulphur-crested one so commonly seen in Western aviaries (protected but considered a pest by most Australians). There are, for instance, handsome black cockatoos like the palm cockatoo of Queensland, besides the red-headed cockatoo ('Gang-Gang') and the pink-and-grey Galah.

The poor galah has entered Strine-talk as a synonym for idiocy—in expressions like 'Mad as a gumtree full of galahs.' If you wish to express your contempt for people, you could refer to them as 'a bunch of galahs'.

We must not forget the Fairy Penguin, resident on Victoria's Phillip Island; their nightly 'parade' is a big tourist draw.

Personal favourites of mine are the stately Pelican found almost everywhere, the majestic 1.5-metre tall Brolga crane, symbol of the Northern Territory, the delicate little Honey-eaters sucking nectar from the red Grevillea flowers in my garden, and the large crow-like Magpie whose bell-like chortling always means 'home' to me when I am in Perth.

Scalies and Slimies

There are exotic lizards in Australia—450 species, including the large dinosaur-like Goanna, or Monitor Lizard (good eating), the dragon-lizards (Agamidae) such as the dramatic Frill-necked Lizard of the north, and the much smaller, ceiling-walking house Gecko. But the reptiles which attract the most attention are snakes and crocodiles.

Snakes are admittedly more alarming in Australia than almost anywhere else: of the approximately 160 species found in the country, the poisonous ones outnumber the harmless ones. And some are among the most dangerous in the world—the Giant Brown Snake and the Taipan of the north, the Tiger Snake of the southeast, the Copperhead and various types of Sea Snake. However, there are only about 15 of these very dangerous snakes.

There are some scary tales about species like the Brown Snake or the Red-bellied Black Snake not only standing their ground against humans, but even attacking or chasing them, in the breeding season. You should certainly give any snakes sighted a wide berth.

Crocodiles are the stuff of Australian legend. Thanks to conservationist policies which have granted them complete protection since the early 1970s, their number has increased dramatically.

The focus of public fear and awe is the Estuarine Crocodile, or Saltwater Crocodile, which will take human beings if they are at hand—and has done so on several highly publicised occasions. The croc grips such larger prey in its jaws and then takes it below water to drown it, rolling over and over in the process, before eating it a few days later. The danger to humans has probably been increased by tourist operators who bait crocodiles by hanging carcasses high above the water from large boat decks, thus teaching the beast to leap ever higher. The average small fisherman's boat then becomes no problem for the crocodile.

Make no mistake about it, the seemingly lumbering 'saltie' can move at an impressive speed on land. Just watch 'show-time' at some of the Northern Territory crocodile farms, when rangers feed huge specimens by offering them dead chickens at the water's edge, and see what you think after that.

If travelling the land, particularly in northern Western Australia,

Daredevil feeding of crocs. Photo by the author.

the Northern Territory and Queensland, you should be careful when approaching coastal inlets, swamps and even large rivers quite far inland. If you are camping near such a spot, I am told it may be advisable to move camp every so often and generally, never to do the same thing twice in the same place at the same time of day. The crocodile apparently is quite cunning and may stalk you for several days to determine your habits before he strikes. The next time you go down to the billabong to fill your kettle for tea, at 5 p.m., the same time as you always do, could be your last.

The Ferals, and Other Unwelcome Guests

Feral domestic animals—in other words, humankind's animals left to go wild in the bush and desert—are some of the great banes of the Australian ecology and a constant reminder of the ignorance of the early white settlers.

There are feral buffalo, horses and donkeys, rabbits and perhaps most startling of all, dogs and cats. If you are a newcomer, do not approach 'pussycats' seen in the countryside with the same affectionate trust you might offer your best friend's pet cat. It could turn out to be a snarling tiger-like thing if it is a 'feral'. The heavier ferals, such as the buffalo, which love to wallow in muddy ground, do immense damage to natural bush vegetation and soils.

Another legacy of thoughtless white Australia is the rabbit. Rabbits came with the First Fleet in 1788 but really took off when some new arrivals were imported in the mid-19th century.

Their multiplication to near-plague proportions and the damage they can do to agriculture by devouring pasture-land grasses provoked the erection of thousands of kilometres of 'rabbit-fences' across the land. The disease myxomatosis was introduced after World War II and successfully controlled the rabbits for some time, although now, the animals are developing resistance to the infection.

Still worse than the rabbit has been the European fox, which was introduced for nothing better than the pleasure of the hunt, in the 1840s. This predator has had a disastrous impact on Australia's many unique small mammals.

Toad Tales

One notorious introduction occurred in relatively recent times, to the nation's great shame: the cane toad, also known as the giant or Queensland toad, was introduced to northern Queensland in 1935, from its South American homeland via a stopover in Hawaii. Americans will be familiar with this creature. The idea was that the toad would control beetle pests in Queensland's economically important sugar-cane plantations.

The toad in fact did not do this job very well, but spread widely across the north and began to eat native animals as well. Because this noxious beast has poison glands in its skin, it is also dangerous to native predators which may take a fancy to it.

Proving that human behaviour is any time more bizarre than any animal can produce, there are reports from the USA of drug fiends actually licking live cane toads for kicks afforded by its poison glands; in Australia, it is suggested that Queenslander drug-freaks may be smoking dried toad-skin as a hallucinogen.

Certainly, there is a mass of folklore surrounding the cane toad. In fact, the cane toad has become a cult object in Australia, regarded with perverse affection. A brilliantly hilarious and surprisingly informative, award-winning documentary called *Cane Toads* has been made. Hire it at your local video shop in Australia; this is a 'must-see' item of really offbeat Australiana. There is even an underground political newspaper in Queensland named after the toad and political satirists regularly cartoon unpopular Queenslander politicians as cane toads.

The Thylacine that Got Away

One of the great zoological puzzles of Australia is the Thylacine, also known as the Tasmanian Tiger or the Marsupial Wolf. It is extinct— or is it?

The last known tiger died in Hobart Zoo, Tasmania, in 1936. White settlers put a bounty on surviving tigers from about 1830 and shot it to extinction when it took to hunting their sheep.

But claims of sightings are regularly made today, often in south-western Western Australia, where the Thylacine may have roamed thousands of years ago—and one of these was seriously discussed and published in the eminent British science magazine, *The New Scientist*, during the 1980s. For the moment, searching for, and reporting on, the Thylacine remains one of Australia's more delightfully silly preoccupations—you might like to join the fun and start an expedition yourself, perhaps.

Sea, Surf, Sun

White Australians love the seas around their land even more actively than they do the land. Which is amazing, considering all the nasty things in those seas—sharks, crocodiles, jellyfish, sea snakes and so on. Unfortunately, there are also other man-made hazards nowadays: the waters off Sydney's famous Bondi Beach, for example, are badly polluted.

Australians who cannot swim are few and far between. So if you are a newcomer and cannot yet swim, start taking lessons to become one of the crowd.

Australian surf life-savers are one of the great macho images of the nation—muscled, bronzed and noble—and perhaps deservedly so. Up to 1988, almost 325,000 people had been saved by the Surf Life Saving Association of Australia. As the *Penguin Australian Encyclopaedia* has pointed out, this is more than the Australian death toll in the two world wars.

The surfing fraternity in Australia has developed an elaborate subculture with its own language, publications and values. Do not let your young son get too involved in this essentially male, macho mystique if you want him to stay at school and pass exams.

Dicing with Death

Australian author John Pilger has said that it is the constant effort of peering through the sun that makes the Australian face look so 'laconic', with its lopsided smile and permanent squint. Certainly, there are a lot of glazed blue-grey eyes set in wrinkle-tracks to be seen in Australia.

The Australian exhibits a strong streak of paganism, laced with hedonism, when it comes to beaches, stripping down at the slightest excuse to catch a suntan. Owning a tan has always been an essential part of the Australian Dream. There are beaches which allow women to indulge in bare-breasted 'topless' bathing, just to help the tanning process along, further bolstering the pagan image. You are not supposed to stare.

Yet newspaper editorials warn, and the skin units of Australian hospitals demonstrate daily, that this is dangerous. Many schools will not allow children to come for class in the summer months now unless they are equipped with a powerful sun-block cream and a hat. Skin cancer is an ever-present bogey.

Older Australian men with many years' exposure to the sun behind them have shown me their arms, gouged deep with sickly white scars where cancers have been cut out. I am told that some cases are sitting in hospital with their scalp-skin rolled down to graft into new noses or foreheads. All the statistics point to a rapid increase in skin cancer cases over the past decade.

Apart from sun-block cream, it is important to wear as thick a cover of clothing as possible. Amazingly, the sight of Australian labourers toiling in the sun in bare chests and shorts, or of young boys cycling half-naked, is still commonplace. Not to mention the amount of flesh exposed on Australian beaches.

Ozone-depletion is a more threatening reality in Australia than elsewhere, because of its proximity to the ozone hole over the southern pole, and because the country's classic blue skies do nothing to filter harmful rays. You need sun-creams with an 'SPF'—Sun Protection Factor—of 15 or more to protect exposed areas of skin against cancer. The fairer your skin, the higher the SPF you need, and the shorter the time you should spend in the sun. Your cream must be water-resistant for swimming, applied to dry skin and re-applied every one to two hours.

The bad news is that it is also possible to get the worst form of skin cancer—melanoma—on parts of the body not exposed to the sun. The back is a danger spot, as few people can see what is going on there. Get a friend to check regularly for any obvious changes. The good news is that skin cancers are easily detected early—they are visible—

and very curable. Simply watch out for changes in your skin. Few skin cancers are painful. The most important thing is to train children in self-protection against the sun from an early age.

At the risk of sounding sexist, women particularly should avoid the Australian sun; the drying and wrinkling effect on the skin can age them by many years. One Aussie medic's test on a 25-year-old surfing life-saver at the beach, who had spent half his life on the beach, rated the youngster's skin with a medical age of 60.

When I am in Australia, I find I need extra moisturiser. Anyone who has lived in a humid tropical climate suffers from flaky skin when at first suddenly deprived of moisture in Australia. The most uncomfortable thing is the way your lips crack up; most Australians carry a stick of lip salve about with them to deal with this.

Needless to say, you also need very 'serious' sunglasses, the sort that really do filter harmful rays such as ultra-violet. And a range of hats, of which there is no shortage of interesting choices in Australia.

Atoning for Past Sins

Just as white Australia has a debt to repay to the Aboriginals, so it also has quite a bit of explaining to do about what it has done to the Australian environment. In both areas, a severe case of guilty conscience is tangible throughout the nation.

Through the combined ravages of habitat clearance, mining extraction and introduced predators and competitors, at least 20 native species of animals have been lost during the period of European settlement. About 30–40 species are still considered under threat.

Although Australia to the casual observer seems a wild and largely untouched land, it is in fact dreadfully scarred by the hand of humankind. Groundwater has been polluted by chemicals; more than half the land requires soil-rehabilitation measures to combat salinity, acidification and erosion.

Recycling bins for bottles at a local supermarket. Photo by Philip Little.

In reaction to the past, the average young Australian or school-child is now well versed in basic environmentalist responsibilities. Small children will lecture you on not using plastic bags, or on recycling aluminium 'tinnies'.

Supermarket shelves are crammed with 'environmentally friendly' goods, including items such as non-phosphate, biodegradable washing powders and dishwashing liquids, and recycled, unbleached toilet rolls or tissue packs. (A wry environmental cartoon by Aussie Mark Lynch has two elderly suburban housewives peering suspiciously at the recycled-paper toilet rolls and remarking doubtfully, 'I don't think my Eric would be too keen on toilet paper that's been used before.') At the checkout counter, they will pack your purchases in paper bags if possible (others may charge for plastic bags). Many responsible shoppers make a point of taking their own, canvas or woven, shopping bags.

Every neighbourhood has its sorted recycling bins for glass, cans, newspapers, old clothing, etc. Local councils arrange for sorted garbage pick-ups, gardening groups teach you how to compost organic waste. There is nothing you cannot recycle if you want to.

Australia was one of the first countries to outlaw leaded petrol and ozone-depleting chlorofluorocarbons, and is a leader in substituting the much cleaner liquefied petroleum gas for conventional gasoline in vehicles, over about a quarter of the transportation sector. The country is of course a major LPG producer.

Solar energy is another exciting form of alternative fuel—a fifth of Western Australian households use solar water heaters, a figure growing to almost three-quarters in the sunny Northern Territory.

A Darker Shade of Green

Over the past three decades, a vociferous, energetic and sometimes militant 'Green' movement has grown up to wield considerable political power in Australia. No Australian politician can really afford to adopt an obviously 'un-Green' position nowadays.

Almost every day, it seems, running battles are fought between environmentalists and mining companies, sawmill and plywood companies, housing and tourism developers, and so on. The 'greens' will man barricades, harass nuclear or fishing vessels in port, tie themselves to trees, bury themselves up to the neck in the ground before advancing bulldozers, you name it. They are committed, serious, and emotional. Unfortunately, the atmosphere often is one of confrontation rather than discussion.

The major conservationist players are the Australian Conservation Foundation (recently headed by singer Peter Garrett, leader of the top-ranking Midnight Oil, a social-conscience campaigning band), the Wilderness Society (born in Tasmania, now national), and Greenpeace, particularly active on issues like whale and dolphin protection and nuclear energy. There are myriad other groups at the state and local levels, besides many less politicised nature-rambling clubs.

Environmentalist politicians—a full-fledged 'Green Party' is very likely to emerge soon—such as Tasmania's Bob Brown (briefly calling the shots in Tasmania after the 1989 state elections), cut their teeth on a number of issues, but most notably on the Franklin River controversy of the early 1980s. The federal Labor Party's support for the environmentalist position on the proposed dam on the Franklin River, one of Tasmania's most dramatic wilderness regions, swung the 'green vote' behind it at the 1983 elections which brought it to power—the dam was scotched.

The Labor government has since then skilfully managed the environmentalist lobby, although there were signs of cracks in this facade in 1991, with the passing of hotly-debated 'resource security' measures designed to guarantee the logging and mining industry future access to national forests.

In the early 1980s, the environmentalists also lost important battles over the Lake Pedder hydroelectric scheme in Tasmania, over the integrity of the Daintree rainforest in Queensland, threatened by a four-wheel drive track, and failed to stop plans for a pulp mill at Wesley Vale in Tasmania.

But they did succeed in getting the north Queensland rainforest and Kakadu National Park in the Northern Territory declared World Heritage sites. Battles are still being fought, however, over uranium mining in Kakadu. In 1991, in the midst of a terrible recession, the Labor government decided not to go ahead with the potentially lucrative mining of Coronation Hill in Kakadu, to the great dismay of the mining lobby.

SURVIVAL SENSE

Survival in Australia's remote outback and deserts is a skill which really needs to be learned; there are courses and many good handbooks to help you do so. Although the Australian environment is unique, basic survival techniques are much the same as those taught elsewhere, be it the USA, Canada, England or Asia. However, one or two tips may help the casual camper, driver or hiker who finds him or herself in a tight situation.

Fire

First, never go bush-walking if the newspapers, radio and television tell you there is a 'High' fire alert or a total fire-lighting ban. Leave longer walks till after summer is over.

If caught in a bush fire, do not panic, and do not run if you can avoid it—fires are anytime faster than you. Especially, do not run uphill, which is exactly the way fires love to go. Take shelter where you can to avoid radiated heat (more dangerous than flames or smoke), for instance in a depression such as a vehicle wheel-rut, and cover yourself with a blanket, or even just soil.

This may be hard to believe, but your chances of survival are far higher if you *stay* in your car or your house than if you run from them, even if fire is approaching.

The evidence is that your car's petrol tank will *not* explode. You need only survive the climax of the fire passing over you—a maximum of four minutes. If you panic and run, you not only get exhausted, but radiated heat will kill you. Lie low and *cover yourself.*

Snakes

First, wear long trousers and closed shoes when hiking; second do not go near snakes or provoke them.

If bitten, do not perform the old macho ritual of slashing the bite with a razor blade to bleed it and tying a tight tourniquet between the bite and the heart. This is potentially dangerous. Tight tourniquets (which should be released every 30 minutes) are used only for funnel-web spider, blue-ringed octopus and box jellyfish cases.

The important thing is to act quickly and apply firm pressure with a crepe bandage wound extensively around the bitten area; use a piece of shirt if there is no bandage. To hold the bitten limb immobile, it should be splinted using a strong stick, binding the splint over the bandage. The patient must be kept very still.

Bush Ticks

These are common in the wetter parts of the East. Their bite is not fatal but can make you very ill.

Do not try to pull the tick out—you may create a septic wound. Just touch the tick with a hot match head, or dab it with kerosene or methylated spirit. As it backs out of your flesh, seize it with fingers or tweezers, taking care to pull the head out, not just the body.

It is possible not to know a tick has visited you. If you have any problem walking or with body coordination after hiking in the bush, see your doctor. The tick may have left, but not its poison.

Leeches

Relatively harmless in themselves, leeches are bloodsuckers and may leave small open wounds which could get infected. They are found chiefly in wet areas, like rainforests. Keep bite-wounds clean. You can deter leeches with rub-on insect-repellents, but they are quite easy to remove with a touch of salt or tobacco.

Bush-Walking

You are safest if you have taken a course in map-reading. However, compasses and maps do not survival make; they can even go wrong. Ultimately, you will be thrown back on your own common sense, and whether or not you have prepared wisely.

Even in the apparently meek and mild temperate forests of the south, you must take care. For example, there is a rather horrible thing called horizontal scrub, in which vegetation has bent over and layered itself horizontally into a springy 'floor' which may in reality be several feet above the true forest floor. The unsuspecting hiker could fall through this mass and might find it very difficult to get out.

You must have with you a good water container, and preferably water too, of course. Some means of making fire should be with you. Beware of the 'I'm just going for half a day, why bother with food and water and medical kits' syndrome. If you get lost, you are really in trouble without food and water. Always carry at least some, no matter how short you intend your walk. In high temperatures, you may need about five litres of water a day—but do not drink unless you really need to. There is evidence that excessive drinking while walking or otherwise exercising only makes things worse. Sometimes just moistening your lips will do.

Of course, if you have studied 'bush tucker' with the Aboriginals, you may be able to live off the land in an emergency. But better play safe and carry food ...

You should particularly be ready for violent weather changes, common in southern areas like Tasmania, but also encountered elsewhere. Sudden drops in temperature are the greatest threat.

Water purification tablets, salt, wool or string (to mark a path taken), a plastic groundsheet (which can be spread over a sunlit pit packed with vegetation around a centrally placed container, weighted with a stone over the container, and thus used to collect condensation water in the container overnight), a torch, a knife—these could all be useful. But don't take so much that it becomes a misery to carry your pack!

Put the essentials in a body belt, always with you. It is no good having a first-aid kit if you have left it behind in your pack at camp.

If you are lost, leave messages as you walk or at your camp if you leave it—scratched in the earth, for instance. Light a smoky fire to guide rescue aircraft. Construct an SOS message with each letter at least 2.5 metres high so aircraft can see it.

Last of all, don't worry, it won't happen. Take no notice of all this and do go bush-walking! It is one of the best reasons for being in Australia.

Chapter Thirteen

THE PHILISTINE SLANDER

'You're a brave man, but I don't think you can do it.'

— The sacked Danish architect for the Sydney Opera House,
Joern Utzon, to his replacement, Australian Peter Hall,
in the *Sydney Morning Herald*, April 23, 1966.

'Australia? It's a cultural desert!' snorted one of my acquaintances
when I told her I had a home in Australia.

Only the very ignorant—perhaps also the blind and deaf—could
possibly support such a slander about Australia. Especially with

reference to any time after the 1960s. Even before that, there is a case for saying much was going on that the outside world simply did not know about. But the personal commitment to the arts of the 1970s Labor Prime Minister Gough Whitlam did act as an important catalyst to artistic activity.

One of the most stimulating things about the Australian artistic tradition is that, like the continent's ecology, it has often had to evolve in isolation, generating its own forms. At times, that has also been a problem, but more often, distance from the world's more acclaimed artistic centres has been a plus for Australia in terms of achieving a truly singular artistic identity.

Whether the home audience—Australians themselves—always appreciates or understands its own compatriots' artistic achievements is another issue. This is possibly because very few Australian artistic works really address or empathise with ordinary Australian lives as they are today—in a word, urban middle-class. I have mentioned several times the romantic obsession with the land, the environment and the past in which pioneer Australians battled with Nature to create their present.

A problem for Australian art forms, in terms of preserving their separate identity, is pervasive Americanisation, a trend much lamented by pundits and critics, but which apparently few know how to resist. Another problem has been the seeming inevitability of Australia's best and brightest departing for foreign shores to experience a broader cultural milieu with either the excitement of America or the glamour of older cultures, in Europe. And there to sit as expatriates, often publicly sneering at their homeland for good measure, in more than a few such cases.

In recent years, concerns like the environment, feminism and Aboriginal rights, as well as a strong stream of political satire, have been influential themes right across the board of the Australian arts. Development of the arts has been somewhat constrained during the 1990s, however, by the realities of national economic hardship.

But some of the liveliest and richest artistic endeavour can be seen 'on the fringe' or at the community-neighbourhood level, perhaps not as well publicised as the more formal events. You must seek it out for yourself; it is there, tucked away in obscure corners.

On the Australian art scene, small very often means even more beautiful—like the exquisite performance of one of Gilbert and Sullivan's ultra-British, Victorian-era operettas that I stumbled upon one evening in a quiet suburb of Perth, or the laid-back exhibition by young artists in a converted Fremantle warehouse, against the back-drop of Moroccan and Malay drummers, or the Caribbean reggae gig in a Perth pub, or the bouncing Seychellois folk music another evening, the blues musicians in the bars of Fremantle, or …

There is no shortage of cultural things to do, see, hear and experience in Australia—all this in Perth, a city which isn't even near the centre of all that is going on.

Still Pictures

The ancient and sacred tradition of Aboriginal art has already been dealt with in another chapter. It has taken a long time for this school of art to influence the work of white Australian artists; there was no sign of real interchange until after World War II. A turning point was the comprehensive exhibition of Aboriginal art displayed at the Australian National Gallery in 1989, seven years after the Gallery's foundation.

Painters of the 1850s gold rush at last abandoned earlier colonial artists' picturesque, Eurocentric distortions of the Australian land-scape and began to record truly Australian scenes—painters like S.T. Gill on the goldfields or Tom Roberts on the Australian landscape and lifestyle.

The Australian art world remained for the most part resolutely conservative right through the 1920s and 1930s, taking only slight notice of the revolutions of impressionism, cubism, surrealism and so on, abroad. The social-realist depiction of immigrant and working-class suffering favoured by a group of artists led by Noel Counihan and Josi Bergner during the 1950s somehow seemed more 'Australian'.

One expatriate Australian artist who is particularly well known overseas is Sir Sidney Nolan. He has developed a number of styles—abstract before World War II, more topic-oriented after the war, with famous works on Australian historical episodes, such as the ill-fated Burke and Wills expedition.

For the period immediately following World War II, names that leap to mind include Donald Friend, who lived and worked in Bali in 1967–80, producing complex, sensual works until he died in Australia in 1989; Sir William Dobell, a portrait-painter who died in 1970, also famous for the lawsuit brought against him by fellow artist Joshua Smith, who alleged that Dobell's Archibald Prize-winning painting of Smith was a caricature, not a portrait (Dobell won); Sir Russell Drysdale, whose landscapes dwelled on the harsh Australian terrain, on outback lifestyles and the Aboriginal people.

American avant-garde thinking began to influence Australian artists as the 1960s moved into the 1970s. However, there are several men-unto-themselves, like neo-expressionist Peter Booth, who specialises in the frightening, the doom-laden and the bizarre. Women artists have also begun to play a bigger role in cultural life in recent years.

It is interesting to note that the latent puritanism in Australian society could surface in the art world as late as 1982, when New South Wales police raided a Sydney gallery to seize Juan Davila's work, *Stupid as a Painter*, for being 'sexually explicit'. However, the painting was later returned to the gallery.

Tales of Two Cities

Melbourne and Sydney are old rivals and perhaps in no area more than the arts. Goldrush wealth in the 1850s made Victoria rich, hence the rise of its capital city Melbourne as a major cultural centre, well endowed with wealthy merchant patrons of the arts. Victoria's current economic woes, however, may impose a temporary lull in cultural activity.

Melbourne established the country's first public art gallery, the National Gallery of Victoria, in 1861. Today, this gallery, housed in the Victorian Arts Centre, has important collections of Australian art, as well as some impressive European acquisitions.

The Art Gallery of New South Wales, founded in 1875, is housed in what was supposed to be a 'temporary' building back in 1895 and also features a good collection of colonial Australian art.

Canberra, too, has played a role in stimulating fine art. Australian painting got a big boost with the opening of the Australian National Gallery in Canberra in 1982, late though this was for such an institution to emerge for the first time. However, most states had galleries by the end of the 19th century.

Moving Pictures

There were Australian films made before World War II, some of them very good, but for the purpose of this book, what happened after the war is probably most interesting.

The Australian cinema virtually slumbered after the war, until the Labor government of Gough Whitlam set up the Australian Film Development Corporation, now the Australian Film Commission (AFC), in 1970. The AFC created the government's own film-making unit, Film Australia, and also funded other films. Naturally, this immediately stimulated a new rush of cinematic creativity. One of the most active participants was Phillip Adams, also known today as a newspaper columnist and advertising guru. Since then, Australian film-makers and directors have won an undoubted place in world cinema with their unique style.

Among the giants of the Australian industry are names like Peter Weir—*Picnic at Hanging Rock* (1975), *Gallipoli* (1981), *Fearless* (1993), *Dead Poets Society* (1989); Fred Schepisi—*The Chant of Jimmie Blacksmith* (1978), *Six Degrees of Separation* (1993); Bruce Beresford—*The Getting of Wisdom* (1977), *Breaker Morant* (1980), *Driving Miss Daisy* (1990); and Gillian Armstrong—*My Brilliant Career* (1978), and Little Women (1995). But Weir, Schepisi and Beresford have all since removed themselves to the USA.

Many of the more interesting of these films, from the point of view of the non-Australian, are those which deal with the Australian landscape and Australian history or issues. I would rate *Picnic at Hanging Rock, Gallipoli, The Chant of Jimmie Blacksmith* (an indictment of white attitudes to Aboriginals) and *Evil Angels* (based on a true story only just concluding as I write) pretty high as routes to understanding several different aspects of the Australian psyche.

Early Australian cinema was somewhat slow-moving, melancholic even, and this tradition has survived into the 1990s with contributions like that wistful dissection of a failing marriage, *Last Days of Chez Nous*, and *The Sum of Us*, a moving examination of a father's reconciliation with his son's homosexuality.

But more typical of the 1990s crop have been literally punchy works like *Romper Stomper*, a brutal stare at street warfare between Vietnamese gangs and white skinheads in a Melbourne suburb, and delightful comedies such as the bitter-sweet *Strictly Ballroom* starring twinkletoes heart-throb Paul Mercurio, the romantic (straight) *Muriel's Wedding* and the glamorous (gay) *Priscilla, Queen of the Desert*.

New-Zealand-born Australian woman director Jane Campion took the coveted Palme d'Or best-film award with her dark drama *The Piano* at the Cannes Film Festival in 1993, and continues such quality, as in *Portrait of a Lady* in 1997, starring Australia's own Nicole

Kidman. Other notable Australian film actors include Mel Gibson (who also has British origins), Judy Davis, Jack Thompson, Russell Crowe, Michelle Pfeiffer and Cate Blanchett. And does anyone remember that the swashbuckling Errol Flynn himself, darling of the 1930s, was in fact a Tasmanian-Australian?

Following the trail first blazed in America and other foreign parts by the now somewhat dated *Crocodile Dundee* (1986) starring archetypal bushman Paul Hogan, and again by *Strictly Ballroom* in 1992-93, George Miller and Chris Noonan's brilliantly computer-animated tale of a pig wannabe, *Babe* (a must-see) and Scott Hicks' *Shine* have won international accolades—and box-office returns. Playing a mentally ill Western Australian concert pianist who really exists—David Helfgott—Australian actor Geoffrey Rush won his peers' acclaim in Hollywood, taking the Best Male Actor Oscar in 1997 for his performance in *Shine*.

Thespian Things

In theatre as in other arts, government support has been a stimulus, specifically the establishment in 1968 of what is now called the Australia Council, until recently headed by Donald Horne.

Two groups have been important catalysts in the development of indigenous drama—the now defunct Nimrod company (wound up in 1988) and the Australian Performing Group. The latter group advocated 'worker control of the theatre', operating as a cooperative, and based itself in a converted Melbourne press factory, but more or less gave up the ghost in 1979.

Women's theatre has enjoyed much attention during the 1980s and 1990s.

Aboriginal theatre, and dance, experienced similar growth during these decades. A notable debut was that of Jack Davis' *First Born* trilogy, premiered in Perth during the 1980s.

Australia's most productive, best-known playwright now is David Williamson, with plays like *Don's Party* (1973) and *Travelling North* (1980), both also rewardingly produced in film form. Williamson was also the screen writer for major cinema hits *Gallipoli* and *The Year of Living Dangerously*. He is among the few Australian artists who do examine average middle-class Australian life.

This job, however, has been even better done by television in its attempt to comply with rulings setting a quota on the percentage of television drama which must be of Australian origin. This has resulted in homegrown soap operas like the runaway success, *Neighbours*, but also *Home and Away*, *A Country Practice* and *Flying Doctors*. The only 'soap opera' which has tried to step outside this mundane framework, the ABC's *Embassy*, promptly ran into a storm, creating a major 'diplomatic incident' between Australia and Malaysia.

Besides the soap operas, there have been several successful indigenous mini-series screened on television: Channel Seven's *A Town Like Alice* (1981) and *The Thorn Birds* (1984), Channel Nine's *For The Term of His Natural Life* (1983) and *A Fortunate Life* (1986), for example.

Cabaret and Comedy

Australian performers seem particularly adept at cabaret comedy and satire, both of which translate well to the small screen.

King of the field—or should one say, Queen?—is Barry Humphries, who has so immortalised one of his roles, 'Dame Edna Everage' (Everage = Average, geddit?) that the Australian public now perceives her as an entirely real person. Book reviewers no longer tack on any helpful brackets like 'aka Barry Humphries', radio interviewers interview 'Edna Everage' straight-faced without ever referring to Barry Humphries. You need to know this, or else you may swallow Dame Edna hook, line and sinker without ever realising you have been experiencing satire, in drag.

The queen of Australian suburbia, Dame Edna Everage (Barry Humphries), at her ghastly best. Photo courtesy of John Timbers Studio, London.

It is very hard to describe to the non-Australian what it is about Dame Edna that so hypnotises Australians. She embodies all the most awful aspects of Australian suburban values, but she has also grown beyond this, to monstrous and mythic proportions, very much larger than life. 'Housewife-megastar', is how she describes herself.

Physically, the Dame is big-boned and Cartlandesque, and follows the grandest traditions of the English pantomime dame, plus quite a bit. 'She' specialises in huge horned spectacle frames, heavy make-up and a stridently high-pitched voice. She is almost bound to address you as 'Possums' and has a cruel way of probing for the secret hangups of her audience when she is live onstage. Reading the Dame's autobiography, *My Gorgeous Life*, will give you a feel for the character, seeing her on television a little more, but there is nothing quite like seeing her 'live'. Wicked, possums, wicked.

Barry Humphries became a household name in Britain in the 1960s with his creation of another great Australian character, the ultimate 'Ocker', cartoon-strip character Barry McKenzie. The McKenzie character, who spoke broad 'Strine', re-popularised old Australian slang-phrases like 'Point Percy at the porcelain' for the act of urination.

Not content with all this, Humphries has also spawned the horrendous, drunken Australian diplomat, Sir Leslie Paterson, and the quietly tragic hero of outdated, Gallipoli-conscious Melbournian suburbia, Sandy Stone, who usually appears onstage in his dressing gown and bedroom slippers. Sandy is, as reviewer John Doust said in 1990, 'racist, sexist, boring, self-indulgent, suburban and yes, dead'. The essence of Stone is also captured in a book, *The Life and Death of Sandy Stone*.

Television has been a perfect playground for other comedians. Paul Hogan first made his comic mark in this medium, and other names of note now are Wendy Harmer, who hosts the late-night cabaret *The Big Gig*, and Steve Vizard, who is among those to conceive and perform the zappy satirical show, *Fast Forward*.

British readers will also be familiar with the urbanely biting wit of long-time expatriate Australian Clive James, who has hosted his own British television show in recent years and is a former television critic of the London *Observer* (1972–82).

Fancy Footwork

Ballet has always—quite wrongly, of course—been derided by philistines as a 'sissy' art; in this context, it is intriguing that 'macho' Australia should have excelled in this very art form. There are something like 2,500 ballet schools in the country now.

The great dancer, Sir Robert Helpmann, active in the 1920s and 1930s, was an Australian. Other great Australian dancers include Marilyn Jones, most active in the 1950s, and Kelvin Coe, a star of the 1970s. The Australian Ballet, founded in 1962, with the eminent Dame Peggy van Praagh as its first director, has won an international reputation for excellence and also at home, it would seem, since it survives largely on its box-office receipts.

Music—The Serious Stuff

The Australian Opera was established in 1970 and is Australia's largest performing arts organisation, but it is heavily dependent on government subsidies.

Australia has particularly distinguished itself by producing more than its share of world-class operatic singers: sopranos Dame Nellie Melba of the 1880s and Dame Joan Sutherland, 1950–80s, are among the most famous names. They have their male counterparts—singers like John Brownlee, an operatic baritone who died in 1969, and Peter Dawson, a bass baritone who died in 1961 (born 1892), both world famous.

Among composers, another Sutherland, Margaret, stands out—she died in 1984 after a lifetime of classical compositions based on Australian themes. Percy Grainger of *Country Garden* fame (*c.* 1907) was another well-known Australian name after World War II, albeit an expatriate one. Other cherished names are Eileen Joyce, the international concert pianist of the 1950s, and John Williams, one of the world's top classical guitarists.

The most important actor in the development of Australian music was Sir Bernard Heinze, who died in 1982. As musical adviser to the

ABC broadcasting network from its establishment in 1929, he helped to create state symphony orchestras in each state, linked to the public by a radio and television concert network, a system which continues today.

The Other Stuff

You must have heard of the Bee Gees? or the Easy Beats? Perhaps also of INXs, Men At Work, Midnight Oil, Little River Band, AC/DC and Air Supply. Almost certainly of Olivia Newton-John, Kylie Minogue (I swear there is hardly a little girl born in Australia over the past five years who hasn't been christened 'Kylie') and Jason Donovan. They are all Australian pop and rock bands and musicians, of course. It says much for the Australian ability to evolve unique forms that they should all be so very well known outside of Australia. Men At Work are to be commended in particular for having given the world the song *Land Down Under,* containing the immortal words:

> *I said, do you speak my language?*
> *He just smiled and gave me a Vegemite sandwich.*

Midnight Oil is a politically-motivated, environmentalist band, representing a new genre of popular protest music, which often also champions Aboriginal rights.

Among other groups currently rated highly inside Australia are The Black Sorrows, Mental As Anything, Noiseworks, Wa Wa Nee, and the Eurogliders. On the rock and pop vocalist scene, Jimmy Barnes and John Farnham are both big noises.

A very new name is the Melbourne rock group, Hunters & Collectors, one of Australia's many excellent 'pub bands' described by *The Australian's* Clinton Walker recently as 'a deliberately esoteric, sprawling, post-punk, tribal/industrial art-funk ensemble' turned 'populist'.

I have already mentioned the band Gondwanaland in Chapter Five, a white-Aboriginal fusion. But straight from the Aboriginal heartland of Arnhem Land comes Yothu Yindi, an Aboriginal band with a stunning blend of traditional sound and Western technology. Listen to their 'Treaty'.

Kylie Minogue of course is an international pop phenomenon at the moment, along with her male counterpart, Jason Donovan. Kylie reached stardom through the part of Charlene, the 'girl next door' in *Neighbours*. (This Australian suburban-saga soap opera amazingly not only riveted Australia to its living room chairs but has also been watched by as many as 15 million British viewers.) She was only 18 when she took this role, in 1987.

Both Kylie and Jason project an essentially wholesome, simple image, in itself quite Australian. Until recently, that is—media rumour has it that Kylie is trying to copycat Madonna by injecting a bit of sizzle into her act, but apparently without conviction.

Somewhat dated, but still going strong, and undeniably Australian is Rolf Harris of *Tie Me Kangaroo Down, Sport* fame (1960s). ('Play your didgeroo, Blue,' it went.) Another Aussie singer who left her mark on the international scene in a Germaine-Greer way, is Helen Reddy, known internationally for her song *I Am Woman*.

In bars, pubs and restaurants, you will find surprisingly good new groups cutting their teeth. You have to know your way around the scene to find them from one day to the next, however, for Australian bands rarely sit on long-stay contracts at the same venue. They move from spot to spot very frequently.

Be warned, showmanship of the sequins-and-lamé kind is not really part of the Australian performance style. Many a time, a nondescript band in the most unremarkable everyday gear will shuffle onstage, mumble a few inaudible words of introduction, perform brilliantly, then shrug, take a swig of beer and amble off. Only later do you discover by chance that this was one of Australia's top groups. That kind of understatement is very Australian: remember the tall poppy syndrome?

Bushed

Australian folk music is of great interest for its historic roots stretching back into Celtic, especially Irish, and English traditions, including old Victorian sea shanties. The early bush ballads are like libraries of memories about early pioneer life, on the goldfields and the cattle ranges, in the mines and in the outback deserts. Songs like that old favourite, *Click Go The Shears*, for example.

Australian themes have also been converted into the American country-and-western style, which is very popular in rural areas and among the Aboriginals in particular. One of the most famous songs in this genre is *Pub With No Beer* by Gordon Parsons, recorded by Australia's Slim Dusty in 1958.

If you see a 'bush-dance' advertised, do go to sample the down-to-earth fun; among other things, you may catch sight of strange bush-band instruments like the 'lager-phone', constructed of beer-bottle caps. Among the better-known bush bands are the traditionalist Bushwackers and the more political Redgum, also the Mucky Duck Bush Band of Western Australia, while big-name singers include John Williamson and Eric Bogle. Two of Bogle's protest songs are *And The Band Played Waltzing Matilda* (anti-war) and *I Hate Wogs* (anti-racism).

Bush Balladeers

Closely allied with the country and folk music movements is the literary tradition of the folk poets of the past, chief among them Henry Lawson (1867–1922), C.J. Dennis (1876–1938), hailed as 'Laureate of the Larrikin'—see the Glossary in Chapter Two—and bush balladeer 'Banjo' Paterson (1864–1941).

The Literary Tradition

Just as the AFC stimulated growth in the cinema, so the Literature Board of the Arts Council, set up in 1973, promoted Australian writing. Achievements in this field have been considerable, attracting world attention in some cases.

One of the greatest early novels was based on convict life, although published well after the days of transportation—*His Natural Life* by Marcus Clarke, 1874. The bush poets of the late 19th century represented a breakaway from English traditions, in search of a more Australian identity. Backing this trend energetically was the national news-and-views weekly magazine *Bulletin*, founded in 1880 and still going strong.

The novel gained strength from the 1920s onward, with major contributions like *Coonardoo* (1929) by Susannah Prichard, a novel of cattle-station life in the far northwest which, for the first time in Australia, dared to touch on black-white sexual relationships, and *Capricornia* (1938) on a similar theme, by Xavier Herbert. Herbert's very long *Poor Fellow My Country* (1975) is also well regarded.

A giant has been Patrick White (deceased 1990), who won the Nobel prize for literature in 1973, the first Australian ever to do so, for his *The Eye of the Storm*. One reviewer, Greg Sheridan, however, wrote recently that reading White's work, *Riders in the Chariot*, was a 'dread and dire duty that hangs over every Australian'. I myself tend to fall into the Sheridan camp.

Ex-priest Thomas Keneally is another name to conjure up. *Bring Larks and Heroes* (1967) and *The Chant of Jimmie Blacksmith* (1972), also a film, are among his best-known titles, and his *Schindler's Ark* (the book of the movie, 1993) won the Booker McConnell fiction prize in 1982.

Other notable contributions have been the short stories of David Malouf (try *An Imaginary Life*—1978) and the massive six-volume *History of Australia* (1962–87) by the late Manning Clark. This, read in conjunction with Geoffrey Blainey's *The Tyranny of Distance* (1966—on how Australia's geographical isolation shaped the country's history) and Robert Hughes' moving account of the early convict years, *Fatal Shore* (1987), makes for a near-perfect Australian history lesson.

Melbourne-born (expatriate in England) Germaine Greer's *The Female Eunuch* (1970) is one of the bibles of world feminism. I have mentioned Donald Horne's important study of Australian society, *The Lucky Country* (1964), before but it cannot be mentioned too often. Also on the non-fiction side, Blanche d'Alpuget's meaty, warts-and-all biography of Bob Hawke, 1982, is a fascinating read. Finally, she married him.

Gigantic success came to Colleen McCulloch with her epic blockbuster novel, *The Thorn Birds* of 1977, which chronicles the joy and suffering of several generations of an Irish-Australian family.

Nor should we forget Nevil Shute, a British migrant to Australia in 1950, for his famous novel, *A Town Like Alice* on the love story of an Aussie soldier and a British girl (1950).

In more recent times, the big names have been Elizabeth Jolley for her wry comic style, and Peter Carey, most notably for his big-screen novel, 1988 Booker McConnell prize-winner *Oscar and Lucinda* (soon to be a movie), but also for *Bliss* (1981) and *Illywhacker* (1985).

In poetry, the World War II poems of Kenneth Slessor, who died in 1971, and the passion of Aboriginal poet Kath Walker ('Oodgeroo Noonuccal', died 1993), stand out.

To get your own copies of any of these books, go browse in any Angus & Robertson book emporium, a homegrown bookseller established since 1886.

The fount of all wisdom when it comes to publishing Australian reference books such as dictionaries and encyclopaedias, is Macquarie.

Con Artists

Australian writers and artists unfortunately have recently brought a dubious art form to new heights: artistic fraud. Many believe the root cause is excessive political correctness in artistic circles favouring works by ethnic minorities, whether migrants or Aboriginals: white artists have been obliged to masquerade as minorities in order to get

259

noticed. I myself think this flood of fraud, so evident in the 1990s, is as much an outgrowth of the Australian distaste for intellectual pretentiousness and the Australian sense of humour which delights in mocking the over-earnest. Making a bunch of professors awarding prizes for literature look very silly simply warms the cockles of any dinky-di Australian.

Recent scandals of this ilk have ranged from Helen Darville's elaborate reinvention of herself as Ukrainian-origin Helen Demidenko (*The Hand That Signed The Paper*, 1995), through middle-age white male Leon Carmen's briefly successful pose as award-winning Aboriginal woman writer Wanda Koolmatrie (*My Own Sweet Time*, 1995), to eminent painter Elizabeth Durack's 1997 confession to painting under the guise of a highly-rated Aboriginal alter ego, *Eddie Burrup*. Sadly there are several others. But these incidents do illustrate liberal white Australia's current obsession with multiculturalism, and new-found identity crisis.

Bricks and Mortar

Finally, a word about architecture. Australian architects have excelled more in small-scale, detailed works, and especially in the area of heritage conservation. Only gold money brought a degree of pomposity into public buildings, around the mid-19th century.

Among the more monumental buildings are the Queen Victoria Building in Sydney (1893–98), the National Art Gallery in Canberra, which has touches of the style set by the famous Swiss architect Le Corbusier, the Victorian Arts Centre in Melbourne, and of course, the Sydney Opera House. The Opera House, opened in 1973, is the work of a Danish architect, however, although finally completed by Australian Peter Hall; it cost A$100 million.

Canberra in particular has been an architects' playground, as a planned city from the beginning, a fact which gives it something of an artificial look and feeling.

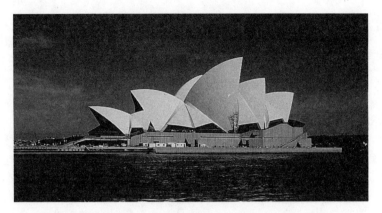

The Sydney Opera House, a national symbol. Photo by Siva Choy.

As noted elsewhere in this book, low-rise sprawl provoked by the bungalow on a quarter-acre block is characteristic of Australian cities. Australian nostalgia surfaces often with the use of rustic features and materials, from exposed brickwork to timber and rammed earth. Revivalist features such as stained-glass windows and panels are also much favoured. The climate has also made possible the wholesale import of many Californian, Mediterranean and tropical Asian styles.

In recent times, architects have directed their attention to issues of energy conservation, recycling and so on. Heritage conservation is a particularly active field, with a very wide-ranging brief, including Aboriginal sacred sites and rock-art treasures.

National trust bodies have existed since 1945, but the real catalyst was the establishment of the Australian Heritage Commission in 1975. Australia's conservation work in areas like Sydney's Rocks, and parts of Adelaide, as well as Fremantle, Perth's port city, to name only three examples, has won world renown. On the other hand, the destruction of old Perth in recent years is also quite remarkable.

Chapter Fourteen

D.I.Y. AUSTRALIA

Eager-to-please author, Ilsa Sharp, at Perth airport, to Customs officer suspiciously inspecting her bulging camera bags:

'I've come to photograph Australia, actually.'

Customs officer: 'Yeah? Well, reckon you'll be needing a wide-angle lens then.'

Every society has a hidden menu of topics—people, events, things—with which all members of that society are supposed to be familiar. Such knowledge serves as a sort of password proving that you are indeed an insider, or almost, and so allows you to enter that society.

Australia is no exception. To help you get your foot past more than just the door, here is a grab-bag of information which once internalised, should allow you to bluff your way through dinner parties, cocktail party small talk and even job interviews, without asking the fatal questions 'Who?' or 'What?'

It's a kind of D.I.Y. kit for constructing 'Instant Australia', for storage in your mental filing cabinet.

I am deliberately excluding any names or events which have been adequately dealt with in earlier chapters, so exclusion from this chapter naturally does not imply that the missing name or event is somehow unimportant.

BASIC FACT-FILE ON AUSTRALIA

Population
17 million. Density about two persons per square kilometre. About a quarter are first or second-generation settlers.

The Capital Cities
Sydney, New South Wales—population more than 3 million.
Melbourne, Victoria—more than 3 million.
Brisbane, Queensland—more than 1 million.
Perth, Western Australia—more than 1 million.
Adelaide, South Australia—about 1 million.
Canberra, Australian Capital Territory—more than 270,000.
Hobart, Tasmania—about 180,000.
Darwin, Northern Territory—close to 70,000.

Time Zones

Using Perth as a benchmark (apologies to easterners), the Western Australian capital is eight hours ahead of Greenwich Mean Time in England, except during Summer Time, when it is nine hours ahead. Perth is experimenting with this eastern system.

Eastern Australia—New South Wales, Victoria, Queensland and Tasmania—is usually two hours ahead of Perth. The eastern states adopt Summer Time (daylight saving) from about November through to February. The Northern Territory and South Australia are one and a half hours ahead of Perth.

You can get an idea of how close Perth is to Asia by noting the fact that the time there (except during Eastern Summer Time) is the same as in Hong Kong, Bali (Indonesia), Singapore and Malaysia.

Government Structure

Australia has a federal system of government, with a Commonwealth and six State parliaments, and representative councils in the Australian Capital Territory and Northern Territory (which are not states).

With the Queen of Australia and her representative, the Governor-General, at the top—and an Executive Council to advise the Governor-General—to give Cabinet decisions legal force, major political decisions and most real government are in the hands of the Federal Prime Minister and his Cabinet. The power of the Federal Government is limited by the Australian Constitution.

The federal House of Representatives is the equivalent of Britain's House of Commons, elected every three years, while the Senate acts as an upper house representing State interests and reviewing legislation, elected every six years (ACT and NT, three years).

State government mirrors this structure, each state with its own Governor, its own Premier and Cabinet, its own constitution, an upper house called the Legislative Council (elected for twice the period of the lower house) and a lower house called either the Legislative

Assembly or the House of Assembly (elected for four years, except in Queensland).

The Northern Territory (self-governing since 1978) and Australian Capital Territory (a federal government territory, with self-government more or less imposed on it against the will of most residents) have a single house of parliament—the Legislative Assembly—which is elected for four years, and the head of the majority party is called the Chief Minister, while the Queen's representative is called the Administrator.

Currency

The Australian dollar—decimal since 1966—consists of 100 cents. Denominations go right down to the small bronze one-cent coin. Curiously, the two-dollar coin is smaller than the one-dollar, both made in aluminium-bronze, and the bevelled-edge 'silver' (cupro-nickel) 50-cent coin is bigger than either, enormous in fact.

HISTORICAL MILESTONES

Even in the 16th century, many Western explorers were convinced that 'a Great South Land' existed. Several among them found parts of Australia but did not recognise the significance of their discoveries: Dutchman Willem Jansz around Cape York Peninsula in 1606, his compatriot Dick Hartog off Western Australia in 1616, and another Dutchman, Abel Tasman, who discovered Tasmania in 1642.

Others include Englishman William Dampier off the northwest coast in 1688, and Willem de Vlamingh, who discovered Perth's Swan River in 1696.

1770 Englishman Captain James Cook lands at Botany Bay and calls the eastern coastline New South Wales.

1788 The First Fleet arrives at Botany Bay under the command of Governor Arthur Phillip, with the first convict settlers from the British Isles—548 males, 188 females.

1793 Arrival of the first free settlers.

1828 First census shows 36,000 convicts and free settlers, as well as 2,549 soldiers.

1840 Abolition of transportation of convicts to New South Wales.

1851 First discovery of gold, New South Wales.

1876 Death of Truganini, last full-blooded Tasmanian Aboriginal.

1883 Silver discovered at Broken Hill, New South Wales.

1900 The Australian states federated; Australia announces intention to become independent from Britain.

1901 Census counts 3.8 million (white) population.

1902 Women get the vote at federal elections.

1908 Canberra chosen as the federal capital.

1914 World War I declared, Australian troops embark for Europe.

1915 Australian and New Zealander soldiers land at Gallipoli on April 25 but are evacuated by December 18.

1920 White population now 5.4 million, according to official figures.

1932 Sydney Harbour Bridge opened.

1940 Australian troops detailed for service abroad in World War II.

1942 Darwin in the Northern Territory bombed by the Japanese, and Japanese submarines enter Sydney Harbour.

1947 Australia's new drive for immigration begins, focusing mainly on Britain and Europe at first.

1949 Australian citizenship comes into being and is granted to all Australians.
Robert Menzies' Liberal government comes into power.

1952 Discovery of uranium in the Northern Territory.

1956 The Olympic Games held in Melbourne.

1961 Iron ore deposits found at Pilbara, Western Australia.

1964 Australia's first truly national newspaper, *The Australian*, is born.
National Service was introduced, a two-year scheme. For the first time, army conscripts could also be sent anywhere, opening up the possibility of their participation in Australia's Vietnam War commitments.

1965 Australian infantry battalion sent to Vietnam.

1966 Prime Minister Sir Robert Menzies, Australia's longest-serving leader (1939–66, except for 1941–49), retires.

Decimal currency is introduced and the metric system of weights and measures phased in.

1967 Australians vote in a referendum to abolish all forms of discrimination against the Aboriginals.

Convicted gambler-thief Ronald Ryan is the last person to be hanged in Australia, for stabbing a prison warder to death when trying to escape, provoking enormously emotional public protest and street demonstrations against the sentence.

Prime Minister Harold Holt disappears at sea off Victoria.

1968 John Gorton, Liberal Party leader, becomes prime minister of Australia.

1969 Bob Hawke is elected president of the Australian Council of Trade Unions.

Women are granted equal pay for equal work.

1972 Labor Party wins elections under the leadership of Gough Whitlam, after 23 years in opposition, riding on the public's desire for change, and the slogan 'It's Time'.

The 'White Australia' policy is formally ended.

Conscription for military service is abolished in favour of a small professional volunteer army.

1973 18-year-olds get the vote.

Queen Elizabeth II of Great Britain to be known as 'Queen of Australia'.

The Sydney Opera House opens, 16 years after the initial design had been selected.

1974 Cyclone Tracy hits Darwin in the Northern Territory on Christmas Day with wind speeds of up to 300 kilometres an hour, and inflicts terrible devastation (at least 50 deaths, 30,000 evacuated), requiring complete rebuilding of the town.

1975 Dismissal of the Whitlam government by Governor-General

Sir John Kerr. Malcolm Fraser's Liberal-Country Party coalition government takes power.

1979 Aboriginal Land Trust now has title to 144 properties, former Aboriginal reserves.

ACTU calls second general strike in Australia's history.

1980 Campbell Inquiry into Australian financial system.

Nugan Hand Bank collapses.

1982 The Franklin Dam controversy erupts in Tasmania, Australia's biggest-ever 'Green' battle.

1983 Prime Minister Malcolm Fraser is granted a double dissolution of Parliament, followed by an election for both houses. The Labor Party takes power under the leadership of Bob Hawke.

'Ash Wednesday' bush fires devastate South Australia and Victoria—75 dead, 8,000 homeless.

Australia wins the America's Cup with its yacht *Australia II*. Australia's first AIDS death—since then there have been more than 1,500 reported cases and more than 800 deaths.

1984 Government, business and union leaders sign the 'Accord' on prices and income policy.

Control of Ayers Rock given to the Aboriginals of the area.

1985 The Federal Treasury, as part of general financial deregulation, allows 16 foreign banks to apply for banking licences.

Lionel Murphy, a High Court judge, found guilty of attempting to pervert the course of justice. Cleared at a second trial, he dies of cancer in 1986, aged 64.

1986 Queen Elizabeth II of Great Britain signs a proclamation while in Australia which finally clears the way for Australia's severance from the United Kingdom, expressed in the Australia Act of the same year.

The movie *Crocodile Dundee*, starring Paul Hogan, becomes the highest-earning film in Australian history and also the highest-earning foreign film to be shown in the USA—it took more than A$180 million at USA box offices, and another more than A$110 million with its 1988 sequel.

1987 Labor retains power at federal elections.

1988 White Australians celebrate the bicentennial anniversary of the arrival of Britain's First Fleet, while Aboriginals stage a massive protest against this celebration of the white 'invasion' of Australia.

1990 Labor again retains power at the federal elections.

1991 In December, a coup in the ALP's inner circle ('Caucus') results in Bob Hawke's ouster by Paul Keating, as the government gears up for a tough fight in the 1993 federal elections.

1996 In March, the electorate ends 13 years of ALP rule and returns John Howard's liberal government.

NAME-DROPPING

Robert Dent The world's first terminally-ill person to opt for legal legal euthanasia, under a path-breaking law passed in the Northern Territory, 1996, but quashed at Federal level in 1997.

Tirath Hassaram Khemlani Mysterious Sindhi middleman, recently deceased, accused of being the go-between for Whitlam's government, in search of a A$4 billion Middle Eastern loan to help Australia buy back more of Australia from foreigners. The move was said to have been made without proper discussion and consultation. A scandal resulted, pushing the Senate to block supply of funds to the Whitlam government and finally provoking a constitutional crisis in which the Queen's representative, Governor-General Sir John Kerr, dismissed the government, in 1975.

Carmen Lawrence Australia's first woman Premier 1990-93, in Western Australia, now in Federal (Labor) politics. Dogged by political 'accidents', she would otherwise have made Deputy Prime Minister in a Labor government.

Ray Martin Popular TV presenter with a mild manner but a real knack for revealing his interviewees' private selves.

269

Indira Naidoo One of the new non-white faces on Australian television and a popular presenter, along with others, like ethnic Chinese **Lee Lin Chin** and **Annette Shun Wah.** Another popular TV news presenter, of Greek heritage, is **Mary Kostakidis.**

Jana Wendt Television's most successful, most watched and some say, most watchable, presenter and interviewer. She has a bulldog-like approach, hanging on to questions until they get answered, and a curiously unsettling stare through strangely hooded eyes. She is reckoned to be attractive.

Barlow and Chambers Brian Chambers, 28, and Kevin Barlow, 28, became the first Australians to be hanged for drug trafficking (in heroin) in Malaysia, despite appeals from the Australian government, in 1986.

Joan Kirner Premier of Victoria 1990-92 (Labor) and a very good sport willing to horse around in public.

Dick Smith A successful entrepreneur, founder of a thriving electronic goods chain, Smith uses his money to fund a series of hobbies, from publishing to aviation and exploration, or for plain philanthropy.

In 1983, he was the first person to circumnavigate the world in a helicopter and in 1987, the first to fly a helicopter to the North Pole, and has been trying out ballooning since.

Geoffrey Robertson Impressive English-born barrister dedicated to defending human rights issues in particular, both at home and abroad, and one of the leaders of the republican movement.

Alan Bond Former national hero as English migrant rags-to-riches business tycoon, declared bankrupt in 1992.

Christopher Skase Media and resort billionaire who came unstuck in the 1987 stock-market crash and then 'went walkabout' to Marjoca, evading trial.

Kim Beazley Leader of the ALP party now in Opposition following Paul Keating's defeat in 1996.

Brian Burke Former premier of Western Australia, 1983–87, he resigned to become Australia's ambassador to Ireland, but is now generally discredited and has been jailed for his role in the 'W.A., Inc.' scandal in Western Australia. His stamp-collecting hobby has been a particular point of interest during these investigations.

Laurie Connell The failed Rothwells merchant banker at the centre of the 'W.A., Inc.' storm about political patronage of big business. Jailed in 1995.

Rupert Murdoch Melbourne-born, Murdoch took American citizenship in 1985 to expand his US media investments. The world's most powerful, and richest, press baron, he is owner of *The Times* in London, *The Australian* in Australia, and others worldwide under his News Corporation banner.

Rose Hancock The Filipina widow of octogenarian iron ore tycoon Hancock once lived in an A$30 million fantasy palace in Perth, Western Australia, and is now remarried and lives in another one, in the USA.

Elle Macpherson Delectable top Aussie model.

Robert Gordon Menzies Australia's longest-serving Prime Minister 1939-41 and 1949-66 and the founder of the Liberal Party. A symbol of the old 'Anglo' Australia.

Kerry Packer Another media baron through his Consolidated Press empire, and Australia's wealthiest man. In the 1970s, he transformed cricket with his World Series of one-day matches and unorthodox coloured clothing, etc.

Geoffrey Blainey A distinguished historian and columnist who provoked controversy with his steady criticism of Labor's Asian immigration drive during the 1980s.

Kamahl Extremely popular with middle Australia, from tiny tots to grandmas, this very successful Indian singer who came originally from Malaysia is an Australian institution, although now somewhat passé.

Bob Santamaria A right-wing Roman Catholic activist and columnist who formed the Catholic Social Studies Movement in 1941 to fight communist influence in trade unions.

Lady Susan Renouf Glam former wife of suave ex-Liberal Party leader Andrew Peacock, this much-married and well-heeled lady pops up all over the media. Peacock is ambassador to the USA and a close friend of movie star Shirley Maclaine.

Ruth Cracknell Leading actress, now ageing but still lively and active, much loved for her role as a scheming doddery mother in TV soap 'Mother and Son'.

Peter Singer Australian philosopher. He is known internationally as the Father of Animal Liberation. See his book 'Animal Liberation', 1975.

Paul Vavies Australian (English-born) Physicist, author of stirring books on the interface of science and religion—*God and the New Physics*, *The Big Questions*.

Ned Kelly Legendary 'bushranger' (bandit) of Victoria in the 1870s, famous for his 40-kilogram home-made suit of armour. In 1880, he was hanged for murder. Lionised in Australian folklore as a kind of Robin Hood, he stands for the ancient Irish hatred of the English.

Recent Federal Prime Ministers

Sir Robert Gordon Menzies	1939–41/1949–66
Harold Edward Holt	1966–67
Sir John McEwen	1967–68
Sir John Grey Gorton	1968–71
Sir William McMahon	1971–72
Edward Gough Whitlam	1972–75
John Malcolm Fraser	1975–83
Robert James Lee Hawke	1983–91
Paul John Keating	1991–96
John Howard	1996–

The Poseidon Incident The Australian share market was feverish in 1970, resulting in a crash limited to Australia alone. Based on over-optimistic reports of a nickel strike in Western Australia, Poseidon shares shot from A$1 in October 1969 to A$280 in February 1970, and eventually crashed. Subsequent investigations revealed malpractice and manipulation.

The Chamberlains Azaria Chamberlain was the baby girl whose death caused uproar in Australia and cast doubt on the fairness of the Australian judicial system. The drama was played out against the almost mystic outback setting of Ayers Rock, where baby Azaria, as her Seventh Day Adventist parents Michael and Lindy always insisted, was taken by a dingo in August 1980. Lindy Chamberlain was convicted of her murder in 1982, even though no body could be found, but was released in 1987 after Azaria's missing jacket was found near Ayers Rock, and pardoned in 1990. See Fred Schepisi's 1988 movie *Evil Angels* (screened under the title *A Cry in the Dark* outside Australia), with Meryl Streep starring as Lindy Chamberlain.

Harold Holt. Australia's Prime Minister in 1966, drowned while swimming off Victoria in 1967. As his body was never recovered, some mystery lingers.

Fred Hollows national hero, almost saint, though New-Zealand born. As an opthalmologist, even when suffering from terminal cancer he continued his mission to bring simple eye-surgery techniques such as intra-ocular lens implants for cataract victims, to the developing world, including Aboriginal Australia as well as Africa, Vietnam and Nepal. He died in 1993 but his widow Gaby carries on his work.

Joan Sutherland Sydney-born, internationally recognised soprano opera singer, born in 1926.

Don Bradman Australian-born cricketer, a brilliant batsman whose record of 452 runs not out in 1930 survived until 1994. He was knighted in 1979.

Norman Gunston Alias Garry McDonald (the actor's real name)—
a cringing fictional Australian character of wild mien, with strands
of hair dragged over his bald pate. McDonald was also the
longsuffering son in the popular TV serial *Mother and Son*.

Paul John Keating Australia's Labor Prime Minister 1991–96,
notable for his determination to bring Australia closer to Asia, and
Indonesia in particular, for his commitment to the cause of Aboriginal land rights and reconciliation, and for his transformation
of the Australian economy, although a self-taught economist who
left school in his teens. A brilliant and vicious parliamentary
street-fighter with a talent for abusive language, his 'big picture'
vision and penchant for the international stage eventually undid
him, as the ordinary Australian apparently was more concerned
with the "small picture" in his own backyard.

Phar Lap A race-horse known to almost every Australian. A
consistent winner, notably in the 1930 Melbourne Cup event, he
was found dead in April 1932. Speculation on the causes continues.

Jeff Kennett Hard-edged but witty and sharp Liberal Premier of
Victoria.

Martin Bryant The disturbed lone gunman who massacred 35
innocents at Port Arthur in Tasmania, April 28 1996, provoking
the government to sweeping gun-control law reforms. He got 35
life-terms in jail.

A Selection of Public Holidays and Special Dates

January 1	New Year's Day
26	Australia Day (public holiday on the following Monday)
	Festival of Sydney
January-February	Festival of Perth
March	
1st Monday	Labour Day, Western Australia
2nd Monday	Labour Day, Victoria, and Moomba Parade
	Labour Day, Australian Capital Territory (ACT)
3rd Monday	Canberra Festival
	Adelaide Festival of the Arts (even-numbered years)
	Perth Swan Valley Wine Festival
April	
Easter holiday	Good Friday until following Monday, or Tuesday in some states
at Easter	Clare Valley Wine Festival, South Australia
	Barossa Valley Vintage Festival (odd-numbered years)
25	Anzac Day
May	
1st Monday	Labour Day, Queensland
	May Day Holiday, Northern Territory
June, 2nd Monday	Queen's Birthday (except Western Australia)
	Brisbane Festival of Creative Arts
	Darwin Beer Can Regatta, Northern Territory

August 1	Wattle Day (not all states)
1st Monday	New South Wales Bank Holiday
	Broome Shinju Matsuri Festival (multicultural), Western Australia
August, 1st Monday	Henley-on-Todd Regatta, Alice Springs (yacht race on the dry bed of Todd River)
September 1	Wattle Day (not all states)
October	
1st Monday	Labour Day, New South Wales, ACT
6	Queen's Birthday, Western Australia
2nd Monday	Labour Day, South Australia
November	
1st Tuesday	Melbourne Cup Day, Victoria
11	Remembrance Day
December 25	Christmas Day
26	Boxing Day (not South Australia)
28	South Australia Proclamation Day
	Sydney-Hobart and Melbourne-Hobart yacht races/Tasmanian Fiesta (start)
	Hobart-Salamanca Arts Festival

CULTURAL QUIZ

Can you be Australian enough to merge into the background? Here are a few test situations to try yourself out.

SITUATION 1

The Australian office you work with is having some problems with a document in French which needs translating. You have a post-graduate degree in French language and literature. Do you:

A Announce the fact loud and clear and proceed to do the translation?

B Keep quiet until someone else says, 'Hey, Bill knows a bit of French, doesn't he?' and asks you to do it?

C Offer rather tentatively to do the translation, saying, 'Look, I'm not sure I can handle it, but let me take a look at it,' and then translate it, but deliberately take a little more time than you really need, and include a few mistakes which the boss can spot, to make him feel proud?

Comments

Of the three options, C is definitely the most Australian. The idea is not to stand out too much, not to excel too obviously—not to risk becoming a tall poppy asking to be mown down. However, B is a good alternative, while A is definitely not on. Oh, and if by any chance you get a promotion as a result of this performance, remember not to throw a party to celebrate it—that would be crowing too much.

SITUATION 2

You've landed a date with this gorgeous Australian blonde at last. Do you:

A Take her to the most expensive restaurant in town to wine and dine her, opening the car door and the restaurant door for her, as well as pulling out her chair for her, and pay the whole bill before escorting her right to her front door?

B Take her to a medium or low-budget restaurant, let her largely fend for herself and split the bill with her before seeing her to her own car or taxi so that she can drive herself home?

C Take her to the local footy match after a quick fish-and-chips snack at the neighbourhood takeaway?

Comments

Choice B is probably about right for the first date. Falling over yourself to charm her as in A will probably alarm her and convince her you 'want to get into her knickers' as the saying goes. On the other hand, choice C is just too Aussie male for a real date, although it is an option by no means unheard-of or untried among Aussie males. You can step up the charm on subsequent dates if you like, once she gets used to your foreign ways.

SITUATION 3

The chairman of an important business associate company in Australia, whom you have never met, has written to you for some information which he says he needs 'soonish'. Do you:

A Compose a letter beginning, 'Dear Sir, with reference to yours of the 18th inst, re data required ...', etc., and fax it forthwith, mailing the original by express airmail?

B Put it in your KIV tray for a few days and then answer it by ordinary airmail, writing, 'Dear Joe, it's been a bit of a problem finding what you need, but no worries, this should be about right...'?

C Forget about it?

Comments

Option A will do you little good, maybe some harm, while B is correct and non-threatening in terms of over-efficiency. It is quite essential that you address your correspondent by his first, given name to get the right Australian tone. If possible, do remember to include a few spelling mistakes. Option C, while it does occur, is just too unfriendly for an Australian.

SITUATION 4

Just to prove you can speak the lingo, now translate this short passage (courtesy of writer Frank Devine's 'That's Language' column in *The Australian Magazine*, 28–29 May 1994, which is circulated nationally with *The Weekend Australian* newspaper, a marvellous source of information for all Australia-watchers):

'At Chrissie, me and my sister went to Brizzie to see our rellies. I got an eleckie blankie for a prezzy and she got some lippy. We both got sunnies and pushies. For brekky, we had mushies and chocky bikkies.'

Answer:

' At Christmas, me and my sister went to Brisbane to see our relatives. I got an electric blanket for a present and she got some lipstick. We both got sunglasses and pushbikes. For breakfast, we had mushrooms and chocolate biscuits.'

FURTHER READING

The 'Hard Core'

Here is the minimum reading and reference list of key titles, to achieve that 'Instant Australia' confidence:

The Lucky Country. Donald Horne, Penguin, Australia 1964/1988. This is the definitive study and should be your 'Bible' on Australia; it hardly seems outdated to me, even today.

A Short History of Australia. Manning Clark, Mentor paperback, NAL Penguin Inc, USA 1964/1987. The big historical picture, right up to the 1980s. (The full version, *A History of Australia,* comes in six volumes.)

The Fatal Shore. Robert Hughes, Collins Granville, London 1987/Pan Books, London 1988. Sobering detail on the terrible years of convict transportation to Australia.

The Australians, In Search of an Identity. Ross Terrill, Bantam, London 1987.

A Secret Country. John Pilger, Jonathan Cape, London 1989/Vintage, London 1990. A thought-provoking assessment of the darker side of contemporary Australia, touching on politics, business, sociology and the environment.

The Little Aussie Fact Book. Margaret Nicholson, Pitman Publishing, London 1985/1989. Everything you could ever want to know about anything Australian, in neat concise form, pocket-sized.

A Dictionary of Australian Colloquialisms. G.A. Wilkes, Sydney University Press, 1978/1985. A flashlight in the maze of 'Strine'.

The Australian National Dictionary—A Dictionary of Australianisms on Historical Principles. Editor W.S. Ramson, Oxford University Press, Melbourne 1988.

The Macquarie Dictionary of Australian Quotations. Eds. Stephen Torre & Peter Kirkpatrick, The Macquarie Library, Sydney 1990.

The Penguin Australian Encyclopaedia. Ed. Sarah Dawson, Viking/ Penguin Books, Melbourne 1990. A crash course in Australia ...
The Book of Australia, an almanac. Hodder & Stoughton, Sydney 1990.
The Macquarie Book of Events. Ed. Bryce Fraser, The Macquarie Library, Sydney 1990.

On Aboriginal Australia

My Place. Sally Morgan, Fremantle Arts Centre Press, Western Australia 1987. A personal search for lost Aboriginal 'roots'.
The Other Side of the Frontier. Henry Reynolds, James Cook University of Queensland, Australia 1981. White settlement of Australia seen from the other side, by the Aboriginals.
Seeing the First Australians. Eds. Ian/Tamsin Donaldson, George Allen & Unwin, Sydney 1985. A well illustrated and researched account of how the first European settlers and later Australians have viewed the Aboriginals of Australia.
The Chant of Jimmie Blacksmith. Thomas Keneally, Fontana, Australia 1972. A novel dramatically depicting the Aboriginal plight.
The Songlines. Bruce Chatwin 1987, Picador/Pan Books/Jonathan Cape, London 1988. This mystical work tells of the ancient paths travelled by the Aboriginals while singing the songs of their ancestors.
My People. Kath Walker, Jacaranda Wiley, Australia 1981. Collected verse by this established, campaigning Aboriginal poet.
Charles Perkins. A Biography. Peter Read, Viking, Australia 1990.
Being Whitefella. Ed. Duncan Graham, Fremantle Arts Centre Press, Western Australia, 1994. Essays by thinking whites on their relationships with the Aboriginals.

More History and Current Affairs

The Tyranny of Distance. Geoffrey Blainey 1966, Sun Books, Australia 1975. How the geography and sheer vastness of Australia have shaped the country's history. For more historical insight, try also Blainey's *Triumph of the Nomads,* a history of ancient Australia, *The Rush That Never Ended* and *A Land Half Won.*
A Fortunate Life. A.B. Facey, Penguin Books Australia 1981. The

moving autobiography of a completely ordinary white Australian, born in 1894, who helped pioneer the harsh West, survived Gallipoli, saw and experienced the lot.

For the Term of His Natural Life. Marcus Clarke, Angus & Robertson, Australia 1874/1980. A pioneering novel of colonial times depicting the horrors of Australia as a penal colony.

The Horne Trilogy: *The Education of Young Donald, Confessions of a New Boy, Portrait of an Optimist.* Donald Horne, Penguin Australia 1975. An intellectual autobiography and indirectly an intellectual history of three decades in Australia.

Robert J. Hawke. Blanche d'Alpuget, Schwartz/Penguin, Sydney 1982. This substantial warts-and-all biography of Australia's second-longest-serving prime minister, up to his first election victory in 1983, paints a revealing picture of Australian political life.

Women in Australia

Damned Whores and God's Police. Ann Summers, Penguin Australia 1975. A startling and revealing feminist history of Australia.

Tracks. Robyn Davidson, Jonathan Cape, London 1980. An incredibly brave desert solo trek in which the camels star as much as this intrepid female explorer.

Pioneer Women of the Bush and Outback. Jennifer Isaacs, Lansdowne, Australia 1990. The women pioneers' story—European, Chinese, Aboriginal—as researched through archival records.

No Place for a Nervous Lady, Voices from the Australian Bush. Lucy Frost, McPhee Gribble/Penguin Books, Melbourne 1984. The letters and diaries of 13 white women struggling with 19th century Australia.

Fiction

Power Without Glory. Frank Hardy, Angus & Robertson, Australia 1950/1982. A novel based on the true story of a businessman's life, this book gave rise to an unsuccessful suit for criminal libel.

Voss. Patrick White, Penguin, Australia 1960. A novel of exploration, dwelling on the landscape. Difficult, dense reading. The author was a Nobel prize winner in 1973. If you like it, try also White's *The Tree of Man, The Aunt's Story* and *Riders in the Chariot.*

Don's Party. David Williamson, Currency Press, Australia 1978. A novel of rumbustious postwar, pre-Whitlam Australia in the raw.

Oscar & Lucinda. Peter Carey, University of Queensland Press, Australia 1988. Like White's works, a difficult, dense piece of writing which yields magic if you concentrate. This novel won the Booker McConnell prize for fiction. Carey's complex narrative has epic shape and surrealistic, nightmarish qualities. His characters are very strange indeed. If you like this one, try also his *Bliss* and *Illywhacker.*

A Town Like Alice. Nevil Shute, Heinemann, London 1950. This wartime romance of an Englishwoman and an Aussie soldier tells much about Australia.

The Thorn Birds. Colleen McCulloch, Harper & Row, USA 1977. An epic family 'dynasty' romance, through the generations of an Irish-Australian family, some 20 million copies sold.

Kangaroo. D.H. Lawrence, England 1923.

Cloudstreet. Tim Winton, Penguin Books, Australia 1991. Like many Australians, this West Australian novelist is in love with beaches and the sea, and it shows. An award-winner, this one.

Australiana: Bush Ballads and Satire

The Best of Henry Lawson. Henry Lawson, Angus & Robertson, Australia 1981. Favourite bush ballads and poetry.

The Prose Works of Henry Lawson. Angus & Robertson, Australia 1948/ 1980s.

Collected Verse. A.B. 'Banjo' Paterson, Angus & Robertson, Australia 1982.

The Songs of a Sentimental Bloke. C.J. Dennis, Angus & Robertson, Australia 1977.

Australian Bush Ballads. Eds. Douglas Stewart & Nancy Keesing, Angus & Robertson's Australian Classics series, Australia 1955/1981.

Great Australian Legends. Frank Hardy (in association with Truthful Jones), Hutchinson Australia 1988.

My Gorgeous Life, An Adventure. Dame Edna Everage (alias Barry Humphries), Sun MacMillan, Australia 1990. To quote a W*eekend*

Australian review: 'Scorned at school for her mauve hair, little Edna eventually triumphs as an international megastar.' A spoof, of course.

The Life and Death of Sandy Stone. Barry Humphries, MacMillan Australia 1990. Moribund suburban Australia captured with lugubrious accuracy.

Keating: 'Shut Up and Listen and You Might Learn Something!' Compiler Edna Carew, New Endeavour Press, Sydney 1990. True sayings of the former Treasurer. It was a toss-up whether to categorise this book under Humour, Current Affairs, or what ...

Culture Shock Humour

How to Survive Australia. Robert Treborlang, Major Mitchell Press, Sydney 1985.

How to be Normal in Australia. Robert Treborlang, Major Mitchell Press, Sydney 1987.

They're a Weird Mob. Nino Culotta (John O'Grady), Sydney 1957. A big hit at the time, this is a lighthearted account of early migrants' lives.

At Home and Outdoors

Traditional Australian Cooking. Shirley Constantine, McPhee Gribble/ Penguin Books Australia, 1991. Replete with fascinating social history, this is more than a cookery book, but it is also that.

Australian Bushcraft. Richard Graves, Taylor-Type Publications (Australia)/Dymocks Publishing 1984.

Stay Alive, A Handbook on Survival. Maurice Dunlevy, Australian Government Publishing Service, Canberra 1981.

Bushwalking in Australia. John/Monica Chapman, Lonely Planet Publications, Melbourne 1988.

What Bird Is That? Neville W. Cayley (revision A.H. Chisholm, K.A. Hindwood, A.R. McGill, abridged Peter Roberts), Angus & Robertson, Sydney 1931/1986. The classic birdwatcher's field guide.

The Slater Field Guide to Australian Birds. Peter/Pat/Raoul Slater, Weldon Publishing, Sydney 1986/1989. Very clear colour illustrations in this handy small-and-tall guidebook.

ACKNOWLEDGEMENTS

This book would not have been possible without the help of the Australian people in general, or of many published writers already well established in the field of 'Australia-watching', besides numerous friends and acquaintances. If I have inadvertently omitted anyone's name, my sincere apologies.

I particularly want to acknowledge my debt to several reference works (for details of publishers, etc., refer to 'Further Reading', page 279):

The Penguin Australian Encyclopaedia
The Little Aussie Fact Book, Margaret Nicholson
A Dictionary of Australian Colloquialisms. G.A. Wilkes
The Macquarie Dictionary of Australian Quotations
The Macquarie Book of Events
The Lucky Country. Donald Horne

Permissions

The Daily News, Western Australia—Barry Thornton, Deputy Editor, for the meat pies picture.

Mark Lynch, Sydney, for his cartoon of tall poppy-cutting, first published in *The Australian*.

John Timbers of John Timbers Studio, London, for his photograph of Dame Edna Everage.

Kookaburra Productions, Brisbane—Sean Leahy, for reproduction of the Saltwood comic strip.

Quotations from the *Macquarie Dictionary of Australian Quotations*, reprinted with permission of the publisher, The Macquarie Library Pty Ltd.

In Perth, Western Australia

Siva Choy, for patience beyond the call of marriage, yet again.

Dan and Cally Nelson, for too much to list here, besides a smooth landing in Oz.

Sandra and John Theseira, for much besides food, but the food *was* good!

Danny and Jocelyn Stacey, and Joyce, for unfaltering mateship.

Members of the Eurasian Club of W.A. Inc., for fellowship and good times, especially Ivan and Veronica Fitzgerald, Harvey and Heather Fitzgerald, George and Kay Bentley, Colin Clark, Eddie and Barbara Fernandez, Uncle Ivan and Peter Richards, Patrick Cornelius, Priscilla and Max Clutton, Jim and Monica D'Oliveiro, Royston Sta. Maria and family, Maurice and Estelle Pestana, Teresa and Bernard Noronha, Maureen Lewis, Ivy and Harry Klass, Derek, Yvonne and Elsie Nunis.

Brian and Vivienne Ward.

'Lace'.

Herman and Wilma Aroozoo.

Faridah Ali.

Tony and Marilyn Shotam.

Herbert and Angela Teo.

Alfonso and Pat Soosay.

Carlos Eapon and Ruth Jarvie.

Ismail and Geraldine Ahmad.

Manjeet Kaur.

Narinder Kaur.

Matthew and Joyce Chin.

Gudrun and Edward Benjamin.

Lorna Ollson and John O'Brien.

Hema, Lucia and Claudia Peiris.

Rudy and Chris Riduan.

Roland and Isabelle Sharma.

Jilly and Terry Jordan.

Helen Stirling, Steve Rattenbury, Sreetha Rajalingam and Roger White, our faithful house-sitters.

Frank and Yolanda Caddy, our favourite neighbours.
Alastair Annandale and Nicky Lim.
Sarjit Singh Gill, cobbler-philosopher.
Kerryn Franklin.
Kenny and Anne Barker.
Brian Dukes, for patient advice.
Chris Lewis and Janis Hadley, for help and hospitality.
Lorraine and Wesley McMillan, Babs Lawson.
Dr Eric Tan and the Chung Hwa Association.
Professor David S.G. Goodman (Director), Dr Garry Rodan and staff of the Asia Research Centre, Murdoch University.
Magdalene Lee and staff, Singapore Tourist Promotion Board, W.A.
The Western Australian, Syndication Department.

Outside Western Australia
Hugh Mabbett, sorely missed friend and adviser.
Christine Moulet and Ted Knez, Canberra.
Liz Blyth, Queensland.
David and Amanda Landers, Sydney.
Peter and Betty Game and Babe and Peter Mitchell-Dawson of Melbourne; Ian and Pat Newton of Sydney; James Osborne of Diamond Beach Casino Hotel, Darwin; Tony and Chris Lewis of Balfe's Hill Farm, Tasmania, The Australian Tourist Commission, the various State Tourism Commissions, at home and in Singapore, and Qantas—for looking after me so well on my Australian travels 1985–91.
Philip Conn of Singapore, Barry Whalen of Hong Kong, David Townsend of Canberra, Jonathan Stone of Adelaide and Bruce Wilson of Melbourne, for my very first introductions to Australia, way back when.
Iain Finlay and Trish Sheppard, Sydney, for times past.
Angus Finney, Sydney, for being himself.
Arshak and Sophie Galstaun, Sydney.

Kenny Minogue, Darwin, for introducing me to the sounds of
Gondwanaland.
Peter and Ree Dawson, Darwin.
Peter Saltmarsh, Darwin, for showing me wild Australia.
Bronwen and Gareth Solyom, Tasmania/Indonesia/Hawaii.
Sally Taylor, USA/France/Hong Kong, for friendship and advice.
Zainon Ahmad, *New Straits Times*, Malaysia.

In Singapore
Devadas Govindasamy, for a mine of information.
Members of the Singapore Australian Business Council, and staff of the
Australian High Commission and Austrade.
Sam and Winnie Davamoni.
Margaret and Ben Cunico.
Beth Kennedy and Michael de Kretser.

THE AUTHOR

Ilsa Sharp is uniquely well positioned to explain culture shock in Australia. She comes to the subject from many different directions: British-born, she has worked as a journalist for 26 years in Southeast Asia, based chiefly in Singapore. She holds a degree in Chinese Studies from Leeds University, England, and is married to a Singaporean-Tamil. In 1989, she and her husband became migrants to Western Australia, and a new love affair with Australia began.

Ilsa is the author of several books ranging from histories of Raffles Hotel (1982/86) and the Singapore Cricket Club (1986/93) in Singapore, and a privately commissioned Indonesian family history (1992), to wildlife/nature books such as *Green Indonesia* (Oxford University Press 1994), the story of the Singapore Zoological Gardens (1994) and *A View from the Summit*, the story of Singapore's Bukit Timah Nature Reserve (Ban Hin Leong/Nanyang Technological University 1994).

INDEX